National Identities and the Right to Self-Determination of Peoples

Studies in International Minority and Group Rights

Editors-in-Chief

Gudmundur Alfredsson and Kristin Henrard

VOLUME 12

The titles published in this series are listed at *brill.com/imgr*

National Identities and the Right to Self-Determination of Peoples

"Civic -Nationalism -Plus" in Israel and Other Multinational States

By

Hilly Moodrick-Even Khen

TUTA SUB AEGIDE PALLAS · 1683 ·

BRILL
NIJHOFF

LEIDEN | BOSTON

Library of Congress Cataloging-in-Publication Data

Names: Moodrick-Even Khen, Hilly, author.
Title: National identities and the right to self-determination of peoples : 'Civic-nationalism-plus' in Israel and other multinational states / By Hilly Moodrick-Even Khen.
Description: Leiden : Brill Nijhoff, 2016. | Series: Studies in international minority and group rights ; 12 | Includes bibliographical references and index.
Identifiers: LCCN 2016014300 (print) | LCCN 2016014617 (ebook) | ISBN 9789004294325 (hardback : alk. paper) | ISBN 9789004294332 (E-book)
Subjects: LCSH: Self-determination, National. | Nationalities, Principle of. | National characteristics, Israeli. | National characteristics, Palestinian. | Nationalism. | National characteristics. | Jewish-Arab relations.
Classification: LCC KZ1269 .M83 2016 (print) | LCC KZ1269 (ebook) | DDC 341.26--dc23
LC record available at https://lccn.loc.gov/2016014300

Want or need Open Access? Brill Open offers you the choice to make your research freely accessible online in exchange for a publication charge. Review your various options on brill.com/brill-open.

Typeface for the Latin, Greek, and Cyrillic scripts: "Brill." See and download: brill.com/brill-typeface.

ISSN 2210-2132
ISBN 978-90-04-29432-5 (hardback)
ISBN 978-90-04-29433-2 (e-book)

This book is printed on acid-free paper and produced in a sustainable manner.

"Train the youth according to his way;
even when he grows old, he will not swerve from it." (Proverbs, 22:6).
Artscroll Complete Hebrew Bible Translation, 2000.

•••

To my dear parents, Sarali and Oded, whose training I will never swerve from
and whose love I will cherish forever.

Contents

Acknowledgements

My aspirations in deciding to pursue an academic career after going to law school were to step beyond the borders of the academic ivory tower. I wanted to be engaged in research of practical issues, through which I could have an effect on societal and legal developments. While I hope I succeeded in doing this with my previously published articles, this work marks my first opportunity to offer an internationally published book (as my first book was published in Hebrew). Indeed, I selected a theme I believe will be on the minds of every Israeli who is anxious about the fate of the state of Israel and the cohesion of its diverse society; it certainly occupied and keeps occupying my own mind. I never aimed to solve the problem—this would be either too naïve or too ambitious—yet, I hope I succeeded in starting down a path that others will be able to continue along.

I am grateful to many who joined me along my way (and I apologize to any who I inadvertently omitted from this list): I thank the colleagues who have read former drafts of this work, especially, Professor Mordechai Kremnitzer, Dr. Tamar Hostovski Brandes, and Dr. Yaniv Roznai, and other colleagues who commented on presentations of parts of this piece in academic conferences. I thank the Academic Center of Law and Science (formerly the Sha'arei Mishapt College), especially Dean Professor Aviad Hacohen, for supporting and encouraging my academic research since I joined the institution as a faculty member in 2006. I would also like to thank the Buffet Institute for Global Studies at Northwestern University, which gave me an opportunity to complete the work on the book in Evanston, US. In addition to the inspiring and fruitful academic atmosphere, I had a chance to experience multiculturalism in an immediate way, especially through my children's experience with their young friends.

The above connects directly to my deep gratitude to my family members, whose advice I always cherished (regardless of their age or longevity of life experience): my parents, Sarali and Oded, whose long-standing support is beyond a literal description; my spouse, Maor, who is my life companion and my deepest soul mate; and Itamar and Yaël, my children, whose open minds and hearts have always kept me on the right track.

Introduction

The following dialogue, which appears in Shlomo Sand's book on the invention of the Jewish people, recounts a conversation between Sand's grandfather, who immigrated to Israel from Barcelona, and an official in the Israeli Ministry of Interior:

> "You are not a Jew," said the official.
> "I never said I was," replied Dov. "We shall have to change your registration," the official said casually.
> "No problem," Dov agreed. "Go right ahead."
> "What is your nationality?"
> "Israeli?" Dov suggested.
> "There is no such thing," stated the official.
> "Why?"
> "Because there is no Israeli national identity," the ministry official said with a sigh. "Where were you born?"
> "In Barcelona."
> "Then we'll write 'nationality: Spanish'."
> "But I'm not Spanish. I'm a Catalan, and I refuse to be categorized as Spanish. That's what my father and I fought about in the 1930's."
> The official scratched his head. He knew no history, but he did respect people. "So we'll put 'nationality: Catalan.'"
> "Very good!" said Dov.
> Thus Israel became the first country in the world to officially recognize the Catalan nationality.[1]

The above dialogue presents, in a nutshell, the controversial issues and dilemmas dealt with in this book: nation and its importance in the 21st century; the right for national self-determination of peoples in multinational societies; loyalty to the state; the emergence of a single national identity in multinational states; and the implications of all of these for the state of Israel. I discuss these issues in the context of the emergence of multinational states that have changed the concept of the nation-state almost beyond recognition.

Since the emergence of the nation-state in the 16th century and the subsequent decline of religious empires, the world has been politically configured

---

1 Shlomo Sand, The Invention of the Jewish People (translated by Yael Lotan) 4–5 (2009).

 | DOI 10.1163/9789004294332_002

through nation-states.[2] In the globalized 20th and 21st centuries, however, the concept of the nation-state has been modified. Not only has the concept of demarcation changed with the establishment of the European Union, but the demography of states all over the world, especially in Europe, Canada, the U.S. and Australia, has undergone major changes due to vast immigration. Hence today very few states are construed upon the original 16th-century model of the mono-national state. Furthermore, globalization and the fluidity of national borders have generated a process that Thomas Friedman calls "the flattening" of the world, in which individuals, rather than states or companies, collaborate and compete globally regardless of their national, religious, or other group attachment.[3]

At the same time, however, we can trace a backlash to this process. Over the last two decades, several European states have limited religious freedom in the public sphere. For example, secular France and Belgium, and also more religious states such as Italy and Spain, have banned to various extents the wearing of the Muslim veil,[4] and Switzerland banned the construction of minarets on mosques in the state through a referendum held in 2009.[5] In other states, such as Spain and the UK, multi-nationalism has been questioned through referenda on the secession of sub-nationalities such as the Catalans and the Scotts, respectively.[6]

What emanates from the above political actions and reactions is that cultural boundaries still matter, making national identity in multinational states a non-resolved issue. Possible solutions, I suggest, emerge from the model of citizenship in multinational states developed in this book. Citizenship is a concept that celebrates the value of the lives of people in a political community,

---

2 Benjamin Akzin, STATE AND NATION (1969); Alfred Cobban, THE NATION STATE AND NATIONAL SELF—DETERMINATION (rev.ed., 1969); BORDER IDENTITIES: NATION AND STATE AT INTERNATIONAL FRONTIERS (Thomas M. Wilson and Hastings Donnan eds., 1988).

3 Thomas L. Friedman, THE WORLD IS FLAT 10 (2005).

4 Among those states, France issued the most comprehensive ban, in 11 April 2011, prohibiting the wearing of the veil in all public places. See, *The Islamic Veil Across Europe*, BBC NEWS, 1 July 2014, available at: <http://www.bbc.com/news/world-europe-13038095>.

5 Nick Cumming-Bruce and Steven Erlanger, *Swiss Ban on Building Minarets on Mosques*, THE NEW YORK TIMES, 29 November 2009 available at: <http://www.nytimes.com/2009/11/30/world/europe/30swiss.html?_r=0>.

6 In Spain the process has earlier roots. See discussion in the third chapter of this book. Scotland rejected secession from the U.K. in a referendum held in September 2014. See, *Scottish Referendum: Scotland Votes "No" to Independence*, BBC NEWS, 19 September 2014, available at: <http://www.bbc.com/news/uk-scotland-29270441>.

according to which the "political community is a good in itself, [that] cannot be reduced to the purposes of individuals or the goals of sub-communities."[7] As Beiner suggests, in theorizing citizenship, we must take into account several issues constitutive of political communities, including membership, national identity, and civic allegiance.[8] According to my theory, citizenship rests upon both the abstract concepts of liberal nationalism and multiculturalism and the tangible element of common national symbols that foster feelings of allegiance and belonging among the citizens of the state.

In Chapter 1, I discuss the first touchstone of the model, that is, nationalism. I survey both of its types—civic and ethnic—as well as its principles. I focus on the principle of unity, expressed through nationalism's capacity to foster allegiance to the state and feelings of belonging among compatriots of the state, and claim that these elements are crucial for a society to become nationalistic.

In the second chapter, I discuss the background for the emergence of the philosophical concept of multiculturalism, examining the political changes that rendered states less mono-national and increasingly more multinational. The liberal concept of multiculturalism was developed to account for the importance and crucial role of groups in human lives and to ensure groups' rights and equal representation in the public sphere. In this way, multiculturalism served as the philosophical basis for the legal right to national self determination of peoples.

Thus, the right to self-determination of peoples in general, and more specifically, the right to internal self-determination of peoples, suggests a partial solution to the question of how national minorities in multinational states can express their own national identity and at the same time be part of the larger nation-state. This right facilitates these minorities' full participation in the political life of the nation by ensuring appropriate representation in every political institution of the state, in this way representing the interests of the minority to which they belong.[9] Such participation in the political life of the state is, in turn, enabled by the political regime of federalism, which practically realizes the right to internal self-determination of peoples. In the third chapter, I discuss this regime using the case studies of Canada, Belgium, and Spain, and

7 Ronald Beiner, LIBERALISM, NATIONALISM, CITIZENSHIP 31 (2003).

8 *Id.*, 166.

9 See, Committee on the Elimination of Racial Discrimination, General Recommendation 21, The right to self-determination (Forty-eighth session, 1996), U.N. Doc. A/51/18, Annex VIII at 125 (1996), 4 [hereinafter *General Recommendation 21*]; Re Secession of Quebec, [1998] 2S.C.R 217 (Can.) 130 [hereinafter *Secession of Quebec Case*].

evaluate both the effectiveness and weaknesses of federalism in securing the national rights of minorities in multinational states, as well as in effectuating minority integration in general society.

In the fourth chapter I begin constructing the model of citizenship I call "civic-nationalism-plus," which serves to maintain overarching identities in multinational societies by strengthening a common civic identity and forging common national symbols. I construe the "civic nationalism" element upon the philosophical and legal concepts of liberal civic nationalism, multiculturalism, and the right to self-determination of peoples. I argue that, in a final analysis, federalism and the right to self-determination of peoples—which embody the nationalistic civic commitment to equality among citizens and allow for equal group representation—express a "legalistic understanding of citizenship."[10] Yet, membership has broader social and cultural aspects[11] that require the formation, motivation, and strengthening of feelings of belonging and allegiance to the state. This can be facilitated by forging concrete and common national symbols with which citizens of the state can emotionally identify.

Hence, I reveal the "plus" element in the fifth chapter in the form of common national symbols and their contribution to establishing binding ties among citizens of the nation-state toward the emergence of a cohesive society. After discussing in general the historical development of national symbols and relating in particular to two fundamental national symbols—that is, the national anthem and the national flag—I complete my model of citizenship by suggesting that civic nationalism must be accompanied by an infrastructure encouraging identification with at least some concrete national symbols: for example, the flag, the national anthem, the national currency, and historical monuments.

However, the emergence of the proposed model of citizenship is dependent upon its being rooted within the citizens of the state, primarily through education. In the sixth chapter, I discuss multicultural education, a pedagogical system that emerged in the second half of the 20th century designed to ingrain the ideals of civic equality and diversity in the younger generation and further the democratic principles of social justice.[12] I evaluate this system's effectiveness and discuss its application in different multinational states,

10 Will Kymlicka, MULTICULTURAL CITIZENSHIP 191–192 (1995).

11 *Id.*, 192.

12 Geneva Gay, *Curriculum Theory and Multicultural Education, in* HANDBOOK OF RESEARCH OF MULTICULTURAL EDUCATION 34 (James A Banks ed., 2nd ed., 2004).

especially states composed of national or religious groups in conflict, such as the state of Israel.

In the last chapter I explore the case study of the state of Israel, whose society is divided in terms of nationality between Palestinian-Arabs and Jews. Israel presents one of the most fraught and complicated cases of a multinational society in search of an overarching identity, especially as it has been long-divided by a vigorous (and even violent) national conflict that impedes such efforts. Nevertheless, I reject the view that adherence to the Zionist ideology—which focuses on ensuring the right of self-determination to the Jewish people in Israel—demands Israel have an exclusively Jewish national character and negates the national rights of the Palestinian-Arab minority.[13] Discussing the implications of my theoretical analysis for the state of Israel as a nation state of the Jewish people with a large Palestinian-Arab national minority, I explore the solutions put forward in this book in the context of the question of the identity of the Palestinian-Arabs in Israel and test the applicability of the "civic nationalism plus" model.

This book thus explores the relationship between political and philosophical theories, legal rights, and the force of national symbols in facilitating the emergence of national identities of national minorities within the nation-state. I claim that while the right for internal self-determination may be sufficient for allocating and accommodating community rights and for fostering the specific cultural characteristics of minorities, it is not a sufficient condition for integrating a minority community within the nation-state, nor can it serve as a basis for strengthening feelings of allegiance of minority community members towards the nation-state. I argue that such allegiance is both desirable and possible: it is desirable in order to form a coherent national identity that is hyphened (including the identity of both the group and the nation state) and yet inclusive; and it is possible if one accepts a typology of nationalism that defines civic nationalism as "an association of human beings living in a common territory under the same government and laws."[14]

Before delving into the first chapter discussing the concept of nationalism, two theoretical clarifications are required. First, the nation-state is regarded both as a historical fact (i.e., that most existing states are indeed nation-states) and as a morally justified phenomenon (i.e., that persons have a right to nationality and therefore are justified in establishing and preserving the

13 Supporters of this view, nevertheless, accept the prevailing legal reality that Arabic has a formal status in Israeli law. See, Alexander Yacobson and Amnon Rubinstein, ISRAEL AND THE FAMILY OF NATIONS 150–151 (2010).

14 Anthony D. Smith, NATIONAL IDENTITY 80 (1991).

nation-state). The goal in the discussion of nationalism is to describe its roots and typologies rather than to morally justify this phenomenon. In addition, while I argue that the characteristics of civic nationalism must be strengthened to enable a coherent national identity that is relevant to members of both the majority and minorities in the state, I do not intend to nullify ethnic nationalism. In fact, I claim for the co-existence of ethnic and civic nationalism, so that even within ethnic-nationalistic states, modes of civic nationalism can and should be developed and nurtured.

CHAPTER 1

Nationalism

Nationalism is considered a predominant social phenomenon of the modern world,[1] and as a result has been at the center of constant debate about its history and sociology.[2] These debates stem from different philosophical and sociological schools and focus, inter alia, on the question of whether nationalism should be regarded as an instinct (primordialism), an interest (situationalism), or an ideology (constructivism).[3] Hence, they have generated extensive analysis of the phenomenon from various angles.[4]

My aim in this book, however, is not to question the challenges of past attempts to formulate an overall definition of nationalism.[5] I accept nationalism as a political phenomenon of modern times that can be defined as "rest[ing] on two principles—the principle of popular sovereignty and the principle

---

1 Ronald Beiner, LIBERALISM, NATIONALISM, CITIZENSHIP 104 (2003). According to some scholars, especially premordialists such as Adrian Hastings and Anthony Smith, the origins of nations and nationalism are deeply rooted in human associational life and hence nations originated long before modern times. See Philip Spencer and Howard Wollman, NATIONALISM: A CRITICAL INTRODUCTION 27, 30 (2002). "Modern times" refers to the period since the 16th century, when the first modern nation, England, was created as a nation in the sense of a sovereign people, a community of equals. See, Liah Greenfeld, *Etimology, Definitions, Types*, *in* 1 ENCYCLOPEDIA OF NATIONALISM 251, 262 (Alexander J. Motyl ed., 2001) [hereinafter *Encyclopedia of Nationalism*].

2 Beiner, *supra* note 1, 104

3 David Brown, CONTEMPORARY NATIONALISM: CIVIC, ETHNOCULTURAL AND MULTICULTURAL POLITICS 5 (2000).

4 Early salient philosophers of nationalism include Ernest Renan, *What is a Nation*, *in*, MODERN POLITICAL DOCTRINES (A Zimmern ed. 1939) and Giuzeppe Mazzini. See A COSMOPOLITANISM OF NATIONS: GIUSEPPE MAZZINI'S WRITINGS ON DEMOCRACY, NATION BUILDING, AND INTERNATIONAL RELATIONS, (Stefano Recchia and Nadia Urbinati, eds., 2010). Twentieth-century writers on nationalism from a Marxist viewpoint include Ernest Gellner, NATIONS AND NATIONALISM (2nd ed., 2006); Eric Hobsbawm, NATIONS AND NATIONALISM SINCE 1780 (1990), and Benedict Anderson, IMAGINED COMMUNITIES (Rev. ed., 2006). Modernist writings on nationalism include Elie Kedourie, NATIONALISM (1993), and John Breuilly, NATIONALISM AND THE STATE (1982). Liberal nationalists include Yael Tamir, LIBERAL NATIONALISM (1993); David Miller, ON NATIONALITY (1995) [hereinafter *Miller, on Nationality*], and Michael Walzer, THINKING POLITICALLY (2007).

5 Two such fundamental writings on nationalism—Gellner, *supra* note 4, and Anderson, *supra* note 4—have been criticized by Greenfeld; see, Greenfeld, *supra* note 1, 257–258.

 | DOI 10.1163/9789004294332_003

of fundamental equality of membership in the community."[6] The community, which is the nation, can be defined as "a community of people with an aspiration to be politically self-determining."[7] In this way, I focus on nationalism as constructing a politicized identity and ask how this identity is formed and what makes it politicized. While I elaborate on this question later in this chapter, my point of departure is Kohn's valuable observation that "the growth of nationalism is the process of integration of the masses of the people into a common political form"[8]—which, as Greenfeld observes, "suggests a prior existence of and focuses attention on a modern, bureaucratic, and centralized government over a large territory."[9]

Ethnic and Civic Nationalism

Another valuable distinction in this book is the traditional division of modern nationalism into two major types: civic nationalism and ethnic nationalism. Each of these is construed upon its own myth. Ethnic nationalism portrays the myth of common ancestry,[10] which serves as a uniting and assimilating myth for ethnic groups to conform to a political community.[11] Civic nationalism rests on the myth of a political commitment to the residential homeland.[12] I elaborate on these contrasting myths in the next two sections.

Ethnic Nationalism

According to ethnic nationalism, described mainly as an "eastern European" nationalism,[13] ethnic identities and communities are crucial for the formation and persistence of nations.[14] Ethnic communities are those communities that "possess a sense of solidarity and whose members have a myth of ancestry that explains their sense of common origins and relatedness, in addition to

6 Greenfeld, *supra* note 1, 262.

7 Miller, on Nationality, *supra* note 4, 19.

8 Greenfeld, *supra* note 1, 258, citing Hans Kohn, The Idea of Nationalism, a Study in Its Origins and Background 4 (1961).

9 Greenfeld, *supra* note 1, 258.

10 Brown, *supra* note 3, 34.

11 Beiner, *supra* note 1, 25.

12 Brown, *supra* note 3, 34; Beiner, *supra* note 1, 25.

13 Its first representative model is Russia in the 19th century, but its paradigmatic case is Germany. See, Greenfeld, *supra* note 1, 260.

14 Anthony D. Smith, Ethno-Symbolism and Nationalism: a Cultural Approach 21(2009). [hereinafter *Smith, Ethno-Symbolism*].

cultural markers and shared memories."[15] According to the ethnic myth, therefore, the nation is built upon an "organic and mystical"[16] nucleus, and is seen as "a seamless, organic unity with a mystical 'soul' and mission."[17] Because what unites the nation, according to the ethno-cultural myth, is the common ancestry of its members, ethnic nationalism stresses the imagery of the biological family.[18] Nationality, hence, seems as

> an ineluctable, biological necessity…transmitted by blood as an inherent, genetic characteristic.[19] This sense of consanguinity evokes in the members of the national community a sense of continuity with past generations and is thought to determine one's interests and sentiments…one's sense of attachment and commitment to a nation.[20]

The sense of attachment to the nation, also described as a sense of national identity that emerges in the members of the ethnic community, is usually understood by ethnic nationalism as being supported by the "widespread acceptance of collective symbols, such as the flag, the national anthem, or national holiday… [embedded] in the rites and ceremonies of public culture."[21] While supporters of ethnic nationalism tend to stress the force of national symbols in sustaining communal bonds within a group construed upon the myth of ancestral kin,[22] I suggest in the fifth chapter of this book that national symbols can evoke a sense of national identity in groups that are rather "civic."

Before turning to the concept of civic nationalism, however, a final remark about the nature of ethnic nationalism is required. The distinction between

---

15 *Id.*, 27.

16 Anthony D. Smith, NATIONAL IDENTITY 80 (1991) [hereinafter *Smith, National Identity*].

17 *Id.*, 81. This resembles the myth underlying almost every constitutional endeavor in modern times. I thank Dr. Yaniv Roznai for this comment.

18 Brown, *supra* note 3, 35.

19 Greenfeld, *supra* note 1, 259–260.

20 Smith, Ethno-Symbolism, *supra* note 14, 25. The "sense of continuity" may link also with future generations. See, Lior Barshack, *Constituent Power as Body: Outline of a Constitutional Theology*, 56 U. TORONTO L.J. 185 (2006).

21 Smith, *supra* note 14, 25.

22 Anthony D. Smith, who analyzes nationalism through the "ethno-symbolic" paradigm, is a prime representative of such a concept. See, *id.*; Anthony D. Smith, *The Rites of Nations: Elites, Masses and the Re-enactment of the "National Past",in* THE RITES OF NATIONS IN THE CULTURAL POLITICS OF NATIONALISM AND NATION-BUILDING: RITUAL AND PERFORMANCE IN THE FORGING OF NATIONS 21 (Rachel Tsang, Eric Taylor Woods eds., 2014).

ethnic and civic nationalism pertains also to a distinction between two aspects of statehood that are reflected in these different types of nationalism. Ethnic nationalism is reflected in a state that is viewed as an agency of a dominant cultural, social, or ethnic group in the society that rules it;[23] civic nationalism, on the other hand, runs parallel to a state that does not represent the interests of a specific group but rather focuses on the character of the state's institutional structures.[24]

Civic Nationalism

Civic nationalism, generally described as "Western,"[25] is construed both upon a rational concept that sees a nation as "an association of human beings living in a common territory under the same government and laws"[26] and upon less rational and more mythical "ideas of the sacred soil of the ancestors and of benevolent love that citizens owe to their *patria* [homeland]."[27] That is, while the myth of ethnic nationalism is that of the ancestral kin, the myth of civic nationalism is that of a homeland kin.[28] At the same time, while the ethnic community is, by its nature, a close, segregated community, the civic myth of nationalism enables the absorption of new members to the community, because they can tie themselves to the community, its institutions and way of life, "as in matrimonial contract,"[29] and consequently become kin to the members of the community. Thus, civic nationalism suggests living in an "open, voluntary political community formed by the recognition that the self-interest of each citizen is promoted by commitment to the common good [of the society]."[30] The national character of the community is the common public culture and way of life to which all citizens in the territorial community adhere, regardless of their ethnic origin.[31]

Civic nationalism in this way evokes a notion of citizenship that Jurgen Habermas refers to as "constitutional patriotism" because "the constitution is

23 Brown, *supra* note 3, 36.

24 *Id.*

25 Its first representative model is England. See Greenfeld, *supra* note 1, 261.

26 Smith, National Identity, *supra* note 16, 80. See also, Emmanuel Joseph Sieyes, *What is the Third Estate?* [1789], *in* POLITICAL WRITINGS 97 (2003).

27 Brown, *supra* note 3, 34.

28 *Id.*, 35.

29 *Id.*, 34.

30 *Id.*

31 Beiner, *supra* note 1, 26.

an historical project that each generation of citizens continues to pursue...and in which those who encounter one another are collective actors contending about collective goals and the distribution of collective goods."[32] It also evokes a sense of permanence in the territorial home.[33]

In its most common expression, civic nationalism is identical to liberal democracy, as the nation according to this type is seen as "a sovereign (fully independent and self-governing) community of fundamentally equal members... [while] this equality is realized in the social and political arrangements."[34] This rationalist concept, which emphasizes the commitment of the members of the civic community to the political arrangements or institutions of the state rather than to the concrete and shared ideals of the nation, is the concept adopted in the modernist view of nationalism and by liberal nationalism.[35]

This modernist view, best expressed by liberal theorists, aims to undermine nationalism's mythmaking and "vindicat[e] nationalist ideas over against the cruder depictions of nationalism as sheer atavism."[36] The liberal version of nationalism, thus, stresses the importance of nationalism's dependence on the notions of popular will and popular sovereignty for the process of forming the national identity, in order to defy nationalism's image as "a reversion to ancient tribalism."[37]

Indeed, the liberal version of nationalism, which focuses on the *jus soli* as the principle of state-formation and hence "identifies co-nationals by historically

32 Jurgen Habrmas, *Struggles for Recognition in the Democratic Constitutional State*, (Translated by Shierry Weber Nicholsen), *in* MULTICULTURALISM, 107–108 (Amy Gutman ed., 1994).

33 Brown, *supra* note 3, 35. See also, Yaniv Roznai, Silvia Suteu, *The Eternal Territory? The Crimean Crisis and Ukraine's Territorial Integrity as an Unamendable Constitutional Principle*, 16(3) GERMAN LAW JOURNAL 542–580 (2015).

34 Greenfeld, *supra* note 1, 260. The types of nationalism can be further sub-divided: in addition to civic nationalism and ethnic nationalism, we find civic/ethnic collectivistic nationalism and civic/ethnic individualistic nationalism. These sub-divisions refer, generally, to the differences between autocratic and democratic regimes, so that individualistic nationalism is the democratic type of either civic or ethnic nationalism and collectivist nationalism is the autocratic type of these forms of nationalism. On a practical level, individualistic ethnic nationalism does not, in fact, exist. See, *id.* In this chapter, however, I refer only to the individualistic types of nationalism since I deal with democratic regimes, which are the ultimate regimes for the application of the right to self- determination of peoples.

35 Beiner, *supra* note 1, 108.

36 *Id.*

37 *Id.*

accidental coexistence on the same piece of land,"[38] may seem to water down the idea of nationalism into a form of "liberalism, with an attention to the ways in which people care about national identity and wish to see it expressed in some version."[39] However, what portrays liberal nationalism as a theory of nationalism and not a form of "attenuated liberalism" are the theories of those liberal nationalists who require a sense of commitment on behalf of the community members both to the institutions of civil society and to love of land and way of life,[40] thereby employing the myth of kinship and home to create a sense of a community among its members.[41] Later in this chapter I will elaborate on the sense of belonging to a community, which I find a fundamental element of both civic and ethnic nationalism.

Lastly, and before describing the common principles of both civic and ethnic nationalism, it should be mentioned that the force of nationalism in most communities is in its ability to integrate the myths of civic and ethnic nationalism. As David Brown notes:

> National communities tend to be depicted as united by civic pride and by ethno-cultural attributes, as having ethnic cores and accommodating ethnic diversity, as being in some respects natural and in some respects political, as being partly ascriptive communities and partly voluntaristic ones. Nationalism is powerful precisely because it can combine the different ideas of kinship and homeland in a way so as to unite individuals to form communities.[42]

The Common Principles of Ethnic and Civic Nationalisms

Both civic and ethnic nationalisms intend to attain and sustain the principles of nationalism, the latter understood as "a political ideology with a cultural doctrine at its center"[43]—that is, "autonomy, unity and identity on behalf of a population deemed by some of its members to constitute an actual or potential nation."[44] "Identity" refers to the national character that each nation must acquire, or in the words of Rousseau, "The first rule which we have to follow

---

38 *Id.*, citing Stephen Holmes *Liberalism for a World of Ethnic Passions and Decaying States*, Social Research 61 (3) 606 (1994).

39 Beiner, *supra* note 1, 108–109.

40 Yael Tamir and David Miller are representatives of such views and their views are discussed in this chapter in depth.

41 Brown, *supra* note 3, 35.

42 *Id.*

43 Smith, National Identity, *supra* note 16, 74.

44 *Id.*, 73.

is that of national character: every people has or must have, a character; if it lacks one, we must start by endowing it with one."[45] This character is described as a "unique genius" of a "collective self…ascertain[ing] an authentic identity beneath the alien accretions of the centuries."[46] However, it is left unexplained how this character is formed; I will address this question below.

The bases for the formation of a national identity are both abstract and concrete. In the abstract sense, nations and their identities are constituted upon the mutual recognition of their members as compatriots, that is, the belief of their members that something holds them together.[47] Added to this abstract notion are concrete elements that sustain the politicized national identity: a historic territory or homeland; common myths and historical memories; common, mass public culture; and common legal rights and duties for all members.[48]

Most of the above concrete characteristics of national identity can be attributed both to ethnic and to civic nationalism. The ethnic perception of the homeland focuses on the historic land, "the cradle of…the people…a repository of historic memories and associations… [whose] rivers, coasts, lakes, mountains and cities become 'sacred'-places of veneration and exaltation."[49] However, the homeland can also be a component of civic nationalism when regarded as "a patria, a community of laws and institutions with a single political will,"[50] a place in which the compatriots live together under a common constitutional or political framework that expresses "their common political sentiments and purposes."[51]

---

45 II Jean-Jacques Rousseau, THE POLITICAL WRITINGS OF RUSSEAU 319, (C.E. Vaughan ed., 1915), cited *id.*, 75.

46 *Id.*

47 The most famous description of this common belief of the compatriots comes from Ernest Renan, who regards the nation as "a daily plebiscite." Renan's essay is considered the classic work on nationalism. See, Renan, *supra* note 4. Benedict Anderson refers to this belief through the concept of an imagined community. See, Anderson, *supra* note 4, 5–7. See also Miller, on Nationality, *supra* note 4, 22.

48 Smith, National Identity, *supra* note 16, 14. Another configuration of these elements is introduced by Miller who states that a nation is "a community constituted by shared belief and mutual commitment, extended in history, active in character, connected to a particular territory and marked off from other communities by its distinct public culture." See, Miller, on Nationality, *supra* note 4, 27.

49 Smith, National Identity, *supra* note 16, 9.

50 *Id.*, 10.

51 *Id.*, 10, and see also David Miller, *Nationality in Divided Societies, in* MULTINATIONAL DEMOCRACIES 299, 306 (Alain-G. Gagnon, James Tully eds., 2001).

Common myths and historical memories seem to be recognized more as ethnic characteristics. These might include the founding fathers of the nation; military victories and defeats, or historical events that shaped the nation; and mass public culture, including language, religious or other rituals and holidays, literature, and art.[52] However, in cases like France (following the French Revolution) or the US, in which the common myth of the nation is, in fact, that of equal rights and freedoms for all citizens, these common myths and historical memories can also be interpreted as elements of civic nationalism. The final element foundational to a national identity—that is, the common legal rights of all members of the nation—is, of course, purely civic, as it focuses on the citizens' recognition of the authority of the political framework.[53]

A civic nationalistic identity can, hence, be understood as entrenched in society's commitment to just institutions and legal mechanisms. It would then account for other cultural characteristics only in guaranteeing fair representation in the public sphere to all of the particular cultures within the state[54]—what has been referred to as "a multinational identity."[55]

The question of whether a national identity could, indeed, be purely civic is fundamental to this book, and will be fully addressed in the fourth and fifth chapters with my discussion of the "civic-nationalism-plus" model. Nevertheless, in order to begin answering this question, I will explore another principle of nationalism, also fundamental to the civic nationalism plus model—the concept of unity.

Unity and the Theory of Belonging

The concept of unity signifies social cohesion, or the comradeship of all nationals in the nation, such as the French patriots *fraternité* during the Revolution.[56] It is this secular concept of citizens that replaces the genealogical

52 Alexander Yacobson and Amnon Rubinstein, ISRAEL AND THE FAMILY OF NATIONS 142–143 (2010).

53 Miller, Nationality in Divided Societies, *supra* note 51, 306.

54 Will Kymlicka refers to this guaranteeing of self-representation as "group-differentiated self- government rights" and claims that "all national groups [should] have the opportunity to maintain themselves as a distinct culture." See, Will Kymlicka, MULTICULTURAL CITIZENSHIP 113 (1995). He also asserts that in order for national minorities to be equally represented in the public sphere, bureaucratic mechanisms within the state should be applied to ensure fair political representation for minorities. See, *id.*, 131–134.

55 Alan Patten, *Liberal Citizenship in Multinational Societies*, *in* MULTINATIONAL DEMOCRACIES, *supra* note 51, 279, 295.

56 Smith, National Identity, *supra* note 16, 76.

concept of the nation[57] and it serves as the principle that facilitates the ideology of nationalism.[58] It is the glue that holds all of the components of the national identity together; without it, the nation state cannot function.

The concept of unity can also be referred to as "the theory of belonging." This theory suggests that feelings of belonging and allegiance to the state and to each other's compatriots are a necessary element of nationalism.[59] The theory of belonging is vested in the philosophy of communitarianism[60] and serves as both a moral and a practical principle of nationalism.[61] Broadly speaking, communitarianism is a philosophical school that challenges the basic moral assumptions of liberalism (represented by John Rawls), the latter which supposes that a theory of justice is universal so that the human condition can be regarded "'from the perspective of eternity,' from all social and temporal points of view."[62] Communitarianism, on the other hand, suggests that "the standards of justice must be found in forms of life and traditions of particular societies and hence can vary from context to context."[63] Therefore, according to communitarian philosophy, the norms that prevail in a specific society are followed

---

57 *Id.*

58 This concept will be later described as generating feelings of belonging and allegiance to the state. See, generally, Miller, on Nationality, *supra* note 4, 65–66; Tamir, *supra* note 4, 95–112.

59 Miller, on Nationality, *supra* note 4, 65–66; Tamir, *supra* note 4, 95–112.

60 For some of the most fundamental texts of communitarian philosophers see, Alsadir MacIntyre, AFTER VIRTUE: A STUDY IN MORAL THEORY (1984); Michael Sandel, LIBERALISM AND THE LIMITS OF JUSTICE (1998); Charles Taylor, *Cross-Purposes: the Liberal-Communitarian Debate, in* LIBERALISM AND THE MORAL LIFE, (Nancy Rosenbaum ed., 1989). It is, nevertheless, important to note that these scholars have different versions for the communitarian project. For example, while MacIntyre can be depicted as a pure "communitarian localist" who focuses on the communities of "schools, farms, other workplaces, clinics, parishes," Sandel refers to a community in a pan-national sense. Beiner even claims that "none of these theorists were prepared to hold fast to the banner of community expressed as a full-blown principle of ultimate philosophical judgment." See, Beiner, *supra* note 1, 67–68. For further analysis of the differences between the theories of the representatives of the communitarian philosophy, see, *id.*, 65–99.

61 Miller, on Nationality, *supra* note 4, 21–27, 65–66; Tamir, *supra* note 4, 95–116. Since the nation is viewed as a community, even though "an imagined" one (see, Anderson, *supra* note 4), the moral and practical principles of the philosophy of communitarianism are relevant for the understanding of nationalism and the factors that sustain this phenomenon.

62 Daniel Bell, *Communitarianism*, STANFORD ENCYCLOPEDIA OF PHILOSOPHY, (January 25, 2012), <http://plato.stanford.edu/entries/communitarianism/>.

63 *Id.*

"not because they lead to virtue or happiness or justice or liberty… [but rather] because these values are those of *my* group."[64]

The moral principle that follows from the communitarianism philosophy of justice and which is relevant for the model promulgated in this book is called "community based morality," or "the morality of community":[65]

> Informal communities cannot be maintained, let alone flourish, unless their members develop some sense of mutual responsibility toward each other… Hence, a sense of mutual care and mutual responsibilities among members [of a community] can be seen as a precondition for the personal enjoyment of all goods derived from communal life.[66]

The mutual care and mutual responsibilities that prevail in a specific community are a consequence of

> the assumption that deep and important obligations flow from identity and relatedness. [Dworkin refers to them] as associative obligations, and views them as obligations that social practice imposes on members in biological or social groups, such as the responsibilities toward family, friends, or neighbours.[67]

When the morality of the community principle is applied to the nation—and particularly the liberal state, which rests upon the concept of mutual and equal rights and duties to all of its citizens—the nation is understood as "a community that generates a particular type of associative obligations, namely, political obligations."[68] In other words, "particular ethical obligations could…be derived from a membership in a national community."[69]

Nevertheless, it may seem as if the political obligations and the ethical obligations in the liberal state are exhausted by "a theory of basic rights,"[70] or more

---

64 Isaiah Berlin, Against the Current: Essays in the History of Ideas 342–343 (1981).

65 Tamir, *supra* note 4, 95. Philosophers such as Tamir and Miller who discuss this principle aim also to justify it morally. See, *id.*, 95–139 and Miller, on Nationality, *supra* note 4, 49–80. My intent in this chapter is to explain this principle and rely on it, not to discuss the question of whether it is morally justified.

66 Tamir, *supra* note 4, 97.

67 *Id.*, 99.

68 *Id.*, 130.

69 Miller, on Nationality, *supra* note 4, 69.

70 *Id.*, 74.

specifically from the perception of "the state as a mechanism of coordination and a protector of [individuals] rights and interests."[71] Yet, the morality of the community principle suggests that the political obligations in a state are based on a sense of belonging that is a "thicker" concept than that of citizenship.[72] "It is not just about membership, rights and duties, but also about the emotions that such memberships evoke."[73]

The morality of the community principle suggests that the compatriots of a nation-state cannot be equated with the people who have accidently discovered themselves together on a lifeboat.[74] They are rather "'contextual individuals,' [i.e.], person[s] who by nature, belong to a particular community and have a variety of attachments and ties."[75] Moreover, these individuals believe that the preservation of their society is "a worthy endeavour"[76] and hence see themselves as "partners engaged in a shared and ongoing effort, which generates mutual responsibilities and obligations, care for future generations and respect for the communal past."[77] In other words, the creation of a national community or a nation as a political unit depends on "will and culture,"[78] as Ernest Gellner identified, so that "in these conditions, men will to be politically united with all those, and only those, who share their culture."[79]

Yet, in order for the endeavour of the citizens of the state to be considered a "common" one, it must be based upon feelings of belonging to a common identity, a concept discussed above. The sense of a specific identity—be it civic, ethnic, or a composite of the two—is what determines the values and needs of the citizens in the state and what designates the shape and form of the institutions that are to be nurtured and developed in a specific nation-state.[80]

---

71 Tamir, *supra* note 4, 137. For one of the most extreme versions of the concept, according to which the state is a coordinative mechanism between its citizens, see Iris Young's theory of "differentiated solidarity," which "specifically recognizes…obligations of collective action to undermine injustice and promote justice among strangers who dwell together in a region." Iris M. Young, INCLUSION AND DEMOCRACY 180 (2000).

72 Nira Yuval-Davis, *Borders, Boundaries, and the Politics of Belonging*, *in* ETHNICITY, NATIONALISM AND MINORITY RIGHTS 214, 215 (Stephen May, Tariq Modood and Judith Squires eds., 2004).

73 *Id.*

74 See Miller's discussion of this example in Miller, on Nationality, *supra* note 4, 41.

75 Tamir, *supra* note 4, 104.

76 *Id.*, 130.

77 *Id.*

78 Gellner, *supra* note 4, 54.

79 *Id.*

80 See the examples given by Miller, on Nationality, *supra* note 4, 74. *Cf.* Young's notion of differentiated solidarity, in Young, Inclusion and Democracy, *supra* note 71, and Charles

Hence, it is "the bonds of nationality [that] give the practice of endowing special rights and obligations a different shape from the one that it would have without them."[81] It is because "the state is a locus of identification and not merely a formal mechanism for the just allocation of resources and protection of rights"[82] that "individuals assume obligations to a state."[83]

Before moving onto a discussion of the third principle of nationalism, a note of clarification regarding the application of the communitarian theories to those of nationalism is necessary. The communitarian philosophy suffers from several flaws, the most important and relevant to our discussion in this book is viewing the ultimate standard of theoretical judgment as "community as an indiscriminate good."[84] Of course, some communities may be narrow-minded, prejudiced against outsiders or corrupt.[85] Yet, what communitarian philosophy suggests is not "to enshrine community as such as a normative standard [but rather to notice] the quality of social practices that various communities enable us to realize."[86]

Therefore, communitarian philosophy is useful in explanations of nationalism by noting issues of substantive good that neutral liberalists have shunned on principle.[87] In other words, communitarian philosophy clarifies that the national community must find some shared ideals to gather around. Supporting the justice of the procedural mechanisms of the liberal state is not enough to form a united community; the state cannot be indifferent to the *content* of the conceptions of the good life its citizens adhere to.

Taylor's commitment to the ideal of "deep diversity," suggesting that "a multinational identity...that would involve a commitment to the ideal of making a social order" could still foster a "willingness to live together under arrangements which reflect and endorse the pluralistic character of their society." See, Patten, *supra* note 55, 295. In Chapter 5 of this book, which discusses the importance of national symbols, I explain that the determination of the specific interests and values of a state are not dependent on a national identity common to all of the state's citizens and that the state's identity can be formed by taking into account the relevant characteristics of all of the groups within the society. Nevertheless, I argue that such a universal attitude cannot by itself foster feelings of belonging and allegiance to the state because these feelings are also generated by the identification with national symbols.

81 Miller, on Nationality, *supra* note 4, 71.

82 Tamir, *supra* note 4, 139.

83 *Id.*, 137.

84 Beiner, *supra* note 1, 67.

85 *Id.*, 87.

86 *Id.*

87 *Id.*, 67.

Autonomy

What enables the state to be "a locus of identification" is the third principle of nationalism, that is, the concept of autonomy or self-determination. This concept is rooted in Kant's "autonomy"': an ethical imperative for the individual, a principle of his being.[88] The late German Romantics related this concept to groups, "and the ideal of autonomy gave rise to a philosophy of national self-determination and collective struggle to realize the authentic national will in a state of one's own."[89] Autonomy is perhaps one of the most fundamental pillars of nationalism, as Smith observes:

> [Nationalism] signifies the awakening of the nation and its members to its true collective "self", so that it, and they, obey only the inner voice of the purified community. Authentic experience and authentic community are therefore preconditions of full autonomy just as only autonomy can allow the nation and its members to realize themselves in an authentic manner. Autonomy is the goal of every nationalist.[90]

It is, therefore, "[self-determination that] strengthens the claim that members of the state share something more than coordinating institutions, something that evokes in them feelings of solidarity and fraternity."[91]

The above analysis of nationalism seems to be carefully tailored for the homogenous nation-state—in which the nation self-determines itself in order to extract a specific identity that the citizens grasp as their own. However, the more interesting and complicated case is that of a multinational state or a state with national minorities: What does the concept of identity refer to in a multinational society? Can the national identity be inclusive for national minorities? How can unity be achieved in such a state? Can feelings of allegiance and belonging be fostered? I will begin my consideration of these questions in the following chapter, with an analysis of the legal principle of self-determination. I argue that while this principle serves as the core theoretical and practical principle for national rights for minorities in multinational societies, it suggests only partial solutions to how to integrate these minorities in the overall society.

---

88 Smith, National Identity, *supra* note 16, 53.

89 *Id.*, 76.

90 *Id.*, 77.

91 Tamir, *supra* note 4, 124.

CHAPTER 2

Living Together in Multinational States: Self-Determination of Peoples and Multiculturalism

The self-determination of peoples is a multifaceted principle—it is historical, political, theoretical-philosophical, and legal. In the previous chapter, I touched upon the principle's philosophical roots and meanings; in this chapter, I focus on its legal development while concentrating on its specific aspect of "internal self-determination." I argue that internal self-determination has crucial implications with regard to the question of the national identity of minorities, serving as both the core principle for the theory of multiculturalism and the practical basis for the political regime of federalism[1] or regionalism.[2] I examine the trajectories minorities can follow to fulfill their national rights without seceding from existing states; however, I first refer briefly to the historical emergence of the principle of self-determination of peoples.

Origins of Self-Determination of Peoples

Antonio Cassese traces the origin of the principle of self-determination to the American Declaration of Independence in 1776 and the French Revolution in 1789,[3] pointing to how these revolutions emphasized peoples' right to be represented and taken care of by a government rather than a monarch.[4] With the advent of the First World War, the principle of self-determination was used both by Lenin and, on the other end of the political spectrum, by US President Woodrow Wilson.[5] Wilson's analysis of this concept related to three major elements: the right of each people to choose the form of government under which they live; the restructuring of the states of central Europe in accordance with national desires; and a criterion for determining territorial change and

1 As we shall see, *infra*, both multiculturalism and federalism allow for minorities to fulfill the right to self-determination without seceding from an existing sovereign state.

2 Ukraine, for example, is a unitary state with a special status for the region of Cremea.

3 Antonio Cassese, Self Determination of Peoples: A Legal Reappraisal 11 (1995).

4 *Id.*

5 *Id.*, 13.

 | DOI 10.1163/9789004294332_004

balancing the claims of colonial states with those of their subjected peoples.[6] These were all aspects of the principle of self-determination of peoples that was later accepted as a binding legal right with the establishment of the United Nations[7]—that is, the right to self-government, the emanating questions of the right of minorities or ethnic or national groups to secede from a sovereign state, and the right of a colonial people to achieve political independence.[8] A discussion of all of these issues is beyond the scope of this book;[9] hence, I will focus only on the question of the rights of minorities within sovereign independent states, using as a legal point of departure an analysis of the principle of self-determination of peoples as a human right.[10]

The right to self-determination of peoples was first referred to as a human right in the two 1966 human rights covenants: the UN Covenant on Economic, Social, and Cultural Rights[11] and the UN Covenant on Civil and Political Rights.[12] Common Article one of these covenants provides the following:

> All peoples have the right to self-determination. By virtue of that right they freely determine their political status and freely pursue their economic, social and cultural development... The States Parties to the [Covenants] ...shall promote the realization of the right of self-determination and

6 *Id.*, 20–21.

7 *Id.*, 41.

8 *Id.*, 42.

9 There is extensive literature on the right to self-determination of peoples. Some of the works are: Milena Sterio, *On the Right to External Self-Determination: "Selfistans," Secessions, and the Great Power Rule*, 19 MINN. J. INT'L. L. 137 (2010); THE SELF-DETERMINATION OF PEOPLES: COMMUNITY, NATION AND THE STATE IN AN INTER-DEPENDENT WORLD (Wolfgang Danspeckgruber ed.,2002); James Crawford, *The General Assembly, The International Court and Self-Determination, in* FIFTY YEARS OF THE INTERNATIONAL COURT OF JUSTICE 585 (Alan.V. Lowe and Malgosia Fitzmaurice eds., 1996); Martti Koskeniemmi, *National Self-Determination Today: Problems of Legal Theory and Practice*, 43 ICLQ, 241 (1994); THE NEW WORLD ORDER: SOVEREIGNTY, HUMAN RIGHTS AND THE SELF-DETERMINATION OF PEOPLES (Mortimer N. Sellers ed., 1996); *Self Determination, in* 1 UNITED NATIONS LEGAL ORDER 349 (Oscar Schachter and Christopher Joyner eds., 1995); James Summers, PEOPLES AND INTERNATIONAL LAW: HOW NATIONALISM AND SELF-DETERMINATION SHAPE A CONTEMPORARY LAW OF THE NATIONS (1974).

10 Malcolm N. Shaw, INTERNATIONAL LAW 210–212 (7th ed., 2014).

11 International Covenant on Economic, Social and Cultural Rights, Dec. 16, 1966, 993 U.N.T.S, 3 [hereinafter *IESCR*].

12 International Covenant on Civil and Political Rights, Dec. 16, 1966, 999 U.N.T.S. 171 [hereinafter *ICCPR*].

> shall respect that right in conformity with the provisions of the Charter of the United Nations.[13]

Ensuing instruments, such as the Helsinki Final Act of 1975[14] and the African Charter on Human and Peoples Rights of 1981,[15] reiterated the peoples' right to determine their political status and to pursue their economic, social, and cultural development.[16] However, the 1970 Declaration on Principles of International Law Concerning Friendly Relations[17] contrasted this principle with the principle of territorial integrity[18] when it determined that "[n]othing in the foregoing paragraphs shall be construed as authorizing or encouraging any action which would dismember or impair, totally or in part, the territorial integrity or political unity of sovereign or independent states."[19] The Declaration on Friendly Relations was also the only instrument that attempted to conflate the contradicting principles, by qualifying that the above principle applied only to

> sovereign and independent States *conducting themselves in compliance with the principle of equal rights and self-determination of peoples as described above and thus possessed of a government representing the whole*

13 ICESCR, *supra* note 11, art. 1; ICCPR, *supra* note 12, art. 1.

14 The Final Act of the Conference on Security and Cooperation in Europe, Aug. 1, 1975, 14 I.L.M. 1292.

15 African [Banjul] Charter on Human and Peoples' Rights, June 27, 1981, OAU Doc. CAB/LEG/67/3 rev. 5, 21 I.L.M. 58 (1982).

16 Shaw, *supra* note 10, 210.

17 Declaration on Principles of international Law Concerning Friendly Relations and Co-operation Among States, G.A. Res. 2625 (XXV), Annex, 25 UN GAOR, Supp. (No. 28), U.N. Doc. A/5217, at 121 (24 Oct. 1970) [hereinafter *Declaration on Friendly Relations*].

18 See Declaration on the Granting of Independence to Colonial Countries and Peoples, G.A. res. 1514 (XV), 15 U.N. GAOR Supp. (No. 16) U.N. Doc. A/4684, at 66, (14 Dec., 1960), which recalls that "any attempt at the partial or total disruption of the national unity and the territorial integrity of a country is incompatible with the purposes and principles of the Charter of the United Nations." Note a possible distinction between territorial integrity and territorial indivisibility. The latter emphasizes negation of secession while the former carries a dual aspect: internal, which opposes secession, and external, which emphasizes protection against foreign aggression or forcible encroachment of the territory. See Venice Comm'n for Democracy Through Law, *Self-Determination and Secession in Constitutional Law*, COUNCIL OF EUR. (Jan. 12, 2000), <http://www.venice.coe.int/webforms/documents/default.aspx?pdffile=CDL-INF(2000)002-e>. I thank Dr. Yaniv Roznai for this reference.

19 Declaration on Friendly Relations, *supra* note 17.

> *people belonging to the territory without distinction as to race, creed or colour*. (Emphasis added)[20]

Hence, the inviolability of the principle of territorial integrity is preserved only for democratic states that ensure equal representation in the public sphere for all of their citizens, including those who belong to national minorities. In that sense, the right of self-determination "provides the overall framework for the consideration of the principles relating to democratic governance."[21]

This aspect of the right to self-determination—that is, creating the infrastructure for the application of all of the "individual human rights which are frequently constitutionally guaranteed by democratic governance"[22]—is regarded as the right to *internal* self-determination. "Internal" means that this right is exercised "inside the boundaries of existing States in various forms and guises."[23] Internal self-determination was described by the Committee on the Elimination of Racial Discrimination as "the right of every citizen to take part in the conduct of public affairs at any level."[24] The Canadian Supreme Court later supported this observation in its discussion of the right of the province of Quebec to secede from Canada by sustaining that internal self-determination is "a peoples' pursuit of its political, economic, social and cultural development within the framework of an existing state."[25]

The principle of self-determination of peoples, thus, avails itself as a governing principle for the common life of national (or other: i.e., religious, ethnic,

---

20 *Id.* However, note that the declaration also provides that colonial occupation and other regimes that subject peoples to alien domination and exploitation violate the right to self-determination of peoples.

21 Thomas Franck, *The Emerging Right to Democratic Governance*, 86 AJIL, 46 (1992) cited by Shaw, *supra* note 10, 212.

22 James Summers, *The Internal and External Aspects of Self-Determination Reconsidered, in* STATEHOOD AND SELF-DETERMINATION: RECONCILING TRADITION AND MODERNITY IN INTERNATIONAL LAW 229, 237 (Duncan French ed., 2013).

23 Separate Opinion of Judge Yusuf in the ICJ Advisory Opinion on Kosovo, cited *id.*

24 General Recommendation 21, The right to self-determination (Forty-eighth session, 1996), U.N. Doc. A/51/18, Annex VIII at 125 (1996), 4 [hereinafter *General Recommendation 21*]. Note also the observation of Professor Higgins, a member of the human Rights Committee from 1985 to 1995, that "external self- determination requires a state to take action in its foreign policy consistent with the attainment of self-determination in the remaining areas of colonial or racist occupation. But internal self-determination is directed to their own peoples." The observation is cited by Shaw, *supra* note 10, 212.

25 Re Secession of Quebec, [1998] 2 S.C.R 217 (Can.) 130 [hereinafter *Secession of Quebec Case*], at 437–438.

social) communities in a democratic state.[26] It governs both the conferring of rights for the different communities in such multinational states and the relationship between the former. On the theoretical level, this principle lies at the foundation of the philosophical school of multiculturalism, developed in the 1980s to serve for the construction of a framework of rights for majority and minority communities in multicultural societies and for determining the relationship between them. On the practical level, the principle of self-determination of peoples has been used for the establishment of a political framework called federalism,[27] according to which a state composed of various national communities allows these communities self-governing mechanisms that function alongside the national government.

In the following section of this chapter I critically analyze the theoretical aspects of the principle of self-determination of peoples, which rests upon the theory of multiculturalism. I will consider the merits and the faults of multiculturalism in order to evaluate its contribution to the construction of a stable political unit (namely, a state) for multinational societies.

Multiculturalism

Since the second half of the 20th century, with the decline of the Westphalian model[28] of mono-national states and the rise of a human rights movement that generated human rights law and discourse, political theorists gradually acknowledged that "the traditional majoritarian models of democracy and difference-blind models of citizenship are inherently exclusionary, marginalizing a wide range of groups."[29] Hence, they developed alternative models to account for minorities' rights, including "deliberative," "agonistic"

---

26 Note, nevertheless, that the 2014 Russian invasion of Cremea and the unwillingness of the international community to allow for Cremea to join the Russian Federation puts into serious question the international community's commitment to the principle of self-determination of peoples. See, Brad R. Roth, *The Virtues of Bright Lines: Self-Determination, Secession and External Intervention*, 16(3) GERMAN LAW JOURNAL 384–385 (2015).

27 Akhil R. Amar, *Of Sovereignty and Federalism* 96 YALE L.J. 1425 (1987).

28 On the term "Westphalian community" see John Erik Fossum, *Citizenship, Diversity, and Pluralism: The Case of the European Union, in* CITIZENSHIP, DIVERSITY AND PLURALISM 203, 215 (Alan C. Cairns et al. eds., 1999).

29 THE POLITICS OF RECONCILIATION IN MULTICULTURAL SOCIETIES 1, 2 (Will Kymlicka and Bashir Bashir eds., 2008).

(contestatory), and "multicultural" democracies,[30] the latter known as the theory of multiculturalism.[31]

Multiculturalism is a theory of cultural pluralism that aims to endow minority groups the rights of recognition of their particular identities by accommodating their cultural differences.[32] The term "multicultural" and the concept of cultural diversity can be used to refer to various groups sharing "distinct customs, perspectives, or ethos"[33]—such as national minorities, indigenous peoples, gays and lesbians, and people with disabilities. However, I will focus on multiculturalism that arises from national and ethnic differences[34] in order to describe this theory's answer to the question of how and why the particular national identity of national groups within the state should be recognized by the state, in this way assessing the right to self-determination of peoples. I begin with describing the philosophical roots of the theory of multiculturalism.

The philosophical–theoretical justification for the demand that national groups within a state be both publicly and equally recognized and supported by the state is grounded in a discourse of identity and recognition, or what Charles Taylor calls "the politics of recognition."[35] This discourse analyzes the connection between individual human identity and the human need for recognition, depicted as a vital human need, in order to make a case for a group right of recognition in the public sphere.

Taylor traces the roots of the idea of individual identity back to 18th-century philosophical theories of Rousseau and Herder, who suggested that human

---

30 *Id.*

31 One of the most prominent scholars on this theory is Will Kymlicka. Some of his most central works are: LIBERALISM, COMMUNITY AND CULTURE (1989); MULTICULTURAL CITIZENSHIP: A LIBERAL THEORY OF MINORITY RIGHTS (1995) [hereinafter *Kymlicka, Multicultural Citizenship*]; THE RIGHTS OF MINORITY CULTURES (Will Kymlicka ed., 1995). For other writings on multiculturalism see, MULTICULTURALISM: EXAMINING THE POLITICS OF RECOGNITION (Amy Gutman, ed., 1994) [hereinafter *Gutman, Multiculturalism*]; Mark Lopez, THE ORIGINS OF MULTICULTURALISM IN AUSTRALIAN POLITICS (2000); Charles Taylor, *Shared and Divergent Values, in* OPTIONS FOR A NEW CANADA 53 (Ronald. L. Watts and Douglas M. Brown eds., 1991) [hereinafter *Taylor, Shared and Divergent Values*].

32 Kymlicka, Multicultural Citizenship, *supra* note 31, 10 (1995). See also, Gutman, Multiculturalism, *supra* note 31, 4.

33 Kymlicka, Multicultural Citizenship, *supra* note 31, 18.

34 *Id.*

35 Charles Taylor, *The Politics of Recognition,* in Gutman, Multiculturalism, *supra* note 31, 26 [hereinafter *Taylor, The Politics of Recognition*].

beings are endowed with a moral sense, an intuitive feeling about right and wrong, that determines their "inner voice," their authenticity.[36] Rousseau emphasized individual peoples' moral contact with themselves; Herder, who also argued that one's loyalty to oneself implies being true to one's own originality, applied this idea to the discussion of groups' identity.[37] According to Herder, in the same way that individuals should be true to their own identities, peoples should be true to their cultural identity.[38]

Yet, the importance of identity, be it individual or group, is not formed in isolation, but rather publicly: through dialogue and exchange with others, or more precisely, what philosopher and psychologist George Herbert Mead calls "significant others" (i.e., those others who matter to us).[39] Therefore, the formation of an identity is, in fact, strongly affected by the reaction of significant others or the public to this identity, which can either demean and project an inferior image or uplift and forge a positive image among the group members.[40]

The theory of personal and group identity generated the importance of equal recognition and was applied in the political public sphere in two different ways. On the one hand, and connected with the modern emphasis on equal dignity to all human beings, equal recognition was expressed, as in classic liberalism, by the principle of universal equality. On the other hand, equal recognition created the "politics of difference," which demanded, in a sense, the opposite: that is, individuals should not always be endowed with an equal set of rights and immunities, but should rather be recognized for their unique identities and their group's distinctions from other groups.[41]

According to the politics of difference, the liberal principle of equal respect demanding blindness to difference negates the idea of identity, as it "forc[es] people into a homogenous mould untrue to them."[42] Moreover, neutrality is an unrealistic ideal, as the mould that is created by the supposedly set of difference-blind principles reflects, in fact, the homogenous dominant culture.[43] Multiculturalism, then, objects to the idea that ethnic or national minorities should be assimilated into the dominant culture of their state, and supports

36 *Id.*, 28–29.

37 *Id.*, 31.

38 *Id.*

39 *Id.*, 34.

40 *Id.*, 36.

41 *Id.*, 37–38. See also, Iris M. Young, Inclusion and Democracy 180, 225 (2000).

42 Taylor, The Politics of Recognition, *supra* note 35, 43.

43 *Id.*

the concept of "deep diversity"[44] between the several groups that compose a specific society by adapting policies of recognition, acceptance, and integration of different cultures.[45] In addition, discrimination is redefined as requiring differential treatment of various groups and not, as classic liberalism demands, blindness to the differences between individuals.[46]

The politics of difference, hence, stresses the crucial role of cultural membership in a person's self-identity and in enabling people to lead a good life, according to their choices. "A secure cultural context" is a precondition for "giv[ing] meaning and guidance to [people's] choices in life."[47] As Margalit and Raz summarize,

> Cultural membership has a high social profile, in the sense that it affects how others perceive and respond to us, which in turn shapes our self-identity... Hence, cultural identity provides an anchor for [people's] self-identification and the safety of effortless secure belonging.[48]

Yet, as explained earlier, while cultural membership refers to a wide range of group-belonging, I will focus on membership in a national or an ethnic group, which Kymlicka identifies as "societal cultures." Societal culture endows its members' lives with meaning across a broad spectrum of activities, "including social, educational, religious, recreational and economic life, encompassing both public and private spheres."[49] Therefore, societal cultures have "a shared vocabulary" of social life embodied in practices that cover most areas of human activity and they are usually concentrated in a specific territory and share a common language.[50]

Societal culture represents an individual's only means of access to a range of meaningful options, and in this sense, individual choice is, in fact, dependent on societal culture; this is because in order to understand the meaning of a social practice (and to decide whether to adopt it as a way of life) one

44 Taylor, Shared and Divergent Values, *supra* note 31, 75–76.

45 Lopez, *supra* note 31, 2–3.

46 Taylor, The Politics of Recognition, *supra* note 35, 39.

47 Gutman, Multiculturalism, *supra* note 31, 4.

48 Avishai Margalit and Joseph Raz, *National Self-Determination*, 87(9) THE JOURNAL OF PHILOSOPHY 436–461(1990), cited by Kymlicka, Multicultural Citizenship, *supra note* 31, 89.

49 Kymlicka, Multicultural Citizenship, *supra* note 31, 76.

50 *Id.*

must understand "the shared vocabulary of tradition and convention... [that is,] understand the language and history which constitute that vocabulary."[51]

Societal cultures can be those of either national minorities or ethnic groups. National minorities are previously self-governing, territorially concentrated cultures integrated within a larger state; these minorities usually wish to preserve themselves as distinct societies alongside the majority culture and hence demand various forms of self-government.[52] In this way, the application of multiculturalism towards national minorities requires allowing them internal self-determination. Ethnic groups, made up of immigrants who require that their ethnic identity be recognized by the state to which they immigrated, do not seek self-governance but rather demand that the institutions and laws of the main society be adapted to acknowledge their cultural diversity.[53]

The preservation of societal cultures requires the establishment of "group-differentiated citizenship,"[54] which means accommodating cultural differences through the protection of civil and political rights of individuals, albeit in a group-like manner.[55] That is, applying group-specific measures to accommodate national and ethnic differences: self-government rights to accommodate national differences; polyethnic rights to accommodate ethnic differences; and special representation rights to accommodate both national and ethnic differences.[56]

Self-government rights are forms of political autonomy or territorial jurisdiction; one such is federalism, a system in which power is divided between a central government and regional subdivisions. Polyethnic rights secure the free expression of minorities' cultural particularities without it impeding their integration within the economic and political institutions of the dominant culture; that is, polyethnic rights are intended for integration rather than self-governance.[57] Special-representation rights are applied to accommodate both ethnic and national differences, as they require proportional representation or more inclusiveness in political parties.[58] Special-representation rights, thus, are a form of self-governance, as they guarantee national minorities representation on any body that can interpret or modify political or social rights.[59]

---

51 *Id.*, 83.
52 *Id.*, 10–11.
53 *Id.*
54 *Id.*, 35.
55 *Id.*, 26.
56 *Id.*, 26–27, 31–32.
57 *Id.*, 30–31.
58 *Id.*, 32.
59 *Id.*, 32–33.

All of the above described mechanisms—self-government, polyethnic, and special-representation rights—are forms of embodying a culture in the social life through institutionalization.[60] In democratic states this institutionalization requires that the state be obligated to help groups preserve their culture against intrusions of majoritarian or mass cultures by adapting policies that acknowledge cultural particularities by public institutions.[61] One such means of this political and institutionalized recognition of cultural differences is, as mentioned above, the political system of governance of federalism—which I will discuss in the next chapter.

In conclusion to this theoretical discussion of multiculturalism, I will note two things. First, I have presented and analyzed the theory of multiculturalism from the perspective of its relevance to questions of solidarity and living together in multinational societies, and not with the intention of discussing all of its various related issues and criticism. For example, I did not consider the question of the tolerance (or limits thereof) of group practices, nor the important question of whether group-differential rights tend to impose internal restriction on group-members.[62] Because such issues are more relevant to ethnic minorities than national minorities, their full analysis is beyond the scope of this book.[63]

The second and final note refers to the connection between the phenomenon of societal cultures and the issue of national solidarity I discussed in the first chapter. Societal cultures are a product of modernization in which a common culture is diffused throughout a society. As Kymlicka notes, "[T]his occurs for a variety of reasons… [among which is] a high level of solidarity within modern democratic states."[64] The importance of solidarity among compatriots expressed through their feelings of allegiance and belonging to a state—which I argued in the previous chapter is a crucial element of national societies—is therefore intensified within the concepts of multiculturalism and societal cultures. What emanates from both discussions is that solidarity among compatriots is essential in forging a common national identity. However, the questions remain whether and how various national groups living in the same state can create a common identity while belonging to different cultural societies. The first step in answering these questions comes in the next chapter, as I turn to discuss the political regime of federalism.

---

60 *Id.*, 76.

61 Gutman, Multiculturalism, *supra* note 31, 4–5.

62 Kymlicka, Multiculutral Citizenship, *supra* note 31, 38.

63 For an analysis of these questions see, for example, *id.*, 38–44, 152–172.

64 *Id.*, 77.

CHAPTER 3

Federalism and Three Case Studies: Canada, Belgium, and Spain

The previous chapter looked at multiculturalism as the ideological basis for the political regime of federalism. Federalism, in turn, sustains minorities' rights for self-governance or autonomy and polyethnic rights that guarantee financial support and legal and political protection from the state for certain practices of those minorities.[1] In this chapter, I will show that federalism sets a political framework both for securing the development of identity, culture, and interests of minorities and for integrating them within the state rather than encouraging segregation. Nevertheless, I will argue that federalism is not a panacea for the problem of how to foster a complex or hyphened identity for national minorities. I will point out its disadvantages and cleavages through the analysis of three case studies: Canada, Belgium, and Spain.

Federalism, which usually means territorial federalism,[2] is a political system or structure that was formed primarily in the West[3] in the 20th century.[4] In some multinational states, the purpose of federalism was to answer the demands of national minorities for self-government in the form of territorial autonomy, allowing "the creation of regional political units, controlled by the national minority, with substantial (and constitutionally protected) powers of self-government."[5] However, federalism is a system that also allows minorities to have it both ways: on the one hand, it enables "territorially concentrated

---

1 Will Kymlicka, MULTICULTURAL CITIZENSHIP: A LIBERAL THEORY OF MINORITY RIGHTS 6–7 (1995) [hereinafter *Kymlicka, Multicultural Citizenship*].

2 This meaning of federalism will also be applied in this chapter, unless otherwise noted.

3 But also in India and in Mexico, for example. See, Alexander Yacobson and Amnon Rubinstein, ISRAEL AND THE FAMILY OF NATIONS, 158–162 (2010); J. Lloyd Mecham, *The Origins of Federalism in Mexico*, 18(2) THE HISPANIC AMERICAN HISTORICAL REVIEW 164 (1938). There are also forms of quasi-federal systems of devolution of powers. For a discussion of such examples see Will Kymlicka, *Justice and Security*, *in* ETHNICITY, NATIONALISM, AND MINORITY RIGHTS 144, 147 (Stephen May, Tariq Modood, and Judith Squires eds., 2004) [hereinafter *Kymlicka, Justice and Security*].

4 Kymlicka, Justice and Security, *supra* note 3, 146.

5 *Id.* Note, however, that there are federal states such as the United States and Germany in which federalism serves to divide sovereignty between political units within the state without allowing special sovereign authorities to minorities groups.

 | DOI 10.1163/9789004294332_005

minorities...to exercise autonomy or self-determination on matters crucial to their identity and continued existence, without the fear of being overridden or vetoed by the majority group";[6] and on the other hand, it enables those minorities to participate in a larger political entity and to enjoy the economic, social or other benefits that such an arrangement provides for.[7]

Federal systems come in different forms, and I shall describe three systems in more depth in this chapter. Nevertheless, three characteristics are common to all kinds of federal systems: (i) ensuring minorities territorial autonomy; (ii) protecting minorities' right to equal recognition in the public sphere; and (iii) allowing minorities veto rights over certain decisions.[8]

With regard to territorial autonomy, federalism, although it accepts nationalism as a concept that is supported by the philosophy of communitarianism, suggests that small communities can exist within larger communities. Through the principle of territorial autonomy, then, federalism serves the purpose of forging communities and stresses the importance of nurturing the culture of a political community to enable social life.[9]

The other two principles of federalism—equal public recognition and veto rights—are mechanisms that address potential inequalities between the minority and majority communities, allowing for the integration of those minorities within the larger community, that is, the state. The right to equal recognition in the public sphere, discussed also in the previous chapter, derives from the understanding that the construction of the public sphere creates disadvantages for people with different identities, ways of life, and tastes.[10] The formal

6 Richard Simeon and Daniel-Patrick Conway, *Federalism and the Management of Conflict in Multinational Societies, in* MULTINATIONAL DEMOCRACIES 338, 339 (Alain-G. Gagnon, James Tully eds., 2001).

7 *Id.*, 340. On the other hand, federalism can be seen as a destabilizing force that could lead to dissolution, as was the case in the former Soviet Union. For the possible implications of federalism in Ukraine, see, Oleh Protsyk, Majority-Minority Relations in Ukraine, 1 EUR. ETHNOPOLITICS & MINORITY ISSUES 8 (2008). I thank Dr. Yaniv Roznai for this note.

8 This description of the characteristics of federalism is based on Kymlicka, Justice and security, *supra note* 3, 147–148 and Charles E. Ehrlich, *Democratic Alternatives to Ethnic Conflict: Consociationalism and Neoseparatism*, 26 BROOKLYN J. INT'L L. 447, 453 (2000). However, what I call "equal recognition in the public sphere" is described by Kymlicka as the state's conferring an official status to the minority's language. See, Kymlicka, Justice and Security, *supra* note 3, 148.

9 Alain-G. Gagnon, *The Moral Foundations of Asymmetrical Federalism: A Normative Exploration of the Case of Quebec and Canada, in* MULTINATIONAL DEMOCRACIES, *supra note* 6, 319, 325.

10 Alan Patten, *Liberal Citizenship in Multinational Societies, in* MULTINATIONAL DEMOCRACIES, *supra* note 6, 285.

language, the official curriculum of the education system, national symbols, the national holidays and days of rest, and the content of broadcasting in national media usually all carry advantages for the majority culture and disadvantages for the minorities' culture.[11] By ensuring a right to equal public recognition, more than one dominant culture is to be "affirmed, accommodated and promoted"[12] by the public institutions and mechanisms of the state.[13] Within such a system, the official languages can be those of the most significant cultural or national communities of the state, and the education system and official media may include the history, culture, or literature of more than one dominant culture.

Iris M. Young takes the concept of equal recognition in the public sphere further and suggests that

> recognition…is more a condition for political discussion and decision-making than one of its goals. It affirms the need for group based organization and voice at the same time that it expresses openness to listening to others and engaging with them in shared public spaces.[14]

Young's ideal of differentiated solidarity "specifically recognizes the obligation of collective action to undermine injustice…among strangers who dwell in a region."[15] Accordingly,

> everyone [should have] their home place, the place of their immediate residence and local community participation [while] no one [would] feel that another part of the city or region is closed to him or her, however, because of the behavior and attitude of its residents.[16]

This concept is related to Young's understanding of the principle of self-determination as one of relational autonomy or non-discrimination, under which "self-determining peoples understand themselves as constituted in

---

11 *Id.*, 286.

12 *Id.*

13 Indeed, the question of what is to be considered "equal" is also important but is beyond the scope of this chapter. We can use Patten's observation that "our intuitions about what constitutes equality in different cases will at least allow us to identify serious inequalities, even if finely tuned discriminations are more controversial." See, *id.*, 287.

14 Iris M. Young, Inclusion and Democracy 180, 225 (2000).

15 *Id.*, 224.

16 *Id.*, 226.

relation to one another [and] recognize that there are many respects in which they live and act together with others."[17] Young's understanding of self-determination as non-domination rather than non-interference[18] thus creates a notion of integration, rather than segregation, of cultures, based on the idea that "because a people stands in interdependent relations with others…a people cannot ignore the claims and interests of those others when the former's actions potentially affect the later."[19]

Federalism sustains the right to equal recognition in the public sphere through several possible means. Some federal states, such as Belgium and Canada, recognize two or three languages as their official languages[20]—some of them going so far as to allow several official texts of the national anthems in these languages.[21] Another way that the right to equal public recognition is federally protected is through state support of the education systems of minorities' communities.[22]

Federal implementation of the right to equal recognition in the public sphere can thus acquire either a more rigid or a more flexible sense of integration, as suggested by Young. In the former, federalism makes all, or at least the dominant, cultures in a specific state visible and present in the public sphere in order to create a combination of them.[23] In its more flexible sense, the right to equal recognition creates a dialogue among all relevant cultures, enabling and respecting the space each culture requires to "dwell" within the overall space of the state.[24] In this sense, recognition is a condition for dialogue rather than one of its goals.[25] Respect for each culture's space is supported and entrenched by the principle that gives minorities veto rights over some of majority decisions, aimed at preventing the majority from ignoring the specific interests of minorities' communities.

---

17 *Id.*, 259.

18 *Id.*

19 *Id.*

20 In Canada, French and English. See, Official Languages Act (R.S.C., c. 31 (4th Supp.) (1985)). In Belgium, the official languages are French, Dutch and German. See, Loi concernant le régime linguistique dans l'enseignement [An Act respecting the language regulations in education], 30 juillet 1963, 22 août 1963, 8210 [Belg.].

21 Such is the case in Belgium and Canada. South Africa's national anthem is composed of the state's five official languages. See discussion in the fifth chapter.

22 Kymlicka, Justice and Security, *supra* note 3, 148.

23 The analysis of the Canadian flag case in the fifth chapter will serve to illustrate how the cultures of different communities can be combined.

24 Young, *supra* note 14, 225.

25 *Id.*

Having presented the general structure of federalism with regard to how it ensures the existence and development of minority communities, I will examine how this goal is realized. I will examine three case studies with the aim of assessing the achievements of the goals of federalism in each case.

Canada

Canada was established as an independent confederation in 1867, at that time made up of four provinces: Ontario, Quebec, Nova Scotia, and New Brunswick.[26] Canada is considered one of the oldest and most stable federations;[27] however, the difficult relationship between English-speaking and French-speaking Canadians (the latter mainly in Quebec) has led to instability in this country.[28]

Quebec's nationalism can be traced back to the establishment of Canada as a confederation and explained by "the compact theory." According to this theory, confederation is described as a compact of provinces, and in the Canadian case it was interpreted as a compact between two nations, French Canadians and English Canadians, "in which each affirmed the right of the other to live according to its own culture."[29]

However, Quebec nationalism took a practical form only in the 1960s during the "Quiet Revolution,"[30] through which Quebec "sought the right as a founding nation to have an equality of opportunity...and equal recognition as one of the founding nations."[31] This political trend resulted in the establishment

26 Today Canada is composed of ten provinces and three territories: Alberta, British Columbia, Manitoba, New Bruswick, Newfoundland and Labrador, Nova Scotia, Ontario, Prince Edward Island, Quebec, Saskatchewan, Northwest Territories, Nunavut, and Yukon.

27 Simeon and Conway, *supra* note 6, 342.

28 *Id.*

29 S.V. La Selva, *The Moral Foundations of Canadian Federalism: Paradoxes, Achievements, and Tragedies of Nationhood*, cited in Jean-Francois Gaudreault-DesBiens, *The Quebec Secession Reference and the Judicial Arbitration of Conflicting Narratives About Law, Democracy and Identity*, 23 Vt. L. Rev. 793, 806 (1999).

30 Henry S. Albinski, *Politics and Biculturalism in Canada: The Flag Debate*, The Australian Journal of Politics and History 169, 172 (1967). For the claim that Quebec's nationalist and separatist motivations are rooted in the differences between the Anglo and French historical narrative and ethos of Canada, see, Gaudreault-DesBiens, *supra* note 29, 793.

31 Albinsky, *supra* note 30, 172.

of the Parti Québécois, a political party with the goal of Quebec's independence.[32] This initiated a destabilization of the Canadian federal system, demanding significant changes in its structure.[33]

The Quiet Revolution was intended to change the "confederation bargain of 1867"—which, although giving Quebec significant autonomy in linguistic, social, and cultural affairs, had left the economy and national politics largely in the hands of English Canadians.[34] Trends of modernism and secularism led Quebec governments to demand more power and to resist federal intrusions.[35] These developments were accompanied by, on the one hand, a strengthening of political "Québécois" identity, and, on the other hand, a strong Quebec presence in the federal government, including the fact that three of the eight prime ministers since 1968 have been from Quebec.[36]

But not all the trends generated by this strengthening of a national Québécois identity have been secessionist. The adoption of the new Canadian flag in 1965, for example, evidenced a unifying effort. This initiative—to adopt a new Canadian maple leaf flag in place of the British Union Jack—was led by liberal party member Lester B. Pearson, who was promoting a concept of "unity... [that should] be based on two races, cultures, traditions and languages; on a full and equal partnership of English and French-speaking Canadians."[37] Indeed, the adoption of the flag was a long process, and it awakened debate in the Canadian public in general and in Quebec in particular over the questions of whether unity between the national communities in Canada could be achieved artificially by the flag, and whether neutral symbols or a combination of representative symbols of both communities should be chosen for that purpose.[38] It also demanded political compromises on behalf of all the parties, and especially among Quebec parties.[39] Despite all of this, however, a unifying flag was finally adopted, and further unifying efforts have been made through the 1982 Patriation of Canada's constitution and the adoption of the Charter of Rights and Freedoms, which rendered the French language equal to

32 Simeon and Conway, *supra* note 6, 342.

33 *Id.*

34 *Id.*, 344.

35 *Id.*

36 *Id.*

37 Albinski, *supra* note 30, 172.

38 The Union Jack for the English-speaking Canadian community and the *fleur de-lis* for the French-speaking community. For a comprehensive discussion of the flag debate see *id.*, and chapter five of this book.

39 Albinski, *supra* note 30, 181–188.

English[40] and gave Quebec representation in the Supreme Court.[41] However, the fact that Quebec was not a party to the agreement[42] left secessionist trends unappeased.

The "Meech Lake Accord" of 1987, proposed by then Prime Minister Brian Mulroney, intended to add more authority to the province of Quebec by recognizing it as a "Distinct Society within Canada [and] placing some limits on the power of the federal government to intervene in provincial jurisdiction";[43] however, when the other provinces objected to the idea that Quebec was a unique and not an equal province, the accord failed and thus did not become law[44]—again strengthening secessionist and independent trends in Quebec. A following proposal to amend the Canadian Constitution and to include the explicit recognition of Quebec's distinctiveness in Canada (that is, the Charlottetown Accord of 1992) also failed when rejected by referenda in Quebec and in the other provinces.[45]

The failure of the Meech Lake Agreement and the Charlottetown Accord intensified the division between French and English Canadians in Canada and encouraged secessionist trends in Quebec.[46] Quebecers interpreted this failure as a refusal, on the part of the English Canadians, to allow for different interpretations of Canadian identity; hence, a clash of narratives between Francophones and Anglophones emerged.[47] Since then, through the second referendum on secession in 1995 and the Supreme Court's ensuing decision that Quebec had no unilateral right to secede from the state,[48] many French Quebecers have increasingly identified with their own provincial government, referring to it as their "national" government.[49]

It seems that federalism itself cannot be blamed for the secessionist tendencies in Canada,[50] as the institutions of federalism remained unchanged from the time of Canada's inception to the Quiet Revolution. It is more likely,

40 Gaudreault-DesBiens, *supra* note 29, 816.

41 Simeon and Conway, *supra* note 6, 342.

42 *Id.*

43 *Id.*

44 Gaudreault-DesBiens, *supra* note 29, 811.

45 *Id.*; Simeon and Conway, *supra* note 6, 343.

46 Gaudreault-DesBiens, *supra* note 6, 812.

47 *Id.*

48 Yet, the Canadian Supreme Court conditioned its ruling upon the obligation of negotiating with Quebec in case the Quebecers had voted for sovereignty. See, Re Secession of Quebec, [1998] 2 S.C.R 217 (Can.) 130 [hereinafter *Secession of Quebec Case*] 88.

49 Gaudreault-DesBiens, *supra* note 29, 812.

50 Simeon and Conway, *supra* note 6, 344.

therefore, that economic and social changes—urbanization, industrialization, and secularization—have generated these trends.[51] Furthermore, the adoption of the Charter of the Rights and Freedoms in 1982 strengthened the process of democratization, rendering the political elite less and less dominant—and thus lessening the influence of the federal system and the provincial governments.[52] This increasingly influential "mobilization from below"[53] influenced the failure of agreements between federal and provincial governments, such as the Meech Lake agreement and the Charlottetown Accord.[54]

Kymlicka claims that democratic federalism reduces the likelihood of secession by allowing representation of secessionist voices on the democratic platform—spread for all participants in the democratic procedure.[55] Nevertheless, in Canada federalism has been an integral part of the political trends of secessionism, as it supplied the infrastructure for political forces to pursue their initiatives and goals.[56] Moreover, the Canadian model of federalism, in which each provincial government is a "self-contained system" with an independent financial basis, will likely promote more bargaining and competitive trends than integrative and cooperative ones.[57] This model of "divided federalism"—with strong independent provinces, weak intergovernmental connections, and low representation of important regions in the government[58]—enhances sectarian rather than integrative trends.

Quebec has not yet attempted to secede from Canada. However, despite the unified flag, Canada's federalism seems to support Charles Taylor's description of "a participatory model in which a single national identity cannot be developed primarily due to the distinctiveness of Quebec."[59] In this sense, federalism in Canada expresses the idea of the federal state as a decentralizing force and a community of communities, in which "member states act as the primary political expressions of popular will."[60]

---

51 *Id.*

52 *Id.*, 345.

53 *Id.*

54 *Id.*

55 Kymlicka, Justice and Security, *supra* note 3, 164.

56 Simeon and Conway, *supra* note 6, 345.

57 *Id.*

58 *Id.*, 346.

59 Alain-G. Gagnon, *The Moral Foundations of Asymmetrical Federalism: A Normative Exploration of the Case of Quebec and Canada*, *in* MULTINATIONAL DEMOCRACIES, *supra note* 6, 319, 334.

60 *Id.*, 335.

Belgium

Belgium, which was founded in 1830 as a constitutional, democratic modern state,[61] has been federalized since 1970 in the form of a consociational democracy.[62] Belgium's society was originally composed of two major national communities: the French-speaking Walloons in the south of Belgium and the Dutch-speaking Flemings in the north. Another small linguistic minority—German-speaking—in the north has also been recognized as a distinct community with the devolution of political authorities that began in 1970.[63]

The nationalisms of the Flemings and Walloons were awakened and expressed in different forms, which I will explore further later. However, it was the demands for autonomy that these communities presented—cultural autonomy for the Flemings and economic autonomy for the Walloons (in the early 20th century)—that motivated the turning of Belgium in 1970 into a federal state of entities with partially overlapping territories: communities and regions.[64] According to the reformed constitution of 1970, Belgium was transformed into a federal state, with three communities in different territories: a French-speaking community in Wallonia; Dutch- and German-speaking communities in Flanders; and the bilingual region of Brussels.[65] The changes thus officially recognized four linguistic regions—the Walloon, Flemish, and German regions and Brussels (a bilingual region)—with territorial jurisdiction over economic and social issues, and three cultural communities whose community councils had jurisdiction over cultural affairs.[66] In the following passages I will describe the process that buttressed these outcomes.

The linguistic border between the French- and Dutch-speaking communities in Belgium has early historic origins.[67] The withdrawal of Roman settlers in the fourth and fifth centuries from southern territories left these Latinized;

61 Louis Vos, *Reconstructions of the Past in Belgium and Flanders*, *in* SECESSION, HISTORY AND THE SOCIAL SCEINCES 179, 180 (Bruno Coppieters and Michel Huysseune eds., 2002).

62 Robert Mnookin and Alain Verbeke, *Group-Conflict Resolution: Sources of Resistance to Reconciliation: Persistent Nonviolent Conflict with No Reconciliation: The Flemish and Walloons in Belgium*, 72 LAW & CONTEMP. PROB. 151, 168 (2009).

63 Simeon and Conway, *supra* note 6, 348.

64 Frank Delmartino, Hugues Dumont, Sébastian Van Droghenbroeck, *Kingdom of Belgium*, *in* 7 A GLOBAL DIALOGUE ON FEDERALISM: DIVERSITY AND UNITY IN FEDERAL COUNTRIES 48–49 (Luis Moreno and César Colino eds., 2010).

65 Mnookin and Verbekee, *supra* note 62, 198; Simeon and Conway, *supra* note 6, 348.

66 Vos, *supra* note 61, 198; Simeon and Conway, *supra* note 6, 348.

67 Delmartino, Dumont and Van Droghenbroeck, *supra* note 64, 53.

whereas the northern part of the country, under the influence of Frankish tribes, was Germanized.[68] Since the Middle Ages and until the 19th century, French has been the predominant language spoken by the political and cultural elite, first in Burgundian Netherlands and later in Belgium.[69] The annexation of what is the current Belgian territory to France between 1795 and 1815 emphasized French dominance, especially for the governing class.[70] The fact that most Flemings in the north of Belgium were Dutch speaking was blurred by Belgian's struggle for independence from the brief Dutch rule (1815–1830), as the Belgians were aiming at a common national identity.[71]

French economic, political, and cultural dominance proceeded until the Flemish national awakening in the 19th century.[72] While the Flemish movement originated as early as the emergence of the Belgian state, the Flemish movement in the mid-19th century had more cultural goals than political ones.[73] Its leaders were intellectuals who aimed to preserve the Flemish culture and language without placing any political demands on the government to secure their goals.[74] In addition, the Flemish movement was quite weak through the 40 first years of Belgium's independence due to the area's impoverishment. Moreover, the Belgian governing elites, even in Flanders, were French speaking.[75]

In the second half of the 19th century the Flemish movement became rooted more deeply in the Flemish rural public, and it emerged as a political movement with practical demands on the government.[76] From the 1870s, Flemish culture and language gradually gained more influence and recognition in Belgian administration and education systems.[77] In 1898, Dutch was recognized as an official language of the Belgian nation, alongside French.[78] These achievements were due to the emergence of Flemish political parties, such as the Catholic party in 1884, and the establishment of the mainstream

---

68 *Id.*

69 *Id.*; Vos, *supra* note 61, 183–184.

70 Delmartino, Dumont and Van Droghenbroeck, *supra* note 64, 54.

71 *Id.*

72 Vos, *supra* note 61, 183.

73 R.E.M Irving, *The Flemings and Walloons of Belgium*, MINORITY GROUP RIGHTS REPORT No. 46, 1980, 7; Delmartino, Dumont and Van Droghenbroeck, *supra* note 64, 54.

74 Irving, *supra* note 73, 7; Delmartino, Dumont and Van Droghenbroeck, *supra* note 64, 54.

75 Irving, *supra* note 74, 7.

76 *Id.*, 8.

77 Vos, *supra* note 61, 184.

78 *Id.*, 187.

Flemish movement, the Vlaamsch Nationaal Verbond (VNV), in 1933.[79] During the First World War, the VNV became prominent as a distinctive political movement with anti-unifying tendencies.[80] Belgian's unified national identity was further eroded in the post–Second World War period. Small Flemish groups and factions that intended to keep Flemish nationalism alight amalgamated in 1954 into the radical Flemish national party, the Volksunie, which propagated the idea of *federalism à deux*, that is, a federal state based on the two regions of Flanders and Wallonia with greater autonomy for Flanders.[81]

A reinforcement of the Volksunie in the 1960s was the result of increasing improvements in the economy and demographics in Flanders in comparison to Wallonia.[82] The Flemings saw a potential to dominate Belgium; however, this required stopping both the spread of French influence into Flemish territories and the expansion of Brussels into the surrounding Flemish country-side.[83] To this end, the Flemings demanded a language frontier between Flanders and Wallonia.[84] These demands were fulfilled with the languages laws of 1962–1963 and constitutional revisions introduced between 1967 and 1971 that "marked the end of the traditional unitary structure of the Belgian state."[85] Yet, it was not only the Flemings but also the Walloons that encouraged sectarianism in Belgium. While Francophone nationalism in Belgium is traditionally depicted as a reaction to the threat to French dominance posed by the Flemish national movement and by Flanders' growing economic strength, other data shows that Walloon nationalism is almost as old as its Flemish counterpart.[86] Like the Flemish nationalist movements, but with the advantage of having the upper hand in terms of linguistic and cultural dominance in the new kingdom of Belgium, the Walloons also focused on linguistic and cultural goals, and intended to ensure that French was the *lingua franca* in Belgium.[87] Yet, the fortification of the Flemish national movement and Flanders area pushed the Walloons into a gradually increasing defensive position.[88] Towards the end of the 19th

79 Irving, *supra* note 73, 8.
80 *Id.*, 7. See also Vos, *supra* note 61, 189–190.
81 Vos, *supra* note 61, 196. And see also Irving, *supra* note 73, 9.
82 Irving, *supra* note 73, 9.
83 *Id.*
84 *Id.*
85 *Id.*
86 *Id.*, 10.
87 *Id.*
88 *Id.*

century, Walloons were willing to accept the Flemings' demands for formal acknowledgment of Dutch in Belgium, even though insisting that French remained the main language of Belgium.[89] From the end of the 19th century and until the mid-20th century, the Walloon movement came and went in response to the strengthening and weakening of the Flemish national demands.[90] With the deterioration in the Walloon economy, which worsened significantly in the 1950s, the Walloon regionalists added a social motivation to their agenda and used it as a plank to demand federalism; these trends were fortified in the 1960s and 1970s with the establishment of parties committed to the defence of Francophone interests.[91]

In response to both Flemish and Walloon sectarian tendencies, the government tried to pacify the situation by creating single-language areas[92]—Brussels became officially bilingual, and in some municipalities in Flanders and Wallonia close to Brussels or adjacent to the language border, special arrangements were introduced for the other language group.[93] However, these new policies, far from fixing the cleavage, rather deepened it. The increasing popularity of the regional and language parties in Flanders and Wallonia and the change in the perception of national identity resulted in changes in the state structures. In 1970, the constitution was reformed and Belgium was transformed into a federal state, with three communities in different territories and four linguistic regions with territorial jurisdiction over economic and social issues, and three cultural communities whose community councils had jurisdiction over cultural affairs.[94]

In 1977 and 1978 two political agreements were concluded between the then four-party coalitions (Social Christians, Socialists, Volksunie and FDF [*Front Democratic des Francophones*]). The agreements determined the division of authorities between the Parliament and the Senate and the establishment of the Regional Councils, which are effectively regional parliaments with a government and a prime minister.[95] The Community Councils that were also established by the agreements received authorities in the fields of culture, education, and health.[96]

89 *Id.*

90 *Id.*

91 *Id.*, 10–11.

92 *Id.*

93 *Id.*

94 Vos, *supra* note 61, 198; Simeon and Conway, *supra* note 6, 348.

95 Simeon and Conway, *supra* note 6, 349.

96 Irving, *supra* note 73, 12.

In 1980, 1988, and 1993, further constitutional reforms allowed for greater autonomy for the regions and communities,[97] and in 1993 Belgium was fully federalized.[98] The constitution defined Belgium as a "federal state, composed [as the above described agreements determined] of Communities and Regions, each of which will henceforth have its own government and prime minister."[99] Currently, the political structure is made up of five councils or parliaments and five governments. However, the Flemish side has only one government and parliament for both region and community, while the German and French communities and the Walloon and Brussels regions have their own bodies.[100] All residual powers have been transferred to the regional and community governments, while "the federal level maintained responsibilities for justice, defence, social security and the Belgian economic and monetary union."[101]

At the national level, the regime functions as a consociational democracy established upon three pillars: mutual veto, proportionality, and segmental autonomy.[102] The cabinet has seven francophone and seven Dutch-speaking ministers and secretaries of state, and a majority in each language group as well as a two-thirds majority in the cabinet are needed to amend any legislation of state organization.[103] Since the Flemings are the majority community in Belgium,[104] the state created a number of mechanisms—including required linguistic majorities for special laws, equal representation in the national government, and a multiparty political system—to prevent Flemish domination through majority rule.[105]

The aim of the federal system in Belgium is to settle the three major issues contributing to the cleavages within Belgian society: the national-linguistic conflict between Flemings and Walloons; Walloon nationalism versus Flanders and Brussels on socio-economic grievances; and the identity of Brussels.[106] Nationalistic identities are formed upon the language issue,[107] which divides

97 Vos, *supra* note 61, 198.

98 Simeon and Conway, *supra* note 6, 349.

99 *Id.*, 349–350.

100 Vos, *supra* note 61, 198.

101 Simeon and Conway, *supra* note 6, 350.

102 Ehrlich, *supra* note 8, 453.

103 Simeon and Conway, *supra* note 6, 350.

104 Composing about 60 percent of the Belgian population. See, *the Kingdom of Belgium*, CultureGrams, World Edition 2010, <http://education.uky.edu/OFE/sites/education.uky.edu.OFE/files/documents/CultureGram-Belgium1.pdf>.

105 Mnookin and Verbeke, *supra* note 62, 161.

106 Simeon and Conway, *supra* note 6, 347.

107 Mnookin and Verbeke, *supra* note 62, 168.

Belgian society between those, particularly Flanders, wanting greater autonomy and devolution to a confederate system and those, particularly Walloons, objecting to further moves toward regional or communal autonomy.[108] The Flemings wish to observe the principle of territoriality with respect to language rights, while the Francophones would prefer language rights to be attached to the persons of citizens, entitling them to speak their own language in dealings with governments.[109]

The linguistic conflict is enhanced by the conflict surrounding Brussels, which is central to the general Flemish/Walloon friction due to Brussels' "physical location, its history and its growth."[110] Brussels is located in Flanders, and in the 19th century most of its inhabitants were Flemings; however, over the years Brussels has become francophone.[111] Because of its importance to both communities, Brussels was set as a separate bilingual region with several anti-majoritarian rules, similar to those in the national government structure, to protect the Flemish minority within Brussels from francophone domination.[112]

However, the Flemings feared that even though they constituted the majority of Belgium's population, the increasing number of Francophones acquiring homes in the surrounding areas would result in two regions for French-speaking Belgians and only one region for Dutch-speaking Belgians.[113] Brussels has extended well beyond its official borders of the Capital Region, with "the nineteen communes of Greater Brussels creating a largely French-speaking island in Flemish territory."[114] This stretched the language border, so that even though Dutch was the official language in these suburban areas, French speakers in Brussels wished to obtain full social and educational facilities in those communes outside Greater Brussels where they constituted a majority.[115] Indeed, some of the municipalities received linguistic "facilities" entitling French-speaking people living there to use French in dealings with municipal authorities.[116] From the Flemings' point of view, this is a violation of the territorial principle, while Francophones used this arrangement to suggest that language

108 *Id.*

109 *Id.*

110 *Id.*, 169.

111 *Id.*

112 *Id.*

113 Mnookin and Verbeke, *supra* note 62, 168; Irving, *supra* note 73, 12.

114 Irving, *supra* note 73, 12.

115 Mnookin and Verbeke, *supra* note 62, 170; Irving, *supra* note 73, 12.

116 Mnookin and Verbeke, *supra* note 62, 170.

rights should adhere to the individual and be a personal privilege anywhere in Belgium.[117]

Nevertheless, Brussels itself seems to distance itself from the national movements' argument surrounding it. In recent years Brussels has become a meeting point for different linguistic communities and social classes, including various foreign cultures.[118] As a consequence, a new "Brussels identity" was formed, according to which "the average Brussels resident no longer recognizes himself or herself in these so-called movements, whether Flemings or Walloons."[119] The common language is indeed French, but the existence of institutions and services for specific linguistic communities makes Brussels culturally diverse, expressing neither French nor Flemish culture and identity.

With regard to economics, and even though the regions and communities lack general fiscal autonomy and are dependent on federal grants and shared tax revenues,[120] Flanders continues to demand more autonomy to secure economic advantage and minimize sharing wealth with the Walloons.[121] The Walloons, on the other hand, adhere to the current centralized economic regulation[122] in order to secure their economic interests.

The national conflict between the communities in Belgium is seen as unique in that "the Flemish and Walloon communities are not in fact minority nationalities seeking greater autonomy or independence but rather social movements struggling for control of the state itself."[123] In this sense, "federalism has created a dynamic of disintegration which seems to feed on itself"[124] and it is unclear whether decentralist constitutional amendments have come to an end[125] or whether secessionist trends will weaken. Indeed, the national conflict was awakened in 2005 by the "Manifesto for an Independent Flanders Within Europe," a dense report analyzing the arguments for dissolution of Belgium.[126] The report called for full independence for Flanders, which, as the wealthier region, would have to bear the burdens of the other regions that were likely to increase in the coming years.[127]

---

117 *Id.*

118 Delmartino, Dumont and Van Droghenbroeck, *supra* note 64, 54–55.

119 *Id.*, 55.

120 Mnookin and Verbeke, *supra* note 62, 169.

121 Simeon and Conway, *supra* note 6, 351.

122 *Id.*

123 *Id.*, 347.

124 *Id.*, 352.

125 *Id.*

126 Mnookin and Verbeke, *supra* note 62, 152.

127 *Id.*

Nevertheless, Belgium has not, up to the present, dissolved, and the federal structure continues to serve as the glue of the two main nationalities. Mnookin and Verbeke identify a number of the factors that are most likely to hold the country together: European integration and the European Union; Flemings fear that Brussels might be lost;[128] a strong Belgian establishment, including a national-political-party elite with experience at problem-solving negotiations;[129] and a national culture that prefers pragmatic compromise to violence.[130] This last factor suggests, in fact, that despite the discrepancies and cleavages that may persist between two different communities or nationalities,[131] some unifying cultural characteristics can be observed. I will refer back to and develop this in the fifth chapter of this book.

Spain

Spain is not formally a federal state but functions as a parliamentary democracy that allows for the regional autonomy of 17 autonomous communities;[132] despite this, I will examine its political structure with reference to federal terms and standards. The devolution of powers to the regions by the Spanish constitution of 1978 was a consequence of the major transformation of the Spanish regime after the downfall of Franco's dictatorship, which had imposed a single Spanish nationality over the entire population of Spain with one language (Castilian), proscribing any public expression of other languages and cultures.[133] With the end of Franco's regime, Spain became a democracy that aimed both to preserve the state's unity and to allow for the expression of culture and language of the different national communities composing it.[134]

---

128 See also Ehrlich's claim that Brussels "hampers the natural split of the country into Wallonia and Flanders, [because] in a complete decentralization, Brussels might tilt the balance in favor of the minority French speakers [who will have] two regions" while the Flemish will have one. Ehrlich, *supra* note 8, 456.

129 See also Vos' discussion of the continuing efforts among intellectual Belgians to foster a unified Belgian identity (*âme belge*) despite Belgium's being composed of two ethnic groups and languages. See Vos, *supra* note 61, 188.

130 Mnookin and Verbeke, *supra* note 62, 173.

131 David Miller, *Nationality in Divided Societies*, *in* MULTINATIONAL DEMOCRACIES 299, 303–307 (Alain-G. Gagnon, James Tully eds., 2001).

132 Simeon and Conway, *supra* note 6, 352; Ehrlich, *supra* note 8, 470.

133 Simeon and Conway, *supra* note 6, 352; Yakobson & Rubinstein, *supra* note 3, 167.

134 Simeon and Conway, *supra* note 6, 353.

The constitution established 17 regions and nationalities by a system called asymmetrical federalism, which provides for "a decentralization of powers and responsibilities [by means of] constitutional recognition of self-rule and cultural diversity."[135] I will analyze this political system further in this subsection following a discussion of the main national cleavages in Spain that led to it.

Two prominent conflicts between the Spanish (Castilian) central government (striving for hegemony) and national communities in Spain (hostile to state power) have both resulted in near-ruptures in Spain: the Basque-Castilian conflict[136] and the Catalan-Castilian conflict.[137] While both the Catalan and the Basque national movements were established in the 19th century, they differed in nature and activities.[138] The Basque national movement was originally more radical and sectarian than the Catalan and has turned to violence since the 1960s;[139] the Catalans were at first "mildly regionalist and pro-Spanish rather than fully nationalist"[140] and hence their actions have been more "accommodative and broadly non-violent."[141]

These distinctions notwithstanding, and despite the more anti-unitary nature of the Basque struggle for independence,[142] it was the Catalan national movement, with its separatist claims and pro-secession movements, that generated a stronger sense of national identity among the Catalans, centering on "a positive assertion of the group's culture"[143] and using the Catalan shared local language and culture as a crucial tool in forming a national identity.[144] The Basque national movement, on the other hand, was based on "negation and

---

135 Luis Moreno and César Colino, *Kingdom of Spain in Global Dialogue*, *in* 7 A Global Dialogue on Federalism: Diversity and Unity in Federal Countries, 289 (Luis Moreno and César Colino eds., 2010).

136 See generally, Daniele Conversi, The Basques, the Catalans and Spain: Alternative Routes to Nationalist Mobilisation (1997); Kenneth Medhurst, *The Basques and Catalans*, The Minority Rights Group, Report no. 9, 1987.

137 See the Declaration of Sovereignty of the Parliament of Catalonia. For an English translation see, The Parliament of Catalonia, Declaration of Sovereignty and of the Right to Decide of the People of Catalonia (22 January 2013). <http://www10.gencat.cat/gencat/binaris/declaration_of_sovereignty_tcm34-239795.pdf>.

138 Conversi, *supra* note 136, 257.

139 *Id.*, 258.

140 *Id.*, 258–259.

141 *Id.*, 259.

142 *Id.*, 222–256.

143 *Id.*, 262.

144 Medhurst, *supra* note 136, 3.

confrontation,"[145] especially since their language, *Euskara*, was extinct. Basque nationalists, then, had to protect a more vulnerable culture than Catalan, and since *Euskara* was less accessible to the Basque people, the Basque's national movement's most important leader, Sabino Arana, neglected the language as a unifying national symbol and focused on ethnicity and religion.[146]

Hence, the Catalans followed a trajectory of cultural nationalism, aiming at "becoming self-determined through language and using linguistic markers in order to disseminate among Catalans the ideal of belonging to the same Catalan nation and to achieve cultural legitimation vis-a-vis Castile,"[147] while at the same time remaining pro-Spanish. By contrast, the Basques chose a trajectory of political nationalism that aimed at separation and independence from Spain.[148] This trend of alienation on behalf of the Basque national movement was further encouraged as a reaction of the working class to industrialization in some parts of Basque territories, which in turn was promoted by a privileged upper-class minority with connections to the central government.[149]

The years of Franco's authoritarian rule contributed to the development of both the Basque and the Catalan national movements, albeit in different trajectories.[150] Franco's monopolistic regime controlled all officially recognized political life and repressed all autonomous cultural expressions.[151] The use of Catalan and Basque in public was prohibited, and the educational system was chosen as a particular target of assimilation. Hence, Basque or Catalan literature, linguistic, legal and historical studies were forbidden.[152] These decrees assisted in fortifying a common Catalan national identity among Catalans' intelligentsia and middle- classes.[153] Pro-Catalan sentiments were reaffirmed through the acute need for defence of culture and hence, "renewed assertion of the regions' distinctive cultural identity."[154] Nevertheless, as was mentioned above, the Catalans did not turn to violent protestation; neither did they encourage secession until the end of the 20th century, a tendency that will be discussed below. The Basques nationalists, in contrast, had difficulties in fostering

145 Conversi, *supra* note 136, 262.
146 *Id.*, 173; Medhurst, *supra* note 136, 3.
147 Conversi, *supra* note 136, 260.
148 *Id.*, 175.
149 Medhurst, *supra* note 136, 4–5.
150 *Id.*, 4.
151 *Id.*
152 *Id.*
153 *Id.*
154 *Id.*, 5.

their own culture, as it was "a culture in retreat."[155] Hence, the leadership of the Basque national movement was inclined to violent and militant activities as a defensive measure.[156] This continuing Basque violence constituted a threat to the reform process in Spain[157] that followed the demise of Franco's regime, and which peaked in the 1978 constitution.[158] The continuing sense of alienation from Spain that was widespread in the Basque territories encouraged nationalists that demanded complete independence.[159]

The differences between the Basque and Catalan attitudes towards the Spanish central government serve to explain the 1977[160] newly elected government's different attitudes towards the two sub-nationalities. Prime-minister Adolfo Suarez prioritized settling Catalonia's future rather than that of the Basque's, mainly because moderating the Catalan's opinion smoothed negotiations with their representative, which was not the case for the Basques.[161] However, the Catalans' trajectory changed near the end of the 20th century and the beginning of the 21st. New strategies, represented mainly by the Democratic Convergence of Catalonia political party (CDC), have affected Catalans' nationalist demands.[162] These, led by the CDC president, Jordi Pojul i Soley, who served as Catalonia's president from 1980 to 2003, aimed at attaining more concessions for Catalonia from the central government and expanding Catalan autonomy without demanding independence.[163] At the same time, Catalonia was striving for an independent presence in the world community—albeit an informal presence, as the Spanish Constitution did not allow for autonomous communities to deal with foreign policy.[164] This was ventured through several activities, such as encouraging cultural and economic exchange with other states, promoting Barcelona as a geopolitical center, developing foreign relations, achieving representation for Catalonia in international institutional bodies, and obtaining full representation within the European Union.[165]

155 *Id.*
156 *Id.*
157 *Id.*, 8.
158 Simeon and Conway, *supra* note 6, 353.
159 Medhurst, *supra* note 136, 8.
160 Two years after General Franco's demise.
161 Medhurst, *supra* note 136, 8.
162 Ehrlich, *supra* note 8, 470.
163 *Id.*, 472.
164 *Id.*
165 *Id.*, 473.

Toward the end of the first decade of the 21st century, both in Catalonia and in the Basque country, independence efforts and initiatives were mainly internally political, focusing on legislative initiatives in the local parliaments.[166] For example, in 2008 the Basque parliament passed a law to poll for a "consultation" concerning self-determination for the Basque country. The poll did not go forward because the Spanish Constitutional Court declared the law unconstitutional and invalid following an appeal by the Spanish government.[167] Catalonia has undertaken several initiatives since 2006, in which year Catalonia's Statute of Autonomy was revised following approval by the Catalan and Spanish parliaments and ratification in a Catalan referendum.[168] Despite this legitimacy, the statute was challenged in the Spanish Constitutional Court by members of the People's Party Parliamentary Group, and in 2010, the court ruled that some articles were unconstitutional and invalid and that others were subject to restrictive interpretation.[169] Against this background, in January 2013 the Catalan parliament issued the "Declaration of Sovereignty and of the Right to Decide of the People of Catalonia," in which it declared its aim to initiate a process of exercising the right to decide Catalonia's future.[170] The process included calling a referendum for the Catalan people to make that decision. The Spanish government appealed to the Spanish Constitutional Court, asking it to determine that the declaration was unconstitutional and invalid. In March 2014, the Constitutional Court partially accepted the Spanish government's appeal, deciding that Catalonia's declaration of sovereignty was unconstitutional.[171] Nevertheless, it accepted the Catalan people's right to decide, because this right did not imply self-determination but rather the principles of democratic legitimacy and pluralism.[172]

---

166 Huw Evans, *Law and Legitimacy: The Denial of the Catalan Voice*, Centre Maurice Coppieters cmc papers (2013), <http://www.ideasforeurope.eu/wp-content/uploads/2013/12/CMC-3249-PAPER-thedenialofthecatalanvoice-2811133.pdf>.

167 *Id.*, 7.

168 See, Statute of Autonomy of Catalonia (2006), cited *id.*, note 11.

169 Evans, *supra* note 166, 7.

170 *Id.*

171 The decision is available in Spanish at: <http://www.tribunalconstitucional.es/es/salaPrensa/Documents/NP_2014_026/2013-01389STC.pdf>. For a report on the decision in English see, *Spain's Constitutional Court rejects Catalan Parliament's Declaration of Sovereignty*, VilaWeb, News From Catalonia, 25 Mar. 2014 <http://www.vilaweb.cat/noticia/4181445/20140325/spains-constitutional-court-overrules-catalan-parliaments-declaration-of-sovereignty.html>.

172 *Id.*

The Constitutional's Court decisions with regard to both the Basque and the Catalan initiatives restrict the constitution's more apparently liberal attitude toward the different communities in Spain. Even though the constitution aims to preserve Spain as the "indissoluble unity of the Spanish nation, the common and indivisible homeland of all Spaniards,"[173] it also intends to "recognize and guarantee the right to autonomy of the nationalities and regions which make it up and [to enable] solidarity among all of them."[174] The constitution thus confirms the official status of the Castilian language and yet allows local languages to acquire official status in autonomous communities. It also allows local flags to be flown together with the national flag at official occasions and on public buildings.[175]

As noted, in order to achieve the above-mentioned goals, the Spanish constitution devolved the powers of the regions through a form of asymmetrical federalism.[176] Although not formally a federal state, the Spanish constitution constructs the Spanish state upon a concept of "'sub-state *nacionalidad*' [in which] political aspirations by sub-state nationalities are articulated around common cultural, historical and political facts"[177] and the constitution protects and preserves these aspirations, in varying degrees.[178] Therefore, the constitution provides for regional self-rule; however, it also proclaims the principle of solidarity that should be implemented by the institutions of the state.[179]

Accordingly, the framework of asymmetrical federalism enabled different degrees of autonomy, and Catalonia and the Basque were given more independent authorities than some other regions.[180] This arrangement persisted over the years, and when in 1980 a law was attempted to harmonize autonomy, the constitutional court eventually ruled that the constitution did not require institutional uniformity and it struck down some of the key provisions of the

173 La Constitución Española, Dec. 29, 1978, BOE núm. 311, art. 2 [hereinafter *The Spanish Constitution*].

174 *Id.*

175 Simeon and Conway, *supra* note 6, citing Articles 3 and 4 of the Spanish Constitution.

176 *Id.*, 353.

177 Moreno and Colino, *supra* note 135, 289.

178 *Id.*

179 *Id.*, 291.

180 For example, while the Basques and Catalans received their own police forces, the Galicians and Andalusians did not; in the Basque Country the regional authorities collected taxes and handed them to the central government, while in the rest of Spain, Madrid collected the taxes and gave regional administrations a part of it. See, Simeon and Conway, *supra* note 6, 354.

law.[181] According to some scholars, the system established by the constitution is "a deliberately vague document which created grey areas where it was not clear whether power ought to be exercised by Madrid or by one or more of the regional administrations."[182] In addition,

> the exact powers to be granted to the regions were deliberately vague although certain guidelines were provided... While most of the internal authorities were left for the regions, Madrid retained control of foreign affairs, external trade, the justice system and defence; other issues such as education were not specifically assigned.[183]

On one hand, this framework provides "a flexibility that can avoid constitutional crisis";[184] on the other hand, as described above, it is not an overstatement to suggest that Catalonia and Spain are on the verge of a constitutional crisis.[185] At the very least, it is likely that the autonomous communities will continue to bargain for more powers, and this is especially true for the Basque and the Catalans.[186]

The above claims support the description of Spain in recent years as a "nation of nations" (in contrast to the constitution's definition of Spain as a nation of *nationalities*) or as a post-national state.[187] Numerous minority nationalists relate to Spain as "merely a state composed of several nations."[188] Some politicians referred to current Spain as a "plurinational state" that requires "some federal and confederal arrangements among Spain's main ethno-linguistic communities."[189] Nevertheless, it is important to note that despite the persistence of the regional identities encouraged by some regional political and intellectual elites[190] and which are practically expressed by on the ground secessionist initiatives, there is also evidence that in the majority of the population the Spanish identity remains strong. Several factors account for this finding, among them, "the vitality of Spanish as a common lingua franca...the

181 *Id.*
182 *Id.*, 355.
183 *Id.*, 353.
184 *Id.*, 355.
185 See *supra* notes 169–172 and accompanying text.
186 Simeon and Conway, *supra* note 6, 355.
187 Moreno and Colino, *supra* note 135, 293.
188 *Id.*
189 *Id.*
190 *Id.*, 314.

integrative role of state-wide parties and [above all, unifying classic national elements, such as] the long-standing shared history and other generally accepted symbols such as the monarchy [or even] mass sports."[191] Therefore, solidarity, as envisioned by the constitution, is not necessarily to be discouraged, and the exacting balance between centralization and decentralization will only be determined in the future.

Federalism: A Final Analysis

The case analyses of Canada, Belgium, and Spain thus allow us to assess the strengths and the weaknesses of federalism towards deciding whether it is, indeed, a viable system for "constitu[ting] a stable accommodation within a divided society."[192] On the one hand, as Kymlicka suggests, democratic federalism reduces the likelihood of secession; however, its success is dependent on the system allowing secessionist political mobilization.[193] National minorities will prefer territorial autonomy only if they are allowed to choose between "a range of options from assimilation to secession."[194] If the state prohibits such a free debate, it may increase the minorities' desires for independence.[195] On the other hand, "federalism can perpetuate and intensify the very conflicts it is designed to manage…because they are institutionalized and entrenched in the very design of the political system."[196] The above cases exemplify this argument, and moreover, the referendums in Canada and the legislative initiatives in Catalonia and the Basque Country in Spain support the claim that federalism "can provide the institutional tools and resources for nation building that can make a move towards secession plausible and viable in the future."[197]

Secession might, therefore, be a plausible option in divided countries, and it will not be prevented even by the international community, despite international law's firm rule of the preservation of national unity and the territorial integrity of a state.[198] It seems that the international community's aversion

191 *Id.*

192 Simeon and Conway, *supra* note 6, 340.

193 Kymlicka, Justice and Security, *supra* note 3, 164.

194 *Id.*

195 *Id.*

196 Simeon and Conway, *supra* note 6, 340.

197 *Id.*

198 Declaration on Principles of international Law concerning Friendly Relations and Co-operation Among States, G.A. Res. 2625 (XXV), Annex, 25 UN GAOR, Supp. (No. 28), U.N. Doc. A/5217, 121 (24 Oct. 1970).

to violent "suppression of democratically elected and nonviolent secessionist governments will lead the community to support 'negotiation' but practically to accept a de facto independence even if the fiction of state unity is maintained."[199]

Moreover, there are indeed cases where secession should be respected and even welcomed as long as it is peaceful and "result[s] in two [or more] healthy, liberal democratic states."[200] It does not follow from liberal thinking that secession is morally or politically wrong. On the contrary, liberalism is concerned with the individual rights and freedoms of individuals, which secession, in case it leads to the establishment of democratic states, should not infringe upon.[201]

Nevertheless, secession is not always politically or morally possible and desirable. As mentioned above, the international community protects the rights of states for territorial integrity, and in cases where states wish to preserve this right and object to secession, the latter will not be a realistic option. This conclusion is reinforced in cases where national groups have competing claims over land and resources that would not allow for a peaceful secession.[202] Lastly, some national minorities, especially indigenous peoples, but not only such minorities, would have economic difficulties in ruling their own states.[203]

Therefore, federalism and the right to self-determination are not sufficient conditions for securing the unity of the states of divided societies. While their value is not underestimated, they do not provide adequate substance for a model of citizenship ensuring the unity of multinational states. In the next chapter, I will discuss in detail the characteristics of the model of citizenship required for stable multinational states.

---

199 Kymlicka, Justice and Security, *supra* note 3, 163.

200 Kymlicka, Multicultural Citizenship, *supra* note 1, 186.

201 *Id.*

202 *Id.* Sunstein mentions some other disadvantages of federalism, especially when it is included as a right in a founding document: "[it] would increase the risks of ethnic and factional struggle, reduce the prospects for compromise and deliberations in government… create dangers of blackmail and strategic behavior and exploitation, and most generally endanger the prospects for long-term self-government." See, Cass Sunstein, *Constitutionalism and Secession*, 58 UNI. CHI. L. REV. 633, 634 (1991). I thank Dr. Yaniv Roznai for the reference.

203 Kymlicka, Multicultural Citizenship, *supra* note 1, 186. For example, one of the reasons the Scottish referendum on secession from Great Britain failed was fear over Scotland's economic dependence on Britain. See, *Scottish Independence It'll Cost You*, THE ECONOMIST, April 14th 2012, <http://www.economist.com/node/21552564>.

CHAPTER 4

A Model of Citizenship (Stage 1): Liberalism, Multiculturalism, and Civic Nationalism

In the previous chapters I discussed two theoretical concepts that are fundamental, in my view, to the common life of citizens in multinational states: nationalism and multiculturalism. I applied them to the legal right of self-determination of peoples and to the political regime of federalism and discovered that the last two do not solve all of the queries and difficulties emanating from communal life in a multinational state. In this chapter and the next, I will formulate a model of citizenship in a multinational state.

The nature of citizenship in a democracy determines how common life in a multinational state can be effectuated, as citizenship determines "the set of rights, duties, and identities linking citizens to the state."[1] It contains three elements that encompass all the aspects of life in a democratic state: civil (i.e., individual rights); political (i.e., the franchise and the right to participate in the political process); and social (i.e., welfare rights and rights to participate in the social life of the state).[2] Most importantly, citizenship is "the ideal toward which nation-states strive, but which they never completely attain."[3] The following suggested model of citizenship ventures to include all of these aspects within a multinational state.

I begin drawing the lines of the citizenship model in this chapter by summarizing the theoretical and practical foundations discussed so far and exposing the difficulties of each concept. I propose, as a first stage, to integrate these concepts in order to enable a shared civic identity.

The focus on a *civic* identity (in contrast to an ethnic one) clarifies the first element of this citizenship model. Bearing in mind that, as Kymlicka notes, currently very few states are mono-national,[4] it seems impossible to base the

1 James A. Banks, *Diversity, Group Identity, and Citizenship Education in a Global Age Diversity, in* DEMOCRACY AND MULTICULTURAL EDUCATION 16 (Farideh Salili and Rumjahn Hoosain eds., 2010).

2 *Id.*, 17, citing T.H. Marshall, CLASS, CITIZENSHIP AND SOCIAL DEVELOPMENT: ESSAYS OF T.H. Marshall (1964).

3 *Id.*

4 Will Kymlicka, *Multicultural States and Intercultural Citizens*, 1(2) THEORY AND RESEARCH IN EDUCATION 147, 149 (2003) [hereinafter *Kymlicka, Multicultural States and Intercultural Citizens*].

 | DOI 10.1163/9789004294332_006

model of citizenship on a common ethnic identity, which is expressed through a myth of common ancestry of state residents, a common culture, and shared language and history. Some scholars suggest, however, that the only viable identity is an ethnic one.[5] According to this viewpoint, the liberal state can only be sustained by allegiances and feelings of solidarity among the citizens emanating from membership in a "pre-political" community—i.e., the social ethnic-national community—rather than from any political membership in the state.[6]

As I discussed in the first chapter, while I do acknowledge the importance of feelings of solidarity and allegiance to the state among compatriots in facilitating the common life of its citizens, I argue, and will hereinafter show, that these feelings of "common destiny" need not necessarily emanate from a common ethnic identity. In addition, in a world where most states are multinational—either because they are composed of two or more historic nations ("homeland communities") or because they have absorbed large communities of immigrants—identity is quite a fluid concept. In the modern world, people may belong to different groups that make up their identity: such as religious and national, but also social. For example, one can be a Muslim-Israeli and at the same time a fan of a foreign sports team with a fan club in Israel. In this way, hybrid identities are formed.[7] Yet, hybrid identities are not only a matter of personal identities; group identities can develop an "autonomous hybrid code."[8] For example, Turkish juveniles in Germany invented a third language with elements of both languages, in this way, developing a new group identity of their own.[9] This means that feelings of belonging do not necessarily emanate from a fixed cultural category,[10] and that the project of forging a citizenship model constructed upon a new concept of identity in multinational states may be tenable.

---

5 See, for example, Anthony D. Smith, ETHNO-SYMBOLISM AND NATIONALISM: A CULTURAL APPROACH (2009); Roger Scruton, IN DEFENSE OF THE NATION, cited by Ronald Beiner, LIBERALISM, NATIONALISM, CITIZENSHIP 24–25 (2003).

6 Beiner, *supra* note 5, 24.

7 Sigrid Luchtenberg, *Multicultural Education: Challenges and Responses*, 4(1) JOURNAL OF SOCIAL SCIENCE EDUCATION 31, 49 (2005).

8 *Id.*

9 *Id.*

10 Note also Jacobsohn's observation that identity is not a static concept. See, Generally, Garry J. Jacobsohn, CONSTITUTIONAL IDENTITY (2010). I thank Dr. Yaniv Roznai for the reference.

Yet, before delving into the "project," I reject two polar viewpoints regarding the life in a multinational state: the pluralist version of multiculturalism and the concept of universalism. As explained in the second chapter, the multicultural state is based on the idea that the state equally belongs to all the citizens and different groups forming it.[11] Therefore, multiculturalism objects to the domination of a particular culture or the requirement of assimilation into one culture; moreover, it demands that in cases of former injustice towards specific groups, the state would compensate them for these former policies.[12] Regarding the political arrangement required to achieve these goals, multiculturalism suggests a variety of options—ranging from federalism and self-governance to representation rights—that help to reduce barriers to integration in mainstream society,[13] thus realizing Charles Taylor's concept of deep diversity, i.e., facilitating citizens' different relationships with the state.[14]

However, the pluralist version of multiculturalism polarizes the idea of the neutral state into a requirement that the state simply be a coordinative mechanism between its citizens, who are in fact "*strangers* dwell[ing] together in a region."[15] Hence, in contrast to the allegiances between compatriots, described by nationalists as crucial for the survival of the liberal state, pluralists suggest applying "differentiated solidarity," according to which the citizens (and the state bureaucracy) cooperate only to the extent required to ensure equal individual and group rights in the public sphere.[16]

The above described diluted concept of cooperation—which posits, in fact, no common goal for the citizens in a multinational state beyond noninterference in the independence of communities in determining their own ways of life—results in a "ghettoization" of cultures with no common denominator in the form of a larger common culture.[17] However, it is seriously doubtful whether such a concept of citizenship can serve as the connecting element required

---

11 Kymlicka, Multicultural States and Intercultural Citizens, *supra* note 4, 150.

12 *Id.*

13 *Id.*, 153; Kymlicka, Multicultural Citizenship: A Liberal Theory of Minority Rights 30–32 (1995) [hereinafter *Kymlicka, Multicultural Citizenship*].

14 Charles Taylor, *Shared and Divergent Values, in* Options for a New Canada 53 (Ronald. L. Watts and Douglas M. Brown eds., 1991) [hereinafter *Taylor, Shared and Divergent Values*].

15 Iris M. Young, Inclusion and Democracy 180 (2000) [hereinafter *Young, Inclusion and Democracy*].

16 *Id.*, 180.

17 Beiner, *supra* note 5, 25.

for the common life of people in a state.[18] If only particular identities matter, there seems to be no reason for specific groups to will to stay together in a state, or as Beiner concludes, "it becomes [more] difficult to sustain an experience of common citizenship."[19]

The concept of universalistic citizenship posits some modification of the difficulties described above. The universalistic concept celebrates the individual's worth as a human being, thus elevating it above any collective identity.[20] Therefore, universalistic citizenship objects to all models of particular citizenship, including the group-segregated model endorsed by radical multiculturalism. However, the universalistic concept cannot account for the fact that people are not altogether cosmopolitan and that they tend to express allegiance to a specific state in which they live or would like to live.

Setting aside the above polarized viewpoints of citizenship, we remain with the concept of liberal civic nationalism. Liberalism alone cannot suffice, as it is relatively similar to universalism, stressing the individual over the community, so that the community or the state matters only in so far as it ensures that each individual receives his or her equal rights. Yet, the civic notion closely pertains to the liberal tradition because it posits that the institutions and mechanisms of the state that guarantee each citizen's equal rights are objects of identification for citizens.[21] In other words, civic nationalism stresses the pride of its citizens in the justice of their shared institutions and procedural mechanisms of the state as the primary element in its model of citizenship. Put slightly differently, by Ronald Beiner:

> Civic nationalism suggests that belonging to a political community is a good in itself. Political traditions constitute living totalities that cannot be reduced to the purposes of individuals or the goals of sub-communities, and our humanity would be diminished if our lives lacked a focus for the civic dimension of existence, even it if were somehow possible to satisfy all of our individual and group purposes without participation in a larger political community.[22]

18 Kymlicka refers to national groups living together with no common denominator as "parallel societies." He does not ultimately doom this kind of living together to failure, but nevertheless questions this model's longevity. See, Kymlicka, Multicultural States and Intercultural Citizens, *supra* note 4, 155–156.

19 Beiner, *supra* note 5, 28.

20 *Id.*, 29.

21 Tamir and Miller are representatives of such views, which are discussed in this chapter in depth.

22 Beiner, *supra* note 5, 31.

This model, can, nevertheless, be criticized or at least modified. Multiculturalism's criticism highlights this model's neglect of the importance of a cultural context to people's lives.[23] The fact that the state allows for equal rights of individuals without taking into account their particular identities does not serve the need for recognition, a vital human need.[24] Because "people need a secure cultural context to give meaning and guidance to their choices in life, [such] cultural context also ranks among the primary goods, basic to most peoples' prospects for living what they can identify as a good life."[25]

The notion of the good life is linked to another modification of the civic nationalistic model—the communitarian criticism. As I suggested in the first chapter, the communitarian philosophy adds to the concept of civic nationalism—which is entrenched in society's commitment to just institutions and legal mechanisms—the idea of commitment to a common good, or a common way of life. Indeed, the mere belonging to *any* community is not a value in itself. Communities may encourage narrow-mindedness, "prejudice against outsiders and a whole range of other deformities including those that arise from a cult of local community."[26] Communities are therefore not valuable merely as such, but only to the extent that they enable the realization of appraised social practices or social values.[27] However, communities have the ability to evoke in compatriots a willingness to maintain a liberal welfare state that embodies the compatriots' belief in a mutual care for each other.[28] That is, in the words of Jurgen Habermas, "[T]he exercise of power in the democratic constitutional state is coded…by the institutionalized handling of problems and the procedurally regulated mediation of interests which simultaneously must be understood as actualizing a system of rights."[29] However, and this surpasses pure civic nationalism, as "in the political arena those who encounter one another are collective actors contending about collective goals and the distribution of collective goods."[30]

What emanates from the above is that civic nationalism's discourse of rights is lacking in its ability to ensure commitment to "shared projects or collective

23 Multiculturalism: Examining the Politics of Recognition 4–5 (Amy Gutman, ed., 1994).

24 *Id.*, 4.

25 *Id.*, 5.

26 Alsadir MacIntyre, *The Spectre of Communitarianism*, cited by Beiner, *supra* note 5, 87.

27 *Id.*

28 See the discussion of Tamir and Miller's works in the first chapter.

29 Jürgen Habermas, *Struggles for Recognition in the Democratic Constitutional State*, (translated by Shierry Weber Nicholsen), *in* Gutman, *supra* note 23, 107–108.

30 *Id.*, 108.

co-involvement,"[31] such as is required for the common lives in a state. Rights are instead "a means of encroaching inviolable boundaries against those (strangers, anonymous officials of the state or estranged spouses) we have some reason to distrust."[32] Therefore, civic nationalism should be developed into a concept that enables the compatriots of a civic nation to share a common identity.[33] This identity can be formed upon compatriots' political obligation to four elements: territorialism, participation, citizenship, and civic education.[34] The citizens' commitment to territory is in fact not a commitment "to particular boundaries…but to a particular special and social location"[35] in which the compatriots live together under the same rule of law. This location endows them with the right to citizenship and turns them into a political community.[36]

The next two elements, participation and citizenship, are connected concepts. Citizens participate in the lives of the nation on a territorial and civic basis; but citizenship is the precondition of participation and inclusion in the nation, and, as a consequence, is the basis for exclusion of those who do not belong in the nation.[37] Legal citizenship—as it marks the boundaries of the nation-state by determining who is to be included within it and to be entitled to legal privileges—is one of the major touchstones of civic (territorial) nationalism,[38] in which the cohesion of the nation is predicated upon the rule of law and common rights and duties of all compatriots.[39]

The last element, civic education, is the most significant in terms of its potential ability to forge and maintain the identity of the compatriots of the nation.[40] Using the tools of the education system in primary schools, and even in secondary education, and holding educative campaigns for the general public,[41] the nation-state can inculcate the norms and values upon which it attempts to define itself and with which it intends to identify.[42] In this manner,

31 Beiner, *supra* note 5, 149.

32 *Id.*

33 *Id.*, 118.

34 *Id.*, 117–118.

35 *Id.*

36 *Id.*

37 *Id.*, 117–118.

38 *Id.*, 118.

39 *Id.*

40 *Id.*

41 *Id.*

42 See, for example, Schnel's discussion of how the education system was used in Israel to forge an Israeli-Jewish identity through the teaching of history, natural history, the bible, and geography. See, Izhak Schnell, *Geographical Ramifications of the Occupation for*

education, by clarifying for compatriots the roots of their common identity, serves to prepare the "glue" that holds them together. It also supplies them with the justification for preserving this identity by maintaining loyal ties with each other and with the nation as a whole.

Yet, as the theory of multiculturalism contends, civic nationalism must account for the sense of integration in societies divided by different ethnic or national identities.[43] According to the multicultural version of civic nationalism, there is more than one political community in a multinational state, and, as a result, citizenship in such a state amounts to a sort of dual citizenship construed of somehow contested national identities. Hence, the means of self-governance endorsed by multiculturalism does not solve the problem of the lack of a gluing element in the society. In fact, it even aggravates it. This assertion is based on the assumption that internal self-determination for minorities—that is, having autonomy in governance and the option to segregate themselves within the boundaries of their own community—may not be sufficient to fulfil their sense of belonging to the state as a whole or to construct strong and meaningful ties to it. As Miller suggests:

> [Minorities] want to feel attached to the place [where they live] and part of its history, even if they also feel some attachment to their place of ethnic origin. So they need a story that they share with the majority, though a story that can be told in different ways and with different emphases by different groups. To see themselves only as bearers of a specific ethnic identity would be to lose the chance to join a larger community ...Their need is for a national identity which can be embraced...as an addition to rather than a replacement for ethnic consciousness.[44]

The above criticism supports my conclusion from the previous chapter, according to which the right to self-determination of peoples and its political expression in federal regimes are not sufficient for a cohesive model of citizenship. As Kymlicka notes:

Israeli Society, *in* THE IMPACTS OF LASTING OCCUPATION 93, 105–108 (Daniel Bar-Tal and Izhak Schnell eds., 2013).

43 Kymlicka, Multicultural Citizenship, *supra* note 13, 173–192.

44 David Miller, ON NATIONALITY, 138 (1995) [hereinafter *Miller, on Nationality*]. Note that Miller discusses emigrant minority communities and not homeland national minorities (i.e., minorities that have long been living in the territory of the state and regard it as their homeland). Nevertheless, I find his argument relevant for the case of homeland national minorities.

> The...arrangements are rarely examples of harmonious cooperation between national groups. They often become mere treaties of cooperation in which quarrelsome groups agree to cooperate only on a limited set of issues if they cooperate at all. The sense of solidarity needed to promote the public goal is lacking.[45]

Beiner takes this idea further and quotes Bernard Yack's critical views on the right of self-determination of peoples:

> History has left us sufficient barriers to establishing broader political identities without multiplying them by using the concept of rights to erect and maintain new ones. When past conflicts and injustices have erected such barriers, it may be wise as a matter of political prudence to offer special national rights... But introducing such cultural rights as a general principle would unnecessarily harden perceptions of cultural opposition and thereby promote greater mutual suspicion and contention within political communities.[46]

Returning to civic nationalism, this concept can indeed supply a way for minorities to "share [a story] with the majority." The shared "story" would be that of commitment to a specific framework of laws intended to confer rights and duties upon the citizens of the state.[47] It focuses on what is common in divided societies rather than on the fissures that are motivated by the different ethnic and cultural characteristics of the various communities making up such societies.

Nevertheless, preferring the common does not mean ignoring the divisive issues mentioned above. Civic nationalism approaches these issues using practices of toleration. It suggests the framework of "a liberal polity...in which group recognition is affirmed alongside a commitment to basic rights but is irreducible to them,"[48] thus ensuring the preservation of cultural resources for future generations.[49]

---

45 Kymlicka, Multicultural Citizenship, *supra* note 13, 186.

46 Bernard Yack, RECONCILING LIBERALISM AND NATIONALISM, cited by Beiner, *supra* note 5, 156.

47 *Id.*, 141.

48 Eamonn Callan, *Discrimination and Religious Schooling, in* CITIZENSHIP IN DIVERSE SOCIETIES 47, 50 (Will Kymlicka and Wayne Norman eds., 2000).

49 *Id.*, 50.

Yet, and especially in light of the tolerating aspect of civic nationalism, this concept on its own may be confused with pluralist (radical) multiculturalism, discussed above.[50] As stated above, the theory of pluralist multiculturalism suggests that the state should not adhere to one concept of "the good" while tolerating minorities who do not share this concept and identity. Rather than eliminating or transcending group difference, radical multiculturalism aims for "equality among socially and culturally differentiated groups, who mutually respect one another and affirm one another in their differences."[51] According to this theory, what holds society together is the equal respect every group acquires and endows upon the other groups.[52] The citizens of the state have no common identity, and the only common interest they share is "a commitment to the ideal of making a social order in which different national groups have different objects of identification and different modes of belonging."[53]

Civic nationalism is on the verge of radical multiculturalism, as it also suggests that the citizens share "an allegiance to a set of institutions and their underlying principles"[54] and a willingness to preserve legal arrangements that will secure equality between citizens and other values such as justice and liberty.[55] Yet, civic nationalism differs from radical multiculturalism in that it does not undermine the importance or the mere possibility of the emergence of a national identity; it rather claims that the common interests of the citizens of a state serve the basis for a common identity, or, in fact, they *are* their identity.[56]

On this point I beg to slightly differ. I claim that civic nationalism is not sufficient for the formation and sustaining of a national identity. Moreover, in order to enable a commitment to a shared national identity, it is necessary, as communitarian philosophy suggests, to foster "ties that bind."[57] It is evident

---

50 For fundamental texts discussing this theory, see, Anne Phillips, THE POLITICS OF PRESENCE (1995); James Tully, STRANGE MULTIPLICITY: CONSTITUTIONALISM IN AN AGE OF DIVERSITY (1995); Iris M. Young, JUSTICE AND THE POLITICS OF DIFFERENCE (1990) [hereinafter *Young, Justice and the Politics of Difference*].

51 Young, Justice and the Politics of Difference, *supra* note 50, 163.

52 See Young's concept of differentiated solidarity discussed in *supra* note 16 and accompanying text.

53 Alan Patten, *Liberal Citizenship in Multinational Societies*, *in* MULTINATIONAL DEMOCRACIES 279, 295 (Alain-G. Gagnon, James Tully eds., 2001).

54 Miller, *supra* note 44, 141.

55 Anthony D. Smith, NATIONAL IDENTITY 80 (1991).

56 *Id.*

57 Kymlicka, Multicultural Citizenship, *supra* note 13, 187. In this context, Kymlicka discusses Rawls' suggestion that the ties of civic friendship rest in a shared conception of justice. Rawls is considered a philosopher of classic liberalism and therefore objects to the idea

that these ties should be tailored specifically to each community: otherwise, why should one commit to one political community over another? Yet, the remaining and crucial question whose answer will complete my proposal for a model of citizenship is how we can achieve such binding ties in ethnically and culturally divided societies.

In the next chapter I argue that the binding ties forming a sense of a civic identity that nurtures "collective narratives of self and other presentations and labeling myths of origin and destiny"[58] are found in common national symbols. I claim that such symbols need to be discovered, developed, and endorsed in addition to the fortification and affirmation of the civic framework, which is, in a sense, abstract. I refer to this combined framework of civic nationalism with fortifying concrete cultural symbols as "civic-nationalism-plus."

But before elaborating on this framework and on the preconditions of its feasibility in the next chapter, a clarification is required. In contrast to the idea that "civic nationalism is [not] a helpful one"[59] and that its effect is merely to "thin...national identities to the point where they cease to have any content that could compete with ethnic or other such cultural identities,"[60] I argue that civic nationalism is an important touchstone in the establishment of a national identity in culturally divided societies. Civic nationalism, especially through education, supports the inclusive ideal of "deliberative democracy,"[61] in which all different viewpoints can be equally represented and respected. Forging loyalty to the values of civic nationalism—including toleration and democratic values that secure equality, liberty, and dignity for every citizen—and doing so by using the *modus operandi* of participation, citizenship, and education in a specific territory can serve as the basis for a cohesive society.

---

that a liberal society should define the common good of its citizens outside adhering to a shared conception of justice. For a discussion of the disagreement between Rawls and communitarians see, *infra*, in the first chapter of this book.

58 Nira Yuval-Davis, *Borders, Boundaries, and the Politics of Belonging*, *in* ETHNICITY, NATIONALISM AND MINORITY RIGHTS 214, 215 (Stephen May, Tariq Modood and Judith Squires eds., 2004).

59 David Miller, *Nationality in Divided Societies*, *in* MULTINATIONAL DEMOCRACIES, *supra* note 53, 299, 306.

60 Miller, on Nationality, *supra* note 44, 141. For a criticism of the idea of civic nationalism and its "alleged neutrality," using the examples of civic nationalistic states such as France, India, and the US, see Alexander Yacobson and Amnon Rubinstein, ISRAEL AND THE FAMILY OF NATIONS 147–148, 158–162, 171–178 (2010).

61 For elaboration on the term "deliberative democracy" see, Callan, *supra* note 48, 64, note 12, and the sources cited there.

However, two arguments can be made suggesting that pure civic nationalism frameworks are too weak to sustain a stable and cohesive multicultural society. First, in practical terms, it might seem difficult to find societies that are purely civic national. This can be seen in even the most obvious example of civic nationalism—the US. Although usually depicted as a society of immigrants that has detached itself from narrow conceptions of cultural identity, the US still has accumulated a history and a culture; it is not merely defined through its citizens' "allegiance to a body of principles embedded in the constitution."[62] The Walloons in Belgium provide another example of this weakness. In contrast to the counter national movement in Flanders, the Walloon national movement was established as a purely politically and economically driven movement;[63] however, it could not function on these bases alone and soon acquired a territorial and cultural dimension, becoming what is known as the *rattachisme*-Belgique, stressing the importance of the French culture and language.[64] These two examples serve to demonstrate that "a regional, national movement [let alone a state], cannot wholly avoid cultural terms in its self-positioning."[65] The second argument suggesting the weakness of pure civic nationalism lies in the significance of symbols in the formation of national societies and identities; therefore, I will develop it further in the next chapter.

62 Miller, on Nationality, *supra* note 44, 141.

63 Maarten Van Ginderachter and Joep Leerssen, *Denied Ethnicism: on the Walloon Movement in Belgium*, 18(2) NATIONS AND NATIONALISM 230, 235 (2012). For another similar example see Yacobson and Rubinstein's discussion of French nationalism and their claim that even though France positions itself as a civic nationalistic state, its identity is in fact constructed upon the cultural characteristics of the majority (i.e., the majority's language, cultural symbols, myths, history, literature, etc.). See, Yacobson & Rubinstein, *supra* note 60, 147.

64 Van Ginderachter and Leerssen, *supra* note 63, 238.

65 *Id.*

CHAPTER 5

A Model of Citizenship (Stage II): Civic-Nationalism-Plus

In the previous chapter I established the first pillar of the civic nationalism plus model of citizenship: a civic nationalistic political system that creates a space for the citizens of the state in which they are all equal and share a belief in the principles of justice upon which their society is set. Yet, as I suggested at the end of the previous chapter, in the absence of a common cultural space that serves as the "social glue" of the citizens,[1] they will feel no emotional attachment to the state and foster no feelings of allegiance or belonging to it. This social space and emotional attachment are facilitated through the use of national symbols.

National Symbols

National symbols are a constituent of public culture and of the public space that facilitates the connection between state and society and creates a space where society can be defined in an autonomous way, unmediated by the state. Public space includes all of the cultural and societal mechanisms, including myths, symbols, and ceremonies, that define its nature and borders.[2]

In a context of nationalism, symbols are defined as

> those images, objects, conditions and activities which involve beliefs, values, and attitudes that are utilized by individuals and groups in social intercourse to achieve objectives through influencing or controlling behavior. Above all, symbols are employed to induce action by forming and maintaining a belief system… [Symbols] constitute an important force for social solidarity transformation, and renewal. [They] appear to be necessary for the establishment of social cohesion, the legitimization of

1 Hizky Shoham, Let's Celebrate! Festivals and Civic Culture in Israel, 185 (2014) [Hebrew], <http://www.academia.edu/7804147/Let_s_Celebrate_Festivals_and_Civic_Culture_in_Israel_Hebrew_>.

2 *Id.*, 17.

 | DOI 10.1163/9789004294332_007

> institutions and of political authority, and the inculcation of beliefs and conventions of behavior.[3]

From ancient times, no known society has operated without the use of symbols,[4] including national societies. However, national societies have adapted the use of symbols to their own political ends. In the era of nationalism's awakening, technological and ideological forces influenced political motivations. This marked the decline of theology and of old elites and governments and the rise of a new community known as "the nation"—supported by the masses and organized in mass political movements.[5] When the old hierarchies lost their power, the symbols associated with them—both concrete and metaphorical—were replaced by new ones.[6] Influenced by the French and the American revolutions, the "divine grace" that justified the old regimes' claims for territories gained new meanings: such as the "natural rights to liberty and self-government, the common destiny of a people with shared culture and language, and a willingness of citizens to die for those ideals."[7] Those ideals created and maintained the new nation-states "through elaborate systems of ceremony and symbolism"[8] that affected the entire strata of political life: "the bureaucracy, armed forces, community organizations, educational systems and other social structures."[9] Symbols functioned to serve several goals: they justified the character of the nation, "they assisted in socializing the masses and mobilizing them for political action and they created a system of rewards and punishments for nationals to encourage them to promote the goals of the community."[10]

The symbols that were and presently are used by nation-states—most notably the flag and the national anthem, but many others as well—take different forms: verbal/aural, concrete, graphic, and abstract.[11] Verbal/aural symbols include the national anthem and language itself; concrete symbols include historic sites, statues, clothing, architecture, monuments, and even cemeteries that honor the virtue of national heroes; graphic symbols include the national

---

3 Whitney Smith, *National Symbols*, *in* ENCYCLOPEDIA OF NATIONALISM 521–522 (Alexander J. Motyl ed., 2001) [hereinafter *Smith, National Symbols*].

4 *Id.* For a historical survey of the use of symbols see, *id.*, 523–526.

5 *Id.*, 526–527.

6 *Id.*, 527.

7 *Id.*

8 *Id.*

9 *Id.*

10 *Id.*

11 *Id.*

flag and the designs on stamps, coins, and bank notes; and abstract symbols include the fundamental texts of the nation, for example, the declaration of independence, the names of streets and squares, literature and art that "vaunt the glories of national history and culture,"[12] and the content of national museums exhibits, public broadcasting, and public school history books.[13]

Hence, symbolism in modern national societies is an expression of the

> civil religion [of the nation which] applies to the set of beliefs and attitudes that explain the meaning and purpose of any given political society in terms of its relationship to a transcendent spiritual reality...expressed in public rituals, myths and symbols.[14]

Through symbols, historical or other meaningful events in the life of a nation are "coded, weighted, and narrated."[15] Thus, symbols "provide perhaps the strongest, clearest statement of national identity"[16] because they can be compared with the totemic rites and symbols that Durkheim identified[17]—that is, "they possess emotive collective qualities"[18] and "bear a special relationship to the nations they represent, distinguishing them from one another and reaffirming their identity boundaries."[19] As Lauren Berlant summarizes:

> National symbols "suture" individuals to the collective of "a people" and "their" territory, and both to a "nation." [The National Symbolic produces] the "law" [whose] traditional icons, its metaphors, its heroes, its rituals, and its narratives provide an alphabet for a collective consciousness or national subjectivity.[20]

---

12 *Id.*; Alexander Yacobson and Amnon Rubinstein, ISRAEL AND THE FAMILY OF NATIONS 142–143 (2010).

13 Yacobson & Rubinstein, *supra* note 12, 143.

14 Smith, National Symbols, *supra* note 3, 522.

15 Jeffrey C. Alexander, *On the Social Construction of Moral Universals: The "Holocaust" from War Crime to Trauma Drama, in* CULTURAL TRAUMA AND COLLECTIVE IDENTITY 196, 204 (Jeffrey C. Alexander et al. eds., 2004).

16 Karen A. Cerulo, *Symbols and the World System: National Anthems and Flags*, 8 (2) SOCIOLOGICAL FORUM 243, 244 (1993).

17 *Id.*, 244; Anthony D. Smith, NATIONAL IDENTITY 77 (1991) [hereinafter *Smith, National Identity*].

18 Smith, National Identity, *supra* note 17, 77.

19 Cerulo, *supra* note 16, 244.

20 NATIONAL SYMBOLS, FRACTURED IDENTITIES, XIX (Michael E. Geisler ed., 2005), citing Laurent Berlant.

Through this process of "suturing" the individuals to the collective of a people, which is the nation, symbolism also manipulates the individuals (even though honored in principle) into becoming a part of the "machine dedicated to promoting the nation."[21] Hence, national symbols serve to bond together individuals who consider themselves as belonging to a certain nation or collective, distinguishing them from others "by virtue of who shares the 'code' needed to identify [the symbols'] meaning."[22] This sense of belonging also ensures that these individuals are willing to bear the burden of national duties and sacrifices, most often in the battlefields, that the nation requires.[23]

Thus, national symbols, by creating "a collective belief system,"[24] not only "define and justify the nation, its political system and its social norms and values,"[25] but also substitute for the role of religion in traditional communities and motivate the "individual sacrifice and obedience which every society demands."[26] The common system of values and beliefs that serves to bond the people of the nation together is expressed by the national symbols and their various functions: reference (recalling, retaining, and ordering data), hortatory (evoking, inciting, coercing, affirming, and effecting), and interpretation.[27]

The above discussion is generally reflective of homogenous national societies, in which the compatriots naturally share the "'code' needed to identify [the national symbols'] meaning."[28] Yet, a more complicated and interesting question is whether national symbols can "provide an alphabet for a collective consciousness or national subjectivity"[29] in multinational societies. In other words, and supposing that those multinational societies want to function as cohesive societies and states, could they use symbols in similar ways to refer, evoke, and interpret?

According to some scholars, national symbols presuppose some kind of national history and carry with them a "freight of national history, its memories,

---

21 Smith, National Symbols, *supra* note 3, 527.

22 Note the example given by Geisler of the German soldiers who fought in the trenches during World War I and who "in an effort to identify their comrades in arms in the chaos that marked that warfare would sing the 'Deutschlandlied' and hold their fire if the foggy figures they encountered were able to respond in kind." See, Geisler, *supra* note 20, XVIII.

23 Smith, National Symbols, *supra* note 3, 527.

24 *Id.*, 522.

25 *Id.*

26 *Id.*

27 *Id.*

28 See, *supra* note 20 and accompanying text.

29 *Id.*, XIX, citing Lauren Berlant.

traditions, symbols and values."[30] As Smith suggests, history and historical context have a vital role in shaping the nation and its rituals:[31]

> The study of "everyday nationhood"—the cultural practices of ordinary citizens in talking about, consuming, voting and symbolically enacting the nation—must be complemented by that of "historic nationhood"—the historical developments in culture, politics and society that have shaped particular national communities across generations and in particular the shared memories, myths, symbols and traditions of those communities.[32]

Yet, it is also argued that although symbols have ethnic or pre-modern cultural origins, they *may be made so* by nationalist movements.[33] Symbols such as nationalist language, rites, and ceremonies may be used "to connect nationalist ideology to the culture of wider segments of the population...so that the nation and national identity become a 'natural' part of culture."[34] Such a view suggests that national symbols have a force of forging a nation. Indeed, it is required that the people have some roots of common history, traditions, and beliefs. However, since without the symbols, national identity would not have been considered an integral part of this culture, the "forging force" of symbols is not to be exaggerated.

This force of national symbols serves as the basis for my argument that multinational societies can use such symbols in the same way that mono-national societies do. I would, nevertheless, contend that this is predicated upon strengthening the framework of civic nationalism in order to create "overarching national identities"[35] serving as the foundation on which the symbols rely

---

30 Anthony D. Smith, *The Rites of Nations: Elites, Masses and the Re-enactment of the "National Past", in* THE RITES OF NATIONS IN THE CULTURAL POLITICS OF NATIONALISM AND NATION-BUILDING: RITUAL AND PERFORMANCE IN THE FORGING OF NATIONS 21, 27 (Rachel Tsang, Eric Taylor Woods eds., 2014) [hereinafter *Smith, the Rites of Nations*], analyzing the role of commemorative and celebratory rites in the formation of a nation.

31 *Id.*, 31.

32 *Id.*, 31–32.

33 John Hargreaves, FREEDOM FOR CATALONIA? CATALAN NATIONALISM, SPANISH IDENTITY AND THE BARCELONA OLYMPIC GAMES 12 (2000), discussing the role of sports in forging national sentiments in Catalans.

34 *Id.*, 14.

35 David Miller, *Nationality in Divided Societies, in* MULTINATIONAL DEMOCRACIES 299, 302 (Alain-G. Gagnon, James Tully eds., 2001). For elaboration, see his discussion of a British identity that can be conferred upon both English and Scots. *Id.*, 307–312.

and from which they develop. In the following subsection I elaborate on this framework, which I call "civic-nationalism-plus" and which, I suggest, could help multinational societies create and maintain valid cohesive ties.

Civic-Nationalism-Plus

In building the model of civic-nationalism-plus, I first return to the end of the last chapter, where I referred to the relative weakness of pure civic nationalism. Indeed, civic nationalism bereft of concrete national symbols lacks a necessary element for the process of compatriots' identifying with the nation, as well as for securing their loyalty to it. This dimension of forming a national identity—i.e., forging common national symbols—cannot, therefore, be ignored.[36]

Yet, the case is much more complicated for multinational societies. The questions that arise are whether and how national symbols could reflect the interests, culture, and heritage of national minorities. How can these minorities participate in the process of forming and adopting national symbols? Is it realistic to think that national minorities will be able to identify with state symbols?

Minorities trying to participate in such a process face several difficulties. First, the pervasiveness of symbols in all aspects of political and civil life cannot be exaggerated. Symbols are found everywhere, from the most heroic and ceremonial, such as the flag and the national anthem, to the most mundane and everyday, such as the spoken language, the names of the streets,[37] coins and bank notes[38] and the nation's geographic map, which turns the territory into an asset of the nation by demonstrating the nation's control of a specific space.[39] Groups that aim to leave their mark on such a ramified and complex system have to adopt different strategies for different cases. In long-established nations, such as most European countries, national symbols are

---

36 An illuminating illustration of this claim is the street demonstrations in Nepal during the civil war (1996–2006) in which citizens demanded a federal state based on ethnic groups, the right to self-determination, and a change in the national animals and color. See, Sudhindra Sharma, Pawan Kumar Sen, *Nepal Contemporary Political Situation-IV—Opinion Poll Report* (The Asia Foundation & Interdisciplinary Analysts, 2007) 4, available at <http://ida.com.np/upload_files/ncps4.pdf>. I thank Dr. Yaniv Roznai for this note.

37 Izhak Schnell, *Geographical Ramifications of the Occupation for Israeli Society*, *in* The Impacts of Lasting Occupation 93, 104 (Daniel Bar-Tal and Izhak Schnell eds., 2013).

38 Yacobson & Rubinstein, *supra* note 12, 142.

39 Benedict Anderson, Imagined Communities 174–175 (2006).

deeply installed in the nation's ancient history and cultural traditions and cannot easily be changed.[40] Moreover, in some states, formal lineaments that are strongly connected to collective identity such as the official language, the flag, the national anthem, the capital, or even the date of proclamation of independence, are protected from amendments as they are referred to as "eternal principles."[41]

However, newly established states allegedly provide more opportunities to consider the historical and cultural heritage of the various groups forming the state[42]—for example, the Indian flag tries to incorporate both Buddhist and Hindu traditions through the symbol of the dharma wheel.[43] In most cases, and especially in long-established nations where minorities must find a way to identify with already existing symbols, it is easier for minorities to accept "passive symbols" that do not require any interaction,[44] for example, graphic symbols on coins and bank notes or even the national flag. More "active symbols" would include singing the national anthem in the national language or learning history and literature according to a public school curriculum, based on the majority's culture.

Identifying with the states' symbols may be easier for groups that are seen as "a nation within a nation."[45] These minorities may identify both with the states' symbols and with the group's unique national symbols.[46] This practice is possible for nations composed of "nested nationalities"[47]—nations that have an overarching identity with which all national minorities can identify, but that at the same time acknowledge and formally respect the different groups'

---

40 Examples include the British royal family and the French flag signifying the colors of the French revolution. For other examples see, Yacobson & Rubinstein, *supra* note 12, 160.

41 See, for example, Bahrain Constitution (1973), Art 120(c); Timor-Leste (East Timor) Constitution (2002), art. 156; Romania Constitution (1991), art. 148; Turkey Constitution (1982), art. 4; I thank Dr. Yaniv Roznai for the reference.

42 Yacobson and Rubinstein, *supra* note 12, 160.

43 However, for the Muslims in India, this may seem a symbol of idolatry. *Id.*

44 The concept of the passive symbol was advocated by the Italian government in Lautsi v. Italy, App. No. 30814/06, Eur. Ct. H.R. (G.C.) (2011). In that case, discussed by the European Court of Human Rights, the Court determined that the compulsory display of crucifixes in Italian state-school classrooms did not infringe upon the right of parents to ensure that the education and teaching of their children is "in conformity with their own religious and philosophical convictions." See, Gregor Puppinck, *The Case of Lautsi v. Italy: A Synthesis*, 3 B.Y.U.L REV. 873 (2012).

45 Miller, Nationality in Divided Societies, *supra* note 35, 306.

46 *Id.*

47 *Id.*

unique national identities through the political structure and the mechanisms of governance.[48] Nevertheless, as I have shown in the above discussion on federal systems, this solution is not always acceptable to all various nationalities; the cases of the separatist Catalan movement and the trends of secession of Belgium's Flemish and Walloon movements and of Quebecers in Canada are relevant examples proving this claim.[49]

As a consequence, alternative symbols systems are sometimes created by interest groups, individuals, and institutions struggling to advance their own programs.[50] These goals can be achieved with the support and acceptance of the state, as seen in the cases of Spanish Catalans, who preserve their own language,[51] flag, and national anthem,[52] as well as of the Walloons and Flemings in Belgium and the Quebecers in Canada, who all maintain their own languages, anthems, flags, and national days.[53] However, such symbols can also be used in protest, as was the case in the spring of 2006 during the outbreak of demonstrations in the Los Angeles area of California, US, when illegal residents sang the American national anthem in Spanish, in this way raising the political question: "To whom does this anthem belong?"[54]

48 See Miller's discussion of the British national identity, which encompasses both English and Scottish identities, *id.*, 307–312. See also his brief discussion of other nested nationalities in Belgium and Spain, *id.*, 305–306.

49 See the discussion in Chapter 3.

50 Smith, National Symbols, *supra* note 3, 527.

51 Catalan was accorded the status of a formal language in the Spanish Constitution. See, LA CONSTITUCIÓN ESPAÑOLA, Dec. 29, 1978, BOE núm. 311, art. 3 [hereinafter *The Spanish Constitution*]. See also, the Statute of Autonomy of Catalonia, Organic Act 4/1979, 18 Dec. 1979.

52 Ehrlich notes that at the opening ceremonies of the Barcelona Olympics in 1992, the Catalan flag was flown and the Catalan anthem was played. See Charles E. Ehrlich, *Democratic Alternatives to Ethnic Conflict: Consociationalism and Neoseparatism*, 26 BROOKLYN J. INT'L L. 447, 473 (2000).

53 Louis Vos, *Reconstructions of the Past in Belgium and Flanders*, *in* SECESSION, HISTORY AND THE SOCIAL SCEINCES 179, 187–188 (Bruno Coppieters and Michel Huysseune eds., 2002).

54 Judith Butler, Gayatri Chakravorty Spivak, WHO SINGS THE NATION-STATE? LANGUAGE, POLITICS, BELONGING 58 (2007). Other examples of an alternative framework of symbols introduced by minority groups are: the aboriginals in Australia, who fly their own flag; the NSA movement in South Africa, which encouraged an alternative framework of symbols for the blacks during the struggle for independence in South Africa; and the undercover and illegal struggle of the Kurds to express their national identity in Turkey. For a discussion of the last example see, Edip Yuksel, *Yes, I am a Kurd*, 7 D.C.L.J. INT'L L. & PRAC. 359 (1998).

The above notwithstanding, the formation of national symbols and modes of association and interpretation of them suggest that it would be possible to integrate national minorities through national symbols. Symbols relate directly to issues of power and authority, incorporating interests such as "the political culture, group unity, political demands and responses by elite and masses, international intercourse and social stability and change."[55] However, creating a coherent body of symbols for a nation is neither simple nor static.[56] The process of forming and maintaining collective memory can be

> ongoing and dynamic [and the] historical symbolic meaning [may be] constantly recycled, actualized, challenged, renegotiated and reconfirmed, or rewritten, depending on changes in public consensus or the ability or inability of a particular hegemonic societal group to maintain its hold on the collective imaginary.[57]

In this way, the symbols themselves may change or the meanings assigned to them may be "subsequently...altered, forgotten, or elaborated upon."[58] Indeed, while the sense of a national identity of a group is considered relatively fixed, the mythology accompanying national identities, comprised of more or less concrete symbols, is much more malleable.[59] This is fortified by the fact that "the emotional meanings associated with a symbol need not have a substantive relationship to it to be effective, and indeed, most symbols, even when sanctioned by tradition, are intrinsically arbitrary."[60] Theoretically, therefore, minority communities can participate in the process of the formation of symbols, which is part of the larger process of the formation of the nation itself—"justifying the moral basis of the nation's claim to statehood, explaining its past and its objectives for the future and defining the acceptable forms of political dialogue."[61]

Moreover, if inclusive models of citizenship like multicultural democracy, contestatory democracy, and deliberative or communicative democracy are used to facilitate political dialogue, there are many more chances for the voices

55 Smith, National Symbols, *supra* note 3, 529.

56 *Id.*, 529.

57 Geisler, *supra* note 20, XVIII.

58 Smith, National Symbols, *supra* note 3, 521.

59 Will Kymlicka, MULTICULTURAL CITIZENSHIP: A LIBERAL THEORY OF MINORITY RIGHTS 185 (1995).

60 Smith, National Symbols, *supra* note 3, 527.

61 *Id.*, 529.

of national minorities to be heard and their interests considered when forming symbols.[62] This is because such multicultural attitudes focus on the processes of deliberation and opinion formation in civil society, giving minorities the chance to influence public opinion and to root their beliefs, culture, and ways of life in it.[63]

This process of listening and hearing the voices of national minorities is strengthened when it is connected to the politics of reconciliation.[64] It is now accepted that a state cannot meaningfully acknowledge diversity without first accounting for historic injustice.[65] Because minority groups that call for inclusion are often responding to past unjustified hierarchies and stigmatization, the accommodations to fulfilling their claims must include a historic dimension and a form of acknowledging and remedying past wrongs.[66]

Minority participation in forming national symbols has practical ramifications. In some states that formally acknowledge various national communities, such as Belgium and Canada, each community sings its own version of the national anthem in its own language.[67] This is extremely significant, as the national anthem reflects the narrative of the nation's birth and development.[68] By allowing a minority to have its own version of the anthem, a state allows it to express its own narrative—that is, its own perspective and notion of the nation's history, tradition, and culture, upon which the nation's overall identity is formed.[69] This narrative, when juxtaposed with competing interpretations of other groups in the state, influences how the "living together" element of civic nationalism is shaped, including the normative, legal interpretation of the rights and duties of the compatriots.[70]

Thus, even the national anthem, one of the most powerful national symbols—encompassing the history, tradition, and legacy of a nation and

---

62 *Struggles for Inclusion and Reconciliation in Modern Democracies*, *in* THE POLITICS OF RECONCILIATION IN MULTICULTURAL SOCIETIES 1, 2 (Bashir Bashir and Will Kymlicka eds., 2008).

63 *Id.*, 9.

64 *Id.*, 5.

65 *Id.*

66 *Id.*

67 Spain has an original solution for that problem: a national anthem with no lyrics.

68 Jean-François Gaudreault-DesBiens, *The Quebec Secession Reference and the Judicial Arbitration of Conflicting Narratives About Law, Democracy and Identity*, 23 VT. L. REV. 793, 798 (1999).

69 *Id.*

70 *Id.* For an analysis of the different narratives that emerge from the two versions of *O Canada*, the Canadian national anthem, see, *id.*, 803–805.

serving as a tool for identification with the nation's past valour and its future hope for prosperity[71]—can become meaningful and unifying for different groups within the nation. This conclusion is strengthened by the fact that national anthems, despite their centrality to the mythology of the nation-state, are not as rigid as they might appear. We find evidence of this in many examples of states that have changed their national anthems when the political circumstances demanded it: Guatemala slightly modified its national anthem in 1934 to soften the bloody context of some of the verses;[72] Nicaragua accepted a new formal version of its national anthem in 1939, after a long period of political upheaval and a civil war;[73] and Austria, Bulgaria, and Rumania changed their national anthems after the Second World War,[74] as did the Soviet Union in 1944 when it replaced the *international* with the State Anthem of the USSR. With the dissolution of the USSR in 1991 the Russian Federation was willing to adopt a new national anthem, and succeeded in doing so in 2000. Lastly, South Africa adopted a new national anthem in 1995 after the revolution and change of regime: a combined version of the "*Die Stem van Suid-Afrika*" (The Call of South Africa), South Africa's national anthem since 1957, and "*'Nkosi Sikelel' iAfrika*" (God Bless Africa), a hymn that was adopted by the African National Congress (ANC) in 1925 as its national anthem and which served as a symbol of the protest against apartheid.[75] The new national anthem is composed of South Africa's five official languages.[76]

The national flag is another significant long-established national symbol that is in some cases enshrined in the constitution and whose change often requires a revolutionary change of government.[77] Like the anthem, the flag bears specific meaning with regard to the characteristics of the nation, such as "its struggle for existence, its natural resources, its ethnic or religious composition and its dedication to such virtues such as peace and progress."[78] However, it also carries messages common to each and every nation: "its vitality,

---

71 For a discussion of the development and significance of national anthems throughout the world see, Joseph Zikmund II, *National Anthems as Political Symbols*, XIII(3) THE AUSTRALIAN JOURNAL OF POLITICS AND HISTORY 73 (1989).

72 *Guatemala*, NATIONALANTHEMS INFO, <http://www.nationalanthems.info/gt.htm>.

73 *Nicaragua*, NATIONAL ANTHEMS OF THE WORLD ORGANIZATION, <http://www.national-anthems.org/history.php#s-africa>. [hereinafter *NAW*].

74 Zikmund, *supra* note 71, 78, note 13.

75 South Africa, NAW, *supra* note 73.

76 *Id.*

77 Smith, National Symbols, *supra* note 3, 529.

78 *Id.*

immortality, sacredness, and supremacy."[79] Furthermore, as Smith observes, many characteristics of a flag make it a powerful symbol suited to myth-building, one that individuals and groups can use to recall certain ideas and events: "the appeal of its colors and emblems, its relative inexpensiveness and ease of manufacture, its hypnotic motion when flying, its long-distance visibility,"[80] as well as its historic legacy.[81]

The significance of the national flag in providing a tool for identification with the nation's mythology and the values it inculcates is therefore not to be exaggerated. As a consequence, and in order to make such identification possible for everyone in the state, some national flags aim to represent the various communities that established the nation: for example, the British flag, with three crosses representing England, Scotland, and Ireland; or the Belgian flag, incorporating both the colors of the Duchy of Brabant (representing the Flemish community) and the vertical design based on the French flag (representing the Walloons). Other state flags reflect the civic nationalistic legacy: for example, the French Tricolour, which adopts the colors used by the Paris militia during the battle of the Bastille; or the American flag, which celebrates the establishment of the US through equally representing all the states of the country.

In addition, a national flag's unique status is usually protected against domestic changes.[82] Indeed, a relatively small number of states have changed their national flags in any significant way, and these changes were usually the consequence of a major revolution or change of regime, as in South Africa in 1994 or the dissolution of the USSR.[83] This observation seems discouraging for underrepresented minorities whose culture and tradition are not reflected in national flags while the majority's are prominent—as is the case of the Israeli flag, which does not represent the Arab minority. However, the replacement of the Canadian flag, discussed below, serves as an inspiring case for national minorities striving for representation through the state's symbols.

---

79 *Id.*, citing Weitman S.R., National Flags: A Sociological Overview.

80 *Id.*

81 *Id.*

82 *Id.*

83 An exception is the Canadian flag, which was modified in 1965 without a political revolution. This case is described below. In February 2014, the New Zealand government suggested a referendum on the question of modifying the national flag, which is composed of the British Union Jack and four stars. One suggestion was to include the silver fern, one of New Zealand's national symbols. See, *New Zealand Considers Flag Referendum*, THEGUARDIAN, Feb. 3, 2014, <http://www.theguardian.com/world/2014/feb/03/new-zealand-plans-flag-referendum>.

The modification of the flag, which formerly represented only the English-Canadian community, into one stripped of the cultural symbols of either the French or English communities required neither a political revolution nor an extreme change of regime.[84] Indeed, this case introduces some trajectories that minorities demanding representation in the state's symbols can follow.

The first Canadian flag, the "red ensign" with the British Union Jack in its left corner and the coat of arms of the Canadian army in its right, was first approved in 1892, according to permission given by the colonial United Kingdom. In 1894, it was determined that this flag would be flown as Canada's formal flag, both inside and outside the country, until the Canadian parliament chose an independent flag.[85] The initiative to design an independent flag for Canada was started in 1964 by Lester Pearson, then a member of the liberal party and later Canada's prime minister.[86] Pearson was motivated by the liberal belief that "national unity [in Canada] must be based on two races, cultures, traditions, and languages: on a full and equal partnership of English and French-speaking Canadians."[87] He intended to base national unity upon the guiding principle of finding a common, broad Canadian base with which diverse groups of Canadians could identify, but through which they could, at the same time, find anew their special place in society.[88] In other words, Pearson believed that the establishment of a unifying Canadian identity demanded a process in which all the various groupings of Canadians (but mainly English Canadians and French Canadians) should participate, and the adoption of a new flag should be the first step in this project.[89]

As a result, the flag's design promoted by Pearson and his partners embodied a neutral Canadian symbol—a maple leaf—and demanded the omission of any cultural symbols of the two major cultures of Canada. Neither the French *fleur de lis* nor the English Union Jack was represented on the flag.[90] This proposal garnered different reactions from various sections of Canadian society. The supporters adhered to the concept of neutral unity advocated by Pearson; however, the objectors, who centered in Quebec, claimed that this unity was an artificial expression of Pearson's wish rather than something that existed in

84 See, Henry S. Albinski, *Politics and Biculturalism in Canada: The Flag Debate*, THE AUSTRALIAN JOURNAL OF POLITICS AND HISTORY 169 (1967).

85 *Id.*, 169.

86 *Id.*

87 *Id.*, 172, citing Pearson.

88 *Id.*

89 *Id.*

90 *Id.*, 170.

reality.[91] The objectors, motivated by the lessons of the Quiet Revolution—that French Canadians should no longer be "servants in [their] own house"[92] and should be "equally recogni[zed] as one of the founding nations [of Canada] ... that is struggling to maintain its culture"[93]—suggested that a recognition of the two deeply entrenched and contributing races to Canada's national identity was required. Otherwise, any construct of a new, but false, identity would fall apart.[94]

Political compromises eventually succeeded in appeasing the objectors[95] and the maple leaf flag was inaugurated on February 15, 1965.[96] The implications of the process of adopting the Canadian flag in order to create a sense of unity and belonging of Canadian citizens to a united Canada need further analysis before any concrete conclusions can be reached. However, the efforts dedicated to the design of the new flag by both supporters and objectors reflect the significance of symbolic representation in nurturing a national identity in general, and within a divided society in particular. Furthermore, the case of the Canadian flag clarifies the dilemmas that divided societies may face when venturing to form a cohesive identity. Should such an identity be construed as a fresh, new concept that detaches itself from the cultural heritages of the comprising communities? Or should it incorporate those cultural characteristics and use them as an integrating tool that does not ignore the differences but tries to mitigate them? Finally, a more deeply rooted question arises regarding the connections between the symbolic and the abstract identity: Which concept should come first: should a cohesive identity be forged before it can be represented by symbolic means, or can the symbolic means create the identity?

The answer to this question connects back to the model of civic-nationalism-plus suggested in this chapter. Concrete symbols are crucial to fostering a sense of belonging in the compatriots of the nation; however, in divided societies that have gone through the processes of deliberative, contestatory or multicultural democratization combined with a politics of reconciliation, the common denominators of such symbolism are built upon a civic identity that disseminates the values of equality, mutual respect, and tolerance among the diverse groups. This combination of civic nationalism and symbolic expression is essential in providing the fertile ground for developing symbols that are

91 *Id.*, 174.

92 *Id.*, 172.

93 *Id.*

94 *Id.*, 174.

95 For an elaboration on the negotiations between the political parties, see, *id.*, 176–186.

96 *Id.*, 169.

meaningful for the compatriots. Only then will compatriots' commitment to those symbols, as well as the sense of belonging that the symbols inculcate among the compatriots of the nation, be genuine.

As a final point in this chapter, I will discuss the role of public institutions in creating and preserving national symbols. National symbols are produced by social institutions. For example, parliaments and governments determine the flag and the national anthem, the most fundamental national symbols; the legal branch of governance is responsible for symbols with legal implications, such as the declaration of independence; and other governmental ministries also influence the character of national symbols, such as the ministry of education, which is responsible for school curricula on history and literature, or the ministry of culture, which is responsible for designing national museums and constructing state historic monuments.

Yet, in multinational states, the role of institutions is quite complicated, as they must refer in their considerations to the "identity politics" of the various national groups. Identity politics is a multicultural process "in which a diverse array of identity groups become politicized and mobilized on the basis of [several group characteristics, nationality among them]."[97] Indeed, identity politics is criticized for the fact that it stresses what distinguishes groups rather than what unites them:[98] "The boundaries that define the group, unite it, and distinguish it from other groups are reinforced and efforts to reconfigure group identity are rejected as forms of fragmentation or even disloyalty."[99] This point is crucial when national symbols that should focus on tying and binding elements are at stake.

It is, therefore, the responsibility of institutions to ensure that while group practices and identity categories are protected, they do not entrench hierarchies and essentialize identities.[100] It is rather "more fluid or hybrid notions of membership...reflect[ing] the nature of people's social attachments and identities" that should be developed.[101] Such methods of incorporation would profit from the benefits of identity politics rather than suffer from its pitfalls. When identity groups become democratically engaged in the broader political community, they can mobilize their identities in contributive ways, such as

---

97 Avigail Eisenberg and Will Kymlicka, *Bringing Institutions Back In: How Public Institutions Assess Identity*, *in* IDENTITY POLITICS IN THE PUBLIC REALM: BRINGING INSTITUTIONS BACK IN 1(Avigail Eisenberg and Will Kymlicka eds., 2011).

98 *Id.*, 6.

99 *Id.*, 20.

100 *Id.*

101 *Id.*

to wage struggles against discrimination and to ensure their interests in the larger society.[102] In the context of fostering national symbols, identity politics applied carefully by governmental institutions can achieve the goals of deliberative democracy and allow minorities to make their mark in the process of creating national symbols.

In conclusion, the civic-nationalism-plus model of citizenship acknowledges that common citizenship cannot be based solely on the abstract commitment to just mechanisms and institutions, but requires identification with tangible objects as concrete national symbols. It also stresses the importance of ways that national minorities can take part in the formation of such symbols. Such processes, however, cannot be artificially construed. They need to be rooted in society's willingness to accept both diversity and a common life of the various groups forming a multinational state. Such willingness requires a solid societal preparation, which can be achieved through education in general and multicultural education in particular. In the next chapter I discuss the concept of multicultural education developed since the mid-20th century, explore its achievements, and apply this to the question of how common citizenship can be entrenched.

---

102 *Id.*, 22.

CHAPTER 6

Multicultural Education and Multicultural Citizenship: Toward Civic Equality

Having framed the model of citizenship in multinational states in the previous chapters, I turn now to explore the societal conditions underlying and effectuating this model. The first condition is a rooted concept of civic equality and multicultural citizenship, which enables implementing civic nationalism's ideal: that is, inculcating within the citizens of a state a commitment to and identification with its just institutions and the basic values of democracy, such as equality and human dignity. The second condition, which in fact precedes and underlies the former, is multicultural education, which ingrains the ideals of civic equality and diversity in the young generation, thereby improving the chances of the citizenship model being rooted and applied.

Civic equality is a democratic ideal according to which "individuals should be treated and treat one another as equal citizens, regardless of their gender, race, ethnicity, or religion."[1] In addition, and according to the concept of multiculturalism, civic equality also includes toleration and recognition of cultural differences.[2] Indeed, not all cultural practices should be tolerated, but those which aid, or at least do not impede, civic equality should be tolerated and recognized.[3] Furthermore, the ideal of civic equality can be actualized only if all of the various groups in the multinational state are committed to this idea.[4]

Democratic states can apply civic equality in two different ways. They can practice assimilation and universalism to ensure citizens relinquish their first languages and cultures (in case these do not belong to the dominant mainstream culture of the nation-state)[5] or they can use multicultural practices of recognition and toleration. Assimilation and universalism with regard to

---

1 Amy Gutman, *Unity and Diversity in Democratic Multicultural Education: Creative and Destructive Tensions, in* DIVERSITY AND CITIZENSHIP EDUCATION: GLOBAL PERSPECTIVES 71 (James A. Banks ed., 2003).

2 *Id.*, 72.

3 *Id.*

4 *Id.*, 85.

5 James A. Banks, *Diversity, Group Identity, and Citizenship Education in a Global Age Diversity, in* DEMOCRACY AND MULTICULTURAL EDUCATION 17 (Farideh Salili and Rumjahn Hoosain eds., 2010) [hereinafter *Banks, Diversity, Group Identity*].

 | DOI 10.1163/9789004294332_008

citizenship were common among nation-states until the mid-20th century.[6] According to these practices, the rights of individuals are paramount, and identity group rights conflict with individual rights because they promote group rights over individual free choice.[7] Therefore, citizenship should transcend particularity and difference and be applied according to laws that are neutral to group affiliation.[8] But since the 1960s,[9] multicultural theories have begun to influence governmental and educational policies, first in the US[10] and later in Europe, Australia, and other parts of the world. According to multiculturalism, citizens should not assimilate into the major culture but should rather preserve the right to realize their own culture and language as long as the practices of their culture do not contradict the democratic ideals of the nation-state.[11] In addition, and according to the policy of recognition, the dominant culture should incorporate aspects of minorities' cultural experiences as well as their languages. In this way, all of the groups to which the citizens belong are entitled to an equal right of representation in the civic culture.[12]

Yet, the challenge for multinational states implementing multicultural policies to sustain civic equality is, as have I mentioned in previous chapters, how to recognize and legitimize diversity and at the same time construct an overarching national identity based on citizens' shared values and goals.[13] This challenge can be addressed by multicultural education.

Multicultural Education

Multicultural education is a pedagogic system that developed out of the 1960s Civil Rights Movement in the US[14] and, as a reform movement, was intended to

6 *Id.*, 17.

7 *Id.*, 19.

8 *Id.*, 21.

9 Banks claims that these theories have earlier roots, and that scholars expressed these ideas already by the beginning of the 20th century. See *id.*, 18.

10 *Id.*, 17.

11 *Id.*, 18.

12 *Id.*

13 *Id.*, 25.

14 Christine E. Sleeter and Peter L. McLaren, *in* MULTICULTURAL EDUCATION, CRITICAL PEDAGOGY, AND THE POLITICS OF DIFFERENCE 11 (Christine E. Sleeter and Peter L. McLaren eds., 1995). Another similar system is "critical pedagogy." For a discussion of this system see *id.*, 1–28.

create social change.[15] It was designed to further the democratic principles of social justice[16] and to endorse civic equality among the educated public[17] both by tolerating different cultural practices, to the extent that they do not conflict with democratic values, and by recognizing the contribution of the cultures of a state's diverse groups in shaping the state's society, culture, and history.[18]

Over the last four decades, multicultural education has developed and spread around the world—from the US to Europe, Australia, and South Africa.[19] During these years, it has been extensively researched and applied, with profound implications for international legal documents determining the right to education in general, and education for cultural minorities in particular. In this section, I will overview this system's goals, achievements, and challenges; however, I begin by surveying its implications in the international legal sphere.

The earliest legal document (in the United Nations era)[20] protecting minorities' right to operate an independent educational system while integrating within the general (majority) state culture was the 1960 UNESCO Convention Against Discrimination in Education.[21] This convention determined "the right of members of national minorities to carry on their own educational activities, including the maintenance of schools and...the use or the teaching of their own language."[22] Yet, it also determined three preconditions for the application of the right. The most important for the purposes of integration is the first:

---

15 Geneva Gay, *Curriculum Theory and Multicultural Education, in* HANDBOOK OF RESEARCH OF MULTICULTURAL EDUCATION 30, 33–34 (James A. Banks ed., 2nd ed., 2004).

16 *Id.*, 34.

17 Usually young children or students, but in other cases also adults. For adult education see my discussion of civic education below.

18 Gutman, *supra* note 1, 71.

19 *Id.*, 72.

20 There have been various agreements with minorities in previous periods, for example the Millet system in the Turkish Empire, which allowed for religious freedoms for the several congregations under the rule of the Empire, and the post–World War I agreements, which allowed for specific group rights for minorities within the new states that emerged after the war. For analysis see, Natan Lerner, *The Minorities Treaties System, in* GROUP RIGHTS AND DISCRIMINATION IN INTERNATIONAL LAW 10 (2003); Michael M. Karayanni, *The Separate Nature of the Religious Accommodations for the Palestinian-Arab Minority in Israel*, 5 (1) JIHR 41, 44 (2007).

21 1960 UNESCO Convention Against Discrimination in Education adopted at the thirtieth plenary meeting, 14 December 1960, available at: <http://unesdoc.unesco.org/images/0013/001325/132598e.pdf>. [hereinafter *UNESCO Convention Against Discrimination in Education*].

22 *Id.*, Para. IV.

> (i) That this right is not exercised in a manner which prevents the members of these minorities from understanding the culture and language of the community as a whole and from participating in its activities, or which prejudices national sovereignty.[23]

The right to education continued to receive increasing attention in international law and was developed in the 1989 International Convention on the Rights of the Child.[24] Following this, two additional international documents emerged referring to the right of education of national minorities. The first was the Hague Recommendations Regarding the Education Rights of National Minorities,[25] which elaborated on the rights of minorities to independent education and expanded the obligations of nation-states by determining that

> where required, special measures should be adopted by States to *actively* implement minority language education rights to the maximum of their available resources, individually and through international assistance and cooperation, especially economic and technical. [Emphasis added.][26]

The second legal document was Council of Europe Framework Convention for the Protection of National Minorities,[27] which expresses similar ideas but does not oblige state parties to provide the means for the establishment and finance of private education of minorities.

It is important to note that all of the above described documents stress the importance of integration within "the wider national society," to use the words of the Hague Recommendations.[28] Integration is interpreted according to a multicultural perception, so that both the majority and the minority are required to become acquainted with each other's cultures. As the Hague Recommendations elaborate:

---

23 *Id.*

24 Convention on the Rights of the Child, Nov. 20, 1989, 1577 U.N.T.S. 3 [hereinafter CRC].

25 The Hague Recommendations Regarding the Education Rights of National Minorities, High Commissioner on National Minorities, 1 October 1996, available at: <http://www.refworld.org/docid/3dde52563.html>. [hereinafter *The Hague Recommendations*].

26 *Id.*, para. 4.

27 Council of Europe, Framework Convention for the Protection of National Minorities, 1 February 1995, ETS 157, available at: <http://www.refworld.org/docid/3ae6b36210.html>. [hereinafter *Council of Europe Framework Convention*].

28 The Hague Recommendations, *supra* note 25, para. 1 and see also Council of Europe Framework Convention, *supra* note 27, art.14, requiring that minorities learn the official language of their state.

> (19) In view of *the importance and value* that international instruments attach to *intercultural education and the highlighting of minority histories, cultures and traditions*, State educational authorities should ensure that the general *compulsory curriculum* includes the teaching of the histories, cultures and traditions of their respective national minorities. Encouraging members of the majority to learn the languages of the national minorities living within the State would contribute to the strengthening of tolerance and multiculturalism within the State. [Emphasis added.]
>
> (20) The curriculum content related to minorities should be developed with the active participation of bodies representative of the minorities in question.[29]

Indeed, the Hague Recommendations reiterate the two fundamental values of multicultural education, that is, tolerance and recognition. In addition, they stress the importance of one of the practical means multicultural education uses to realize these values: curriculum. I elaborate on these basic elements and the other foundations of multicultural education in the following paragraphs.

In addition to tolerance and recognition, multicultural education emphasizes equality and equity in education, as it demands

> equitable education to all students regardless of ethnic and cultural background or religious affiliation, [and it] is implemented to enhance tolerance, respect, understanding, awareness, and acceptance of self and others in the diversity of their cultures.[30]

However, the most fundamental element in multicultural education remains culture. Culture is understood as the substance of living and it penetrates and forms all of the personal and communal aspects of a person's life.[31] It provides for "patterns for interpreting reality, and it consists of behavior, ideas, attitudes, habits, customs, beliefs, values, language, rituals, and ceremonies."[32] All of these aspects of culture are also related to the common life in a multinational state, and they are addressed through multicultural

29 The Hague Recommendations, *supra* note 25, arts. 19–20.

30 Hasan Arslan, *Multicultural Education: Approaches, Dimensions and Principles*, *in* MULTICULTURAL EDUCATION: FROM THEORY TO PRACTICE 15 (Hasan Arslan and Georgeta Raţă eds., 2013).

31 *Id.*

32 *Id.*

education in the school system. Multicultural education aims at reforming schools and other educational institutions in order to promote the values discussed above.[33]

Banks identifies five dimensions of multicultural education in the school system:

> (i) content integration—the extent to which teachers use data and examples from a variety of cultures and groups in the course of teaching their subject area or discipline; (ii) knowledge construction—the procedures by which scientists create knowledge and understand how implicit cultural assumptions, perspectives and biases influence knowledge construction; (iii) prejudice reduction—the characteristics of children's racial attitudes and strategies that can be used to help students develop more democratic attitudes and values; (iv) equity pedagogy—the use of techniques and methods that facilitate the academic achievement of students from diverse racial, ethnic and social-class groups; (v) empowering school culture—the process of restructuring the culture and organization of the school to enable students from diverse groups to experience educational equality and cultural empowerment.[34]

Multicultural education addresses all sorts of diverse groups, ranging from racial and ethnic to social-class and gender, in this way referring not only to issues of toleration and recognition but also those of educational gaps and academic under achievement resulting from past deficiencies of means conferred upon certain groups. However, I will focus here on the aspects of multicultural education that can contribute to the promotion of equal citizenship in multinational states. In addition, I will focus on multicultural educational programs that focus on local diversity, i.e., I take account of the different cultural aspects of communities in a specific nation-state, and do not intend to present an international multicultural perspective. Indeed, the history and tradition of the different cultures of the world, including aboriginal peoples, is relevant and enriching in the cosmopolitan society that has resulted from globalization in the

33 James A. Banks, *Multicultural Education: Historical Development, Dimensions, and Practice*, 19 Review of Research in Education 3 (1993) [hereinafter *Banks, Multicultural Education*].

34 *Id.*, 4–7.

last decades.[35] In addition, global multicultural studies can increase people's general openness towards diversity and improve their intercultural skills.[36]

However, international multiculturalism is crucially deficient in its ability to resolve the tensions between the different communities within the nation-state and to bring about a more cohesive society. Because they are not "inward-looking," global multicultural programs do not enable divided societies to deeply examine their own relationships or cope with their own "historical or political baggage."[37] The goal of local multicultural programs, by contrast, is to cope with exactly those issues that global multicultural programs lack the means to tackle. Hence, my focus hereinafter will be on local multicultural educational programs, specifically on their implementation of three dimensions of multicultural education—knowledge construction, content integration and prejudice reduction—as they are referred to by Banks above.

I begin with the first two dimensions: *knowledge construction* and *content integration* in school's curricula. The potential of schools to promote social cohesiveness, but not at the expense of cultural diversity, depends on whether the school can inculcate among students the idea of perceiving diversity as richness rather than as grounds for separation.[38] This goal is achieved by reforming schools' curricula. In order to form a tolerant and difference-recognizing society, the curricula in multicultural schools should emphasize the implications of how knowledge is constructed and taught. Content should be integrated and knowledge should be constructed in a way that addresses culture and does not ignore it. Such a curriculum construction "would help students understand how cultural, national, regional and global identifications are interrelated, complex and evolving… [and] to critically examine their identifications and commitments."[39]

In addition, knowledge construction and content integration must lead to changes in traditional curricula so as to reflect the way that the history of national groups in the nation-state both (actively) influenced and was (passively) influenced by the nation-state's main or majority history and culture.[40] In other words, school curricula should address both the oppression and the

---

35 Sigrid Luchtenberg, *Multicultural Education: Challenges and Responses*, 4(1) Journal of Social Science Education 31, 40 (2005).

36 Will Kymlicka, *Multicultural States and Intercultural Citizens*, 1(2) Theory and Research in Education 147, 157–158 (2003).

37 *Id.*, 160; Luchtenberg, *supra* note 35, 40.

38 Arslan, *supra* note 30, 16.

39 Banks, Diversity, Group Identity, *supra* note 5, 29.

40 Gutman, *supra* note 1, 78–79.

contribution of minority culture to the nation-state.[41] It should be constructed according to the "politics of representation."[42] That is, school's curricula must reflect how "a specific kind of knowledge, conception, or symbolic image of and about a thing, event, place, or people is constructed"[43] and to confront the supremacy of Western cultural knowledge transmitted in school with "the inherent primacy of the multiple and collective origins of knowledge."[44]

Such curricula construction can help students understand their diverse nature.[45] In addition, as it creates "transformative classrooms in which education is reimagined and transformed,"[46] the curriculum shows "respect for individuals by virtue of their group identity."[47] When students "are taught in a manner that reflects their surroundings [and] personal experiences"[48] education fulfills the purposes of recognition and, as a result, of incorporation of both the majority and the minority culture into the larger state culture. The curricula are, therefore, based on transformative knowledge, taught in transformative classrooms and schools.[49] Transformative knowledge is created when knowledge shifts from a mainstream academic curriculum, which reinforces traditional and established knowledge, to knowledge that provides for "paradigms and explanations that challenge some of the key…assumptions of mainstream knowledge."[50] As deliberation among citizens from diverse groups is essential for a democratic society, transformative knowledge creates transformative classrooms and schools, in which students from different groups "view events from diverse perspectives and [are able] to deliberate [and interact] in equal-status situations."[51]

In addition to the dimension of knowledge construction and content integration handled by redesigning schools' curricula, multicultural education is also based on the socio-psychological dimension that includes *prejudice reduction*. Multicultural education focuses on researching and taking account of children's racial attitudes and strategies, which can be used to help

41 *Id.*, 79.
42 Gay, *supra* note 15, 40.
43 *Id.*, citing S. Nieto, AFFIRMING DIVERSITY: THE SOCIOPOLITICAL CONTEXT OF MULTICULTURAL EDUCATION 101 (3rd ed., 2000) 101.
44 *Id.*
45 Arslan, *supra* note 30, 28.
46 Banks, Diversity, Group Identity, *supra* note 5, 29.
47 Gutman, *supra* note 1, 79.
48 Arslan, *supra* note 30, 28.
49 Banks, Diversity, Group Identity, *supra* note 5, 29.
50 *Id.*
51 *Id.*, 31.

students develop more democratic attitudes and values. One of the goals of multicultural education is, therefore, to improve intergroup relations and to foster positive ones.[52] This is definitely "a formidable task, [as] the negative elements of these relations are deeply embedded in the history of every society, and without intervention, tend to be replicated across generations."[53] Therefore, socio-psychological research and theory provide tools to educators to understand the causes of the processes leading to hostile feelings (such as prejudice, stereotyping, and discrimination) and to cope with and neutralize them.[54] Prejudice is defined as "negative attitudes toward social groups" and it can be founded on any group-based characteristics.[55] Discrimination is the behavioral component of the attitude of prejudice and "it consists of a selectively unjustifiable behavior toward members of a target group."[56] Stereotyping is the categorization of people into groups according to characteristics attributed to categories of people.[57]

Prejudice, stereotyping, and discrimination are more prevalent in situations of resegregation.[58] Even in racially or ethnically mixed schools, there may be situations where students have no meaningful intergroup contact. This can be the result either of a voluntary attitude of group-members or of a school policy that puts students into classes or tracks based on achievement—which often match ethnic or racial division.[59] This phenomenon of absence or near absence of contact is called "resegregation" and strategies to cope with it should be forged. Several socio-psychological theories outline conditions and ways to avoid segregation and the resulting negative attitudes, including cognitive, social structure, and behavioral theories and processes.[60]

One of the most influential behavioral theories is Gordon W. Allport's contact hypothesis.[61] According to the contact hypothesis, three aspects of the

52 Walter G. Stephan, Cookie White Stephan, *Intergroup Relations in Multicultural Education Programs, in* HANDBOOK OF RESEARCH OF MULTICULTURAL EDUCATION 782–798 (James A. Banks ed., 2nd ed., 2004) [hereinafter *Handbook of Research of Multicultural Education*]; Janet Ward Schofield, *Fostering Positive Intergroup Relations in Schools*, *id.*, 799–812.

53 Stephan and Stephan, *supra* note 52, 782.

54 See, generally, *id.*; Schofield, *supra* note 52.

55 Stephan and Stephan, *supra* note 52, 782–783.

56 *Id.*, 783.

57 *Id.*

58 Schofield, *supra* note 52, 800.

59 *Id.*

60 For a review of the theories see Stephan and Stephan, *supra* note 52, 783–793.

61 Schofield, *supra* note 52, 802.

contact situation are particularly important in determining whether positive intergroup relations will develop:

> (i) equal status within the situation for members of all groups; (ii) an emphasis on cooperative activities focused on common goals rather than competitive activities; and (iii) the explicit support of relevant authority figures, laws and customs for positive relations.[62]

Equal status, the first aspect of the contact hypothesis, is the precondition for eradicating stereotypes and beliefs about the superiority and inferiority of the groups involved.[63] Equal status situations should be implemented at the level of both teaching staff and students.[64] Thus, for example, the school should hire equal numbers of faculty and administrators belonging to the various groups comprising the students of the school.[65] A multiethnic school's curricula can also contribute to the equal status of students[66] as can avoidance of grouping students according to academic performance—although the effectiveness of the latter practice remains controversial.[67]

Cooperative activity is the second precondition Allport posits for fostering positive intergroup relations, and in this way eliminating resegregation, and it can be achieved in three ways. The first is to foster superordinate and cross-cut social identities: that is, "creat[ing] and emphasiz[ing] meaningful shared social category memberships for youths of different groups,"[68] for example, by grouping students from different ethnic or racial backgrounds into learning or sports teams. Interestingly, academic research has discovered that forging common signs and symbols, such as school T-shirts and traditions of special songs, improves group interrelations,[69] a finding that echoes the previous chapter's discussion of the importance of national symbols and supports the claim that different national groups should identify with common symbols in order to facilitate a cohesive society. Two other ways to foster cooperative activities are through the personalization of out-group members and the development of intergroup friendships.[70] This involves creating personal relationships

62 *Id.*; see also Stephan and Stephan, *supra* note 52, 787–791.
63 Schofield, *supra* note 52, 802.
64 *Id.*
65 *Id.*
66 See the discussion above regarding school's curricula.
67 Schofield, *supra* note 52, 803.
68 *Id.*, 804.
69 *Id.*
70 *Id.*, 805.

between students that strip the stereotypes from group members and focus on each individual's personality traits and personal skills. Naturally, when people work together they have the opportunity to get more closely acquainted and create intimate personal relationships with out-group members.[71]

The third and final aspect of the Allport's contact hypothesis relates, in the context of a school surrounding, to the interaction between authoritative figures/institutions and the students. It thus refers to the relations between teachers, students, and parents, and to the very way that schools conceptualize the nature of teaching and learning.[72] Indeed, how teachers and administrators think about the populations they serve influences how the students are treated and how they conceptualize themselves.[73] According to organization, social, and political theorists, the trust people have in their leaders determines the effectiveness of the function of systems. It follows, then, that the effectiveness of the relationships between teachers, students, and their parents is conditioned upon the level of trust that students and parents have in the school faculty and administrators.[74] Trust, in turn, is conditioned upon feelings of belonging because "when people feel that they belong, and when they feel connected and cared for, trust is a rational response. [Hence], feelings of trust arise most naturally between people who perceive themselves as having similar backgrounds and characteristics."[75]

One disappointing outcome of the above, however, is that "despite good intentions, when racially and ethnically divided communities are brought together in public schools there are obstacles to trust that educators do not encounter when they mirror their student and parent population."[76] This explains why minority communities distrust dominant white society and, by extension, the school system it controls.[77] Their suspicions of the system are often heightened when they are confronted with demands "of deference and subordination to closed, bureaucratic, systems that do not respond to the specific needs, interests and concerns of their children."[78]

71 *Id.*

72 Gay, *supra* note 15, 34.

73 See the case study of Jefferson Heights High School discussed in Colleen L. Larson, Carlos J. Ovando, The Color of Bureaucracy: The Politics of Equity in Multicultural School Communities (2001).

74 *Id.*, 62.

75 *Id.*

76 *Id.*

77 *Id.*, 84.

78 *Id.*

Like the importance of unifying symbols within the parameters of the contact hypothesis, the notion of trust conditioned upon feelings of belonging also pertains to the theory of citizenship suggested in earlier chapters, as the citizenship theory emphasizes the centrality of feelings of belonging to citizenship. Hence, the connection and the vitality of education in general and multicultural education in particular facilitate the model of citizenship.

Despite socio-psychologists' and educators' support of multicultural education in general and the effectiveness of the above described methods in fostering positive intergroup relations in schools in particular, I should also refer to existing criticism of multicultural education. First, little is in fact known about the impact of multicultural education.[79] Research evaluations with positive findings should be viewed with some suspicion.[80] As Stephan and Stephan have discovered, although multicultural education programs achieve some success in improving attitudes toward out-group members, increasing knowledge of out-groups, and improving multicultural skills, most programs do not fully achieve their goals, and so are less successful than they could be.[81] In addition, there is risk of unintended consequences in multicultural programs, especially given the lack of evidence on whether they reach their goals.[82] Lastly, as Lustig claims, interethnic tensions are aggravated in multicultural educational reforms that highlight each ethnic group both sequentially and in isolation.[83]

Before turning to an overview and evaluation of several specific multicultural programs, I will examine the implications of multicultural educational programs for multicultural capabilities and citizenship education. As noted above, multicultural education endows students with multicultural skills, such

---

79 Zvi Bekerman, *Reshaping Conflict Through School Ceremonial Events in Israeli Palestinians-Jewish Coeducation*, 34(2) ANTHROPOLOGY & EDUCATION QUARTERLY 205, 206 (2003).

80 Stephan and Stephan, *supra* note 52, 793.

81 *Id.*, 793. In the last decade, numerous studies of specific multicultural programs in different countries have been done to assess their success and suggest means of improvement. See, for example, Bekerman, *supra* note 79; Mark Robert, The Construction of Culture in Multicultural Education: Classroom Participation and Teacher-student Interaction in a Jewish-Arab School, Thesis submitted for the degree of Doctor of Philosophy, April 2013; Claire McGlynn, Zvi Bekerman, *The Management of Pupil Difference in Catholic-Protestant and Palestinian-Jewish Integrated Education in Northern Ireland and Israel*, 37(5) COMPARE 689 (2007); Michalinos Zembylas, *Negotiating Co-Existence in Divided Societies: Teachers, Students and Parents' Perspectives at a Shared School in Cyprus*, 25(4) RESEARCH PAPERS IN EDUCATION 433 (2010).

82 Bekerman, *supra* note 79, 206.

83 *Id.* 206.

as openness to other cultures and to diversity. Students who receive multicultural education are thus less self-contained and are capable of "inter-cultural interaction and mutual sharing and learning."[84] Multicultural education is in this way the first stage of citizenship education, or more accurately, transformative citizenship education.[85] Such education endows citizens with various "clarified and reflective" identifications—including cultural, national, regional, and global—and assists them in understanding how these identities are interrelated and constructed.[86] This subtle reflective character of citizenship education requires some clarification. The study of culture can tilt between two polarized modes. One is a superficial acquaintance with a foreign culture—mainly its customs, food, and style of dress—which requires no moral evaluation.[87] The other is a utopian mode that demands respect and appreciation of the foreign culture.[88] Yet, there is a third option that the reflective element of citizenship education seems to aspire to. In this mode, citizens are reflective about every culture they become acquainted with and respect the beliefs held by the people of these cultures.[89] In this sense, citizenship education supplies people with deep skills of cultural learning.

One last point to note about citizenship education is that it develops the social-action skills citizens need to participate constructively in the social life of their communities.[90] Hence, transformative citizenship education makes it possible for citizens to acquire "deep citizenship," which not only endows them with voting rights, but also allows them to be involved in social life at the highest possible level, "to promote social justice [and to] challenge, or dismantle, existing laws, conventions, or structures."[91]

There is a final aspect of multinational education to be accounted for—that is, the personal aspect. Multicultural education supplies skills that contribute to an individual's personal experience and self-development. Being able to have positive interactions with members of other cultures enriches peoples' lives, as it expands their horizons and enables them to think more reflectively and critically about their own beliefs.[92] Multicultural education, therefore,

84 Kymlicka, *supra* note 36, 157.

85 Banks, Diversity, Group Identity, *supra* note 5, 30.

86 *Id.*, 30.

87 Kymlicka, *supra* note 36, 163.

88 *Id.*

89 *Id.*, 164.

90 Banks, Identity, Group Diversity, *supra* note 5, 30.

91 *Id.*, 33.

92 Kymlicka, *supra* note 36, 158.

seems theoretically to have both social and personal advantages. Yet, as mentioned above, on the ground, such education seems to face some challenges, which I explore in the following sub-section.

Multicultural Education Programs

There are several types of multicultural education programs, which are adapted to the kinds of states and populations they are intended for. Generally, multicultural education programs exist in states with two or more homeland communities that live more or less peacefully together, for example, Belgium, Canada, Spain and Switzerland. Such programs are also found in states with large aboriginal populations, including Canada, Spain, the US and Australia. However, multicultural programs can also be found in states whose homeland communities are in conflict, such as Israel, Northern Ireland and Cyprus. These latter types of states will be the focus of the case studies later in this chapter. However, I will begin here with a general presentation of the vocabulary that states use to refer to the different populations they are composed of.

The words people use to refer to diverse populations in states are often ideologically colored and highly influenced by state's history and policy.[93] For example, the term "minorities" in the Netherlands, used to refer to immigrant groups that occupy a lower socioeconomic position, was changed to the more neutral term "*allochtones*" in defining immigrants from outside Netherlands in order to avoid the stigmatizing connotations of the former.[94] In Canada, the term *allochtone* refers to the English- and French-speaking groups that form the major national groups in the state. The term *autochtone*, used interchangeably with "First Nations," applies to the Inuit (Eskimos) and Indians in Canada.[95] In the US, Indian groups are referred to as "natives" or "American Indians." The term "minorities" is used both in the US and in Canada to describe "a cultural deviation from the majority" or to refer to racial characteristics.[96] Yet, while in Canada the majority refers only to the "Charter Groups" (i.e., the groups of English and French origin), this issue is undecided in the US. Some exclusively refer to Anglo-American groups as belonging to the majority culture while

---

93 Lotty Eldering, *Multiculturalism and Multicultural Education in an International Perspective*, 27(3) ANTHROPOLOGY & EDUCATION QUARTERLY 315, 317 (1996).

94 *Id.*, 317.

95 *Id.*

96 *Id.*

others argue that all groups of European origin comprise the majority.[97] Finally, the term "minorities" is detailed further to express what kind of minorities are described: that is, whether they are racial minorities, religious minorities, or national minorities.[98] These explicit definitions are very important when constructing multicultural education programs, as they point to the dividing element that these programs need to address.

Multicultural programs can be categorized in different ways, according to their general approaches, which include (i) the enrichment approach, (ii) the bicultural competence approach, and (iii) the collective equality approach.[99] The underlying assumption of the first approach is that education should take account of the enriching potential that cultural diversity holds for general society.[100] Within this approach, multicultural education is aimed at all pupils, irrespective of their ethnic or cultural origin.[101] The bicultural competence approach has the aim of making pupils competent in two cultures, rather than merely having a general acquaintance with various cultures.[102] The collective equality approach is the most encompassing, as it applies to the whole educational system in the state in tackling inequality. The goals of collective equality can be achieved in two ways. The first is for the state to support diverse cultural groups and facilitate their independent educational systems (e.g., Canada's French and English school systems, or Belgium's French and Flemish school systems[103]); however, this approach does not aim at integration. A second mode is to make the school system more multicultural by changing the curriculum and ensuring that schools have a diverse faculty and staff of representative bodies.[104]

The three approaches outlined above apply different educational methods of multicultural education, which include (i) the liberal multicultural approach; (ii) the plural multicultural approach; (iii) the critical multicultural approach; and (iv) bilingual education.[105] The pluralist multicultural method uses a discourse celebrating diversity, history, and cultural heritage; but because it does not recognize the political context or challenging inequalities in

97 *Id.*
98 *Id.*, 318.
99 *Id.*, 319–321.
100 *Id.*, 320.
101 *Id.*, 320.
102 *Id.*, 321.
103 *Id.*
104 *Id.*
105 See, generally, McGlynn and Bekerman, *supra* note 81; Zembylas, *supra* note 81.

power-relations,[106] it seems to maintain and affirm existing identities rather than enabling the emergence of new ones.[107] By contrast, the liberal multicultural approach aims at "diluting difference and seek[s] to maintain consensus and sameness," thus aiming at a formation of new common identities.[108] Despite this, both plural and liberal multiculturalism belong to mainstream multiculturalism, which emphasizes difference and the importance of recognizing diversity.[109] Critical multiculturalism on the other hand does not focus on diversity or the psychological methods of eradicating prejudice, stereotyping, and discrimination;[110] rather, it emphasizes the political dimension of conflict, the unequal power relationships established and perpetuated within the schools, and the influence of the nation-state's political structure.[111] Critical multiculturalism addresses the impact of collective identity on everyday lives, thus leaving room for competing narratives and different identities.[112] For these reasons, critical multiculturalism assesses plural multiculturalism as being unable to achieve its goals, such as integration, because it avoids the tensions that are inevitably at stake; hence, it "promises an emancipation it can't deliver."[113]

A last theoretical educational approach that often accompanies multicultural education, as they both share many common characteristics and goals, is bilingual education. Bilingual education can be applied in either a one-way or a two-way framework.[114] In the former, minority groups are taught in their own language while the majority group language is taught as a separate subject and increasingly incorporated in their regular studies.[115] In a two-way framework, majority and minority groups are taught each other's languages in the same school.[116] Since bilingual education is one of the characteristics of multicultural education in Israel, its implications will also be accounted for in the three multicultural education case studies—Ireland, Cyprus, and Israel—which I describe and analyze below.

---

106 Robert, *supra* note 81, 41.
107 McGlynn and Bekerman, *supra* note 81, 703.
108 *Id.*, 702–703.
109 Zembylas, *supra* note 81, 437.
110 *Id.*, 449.
111 *Id.*, 449–450.
112 *Id.* 450.
113 McGlynn and Bekerman, *supra* note 81, 702.
114 Robert, *supra* note 81, 36.
115 *Id.*, 36.
116 *Id.*

The case studies I have chosen are located in areas of conflict between two national groups living in the same state, a focus that derives from two related reasons. The first is due to my interest in national groups (rather than racial, religious, or social class groups); groups in conflict areas thus posit the greatest challenge for multicultural education programs because of the high levels of resentment, tension, and previous segregation involved in such relations, leading to prejudice, stereotyping, and discrimination. The fact that multicultural education programs even exist in these areas is surprising, given the assumption that democratic education for civic equality demands as preconditions a peaceful and somewhat unified society.[117] Second, studying multicultural education programs for national groups in conflict areas connects with the following chapter, in which I analyze the case of Israel through the prism of the citizenship model presented in the book—a model that multicultural education aims to support, despite its yet-to-be-solved challenges, discussed below.

Northern Ireland

The conflict in Northern Ireland lies between religious groups (the Catholics and Protestants), but since it is centered in the two groups struggle over rule of the state, it very much resembles a national conflict. Since the Good Friday peace agreement of 1998, the government has taken some initiatives to establish integrated education, which means educating together children from different groups who were usually separately educated.[118] There are currently 62 integrated schools across Northern Ireland, made up of 38 grant-maintained integrated schools and 24 controlled integrated schools.[119] Integration is voluntary and not compulsory, and according to Northern Ireland's department of education, the school year of 2012/13 saw a total enrolment of 21,500 pupils, or 7 percent of total pupils.[120]

The system of the integrated schools in Northern Ireland is based on a liberal approach to multicultural education, in which the question of how much emphasis should be placed on difference is not decided, but there is tendency

---

117 Gutman, *supra* note 1, 91.

118 McGlynn and Bekerman, *supra* note 81, 689, 691.

119 Northern Ireland Council for Integrated Education, NICIE, <http://www.nicie.org/>.; Northern Ireland Department of Education, nidirect, <http://www.deni.gov.uk/index/schools-and-infrastructure-2/schools-management/10-types_of_school-nischools_pg/16-schools-integratedschools_pg.htm>. [hereinafter *Northern Ireland Department of Education*].

120 Northern Ireland Department of Education, *supra* note 119.

to seek consensus and put focus less on difference.[121] It also applies psychological theories, such as the contact theory described above as well as the social identity theory, according to which aspects of the self are derived from the changing social categories people perceive themselves as belonging to.[122]

According to current research on the integrated school system in Northern Ireland, the opportunities that multicultural education provides for children to meet "the other" affect not only the process of molding children's identity, but the process of peacemaking among the conflicted groups. While the experience of these schools clearly shows success in breaking down barriers, developing cross-cutting friendships and broadening horizons of the pupils,[123] the influence upon identity is more complicated. The degree to which teachers should remind the children of their identity is not clearly outlined, but the liberal multicultural education approach does place more emphasis on commonality.[124] This choice is crucial especially because psychological theories of social identity suggest that people in conflict situations tend to perceive themselves primarily as members of a social group and less in terms of the individual components of identity.[125] Hence, an educational approach that plays down difference seems to affect how "individuals…mediate their identities in different social contexts."[126]

Cyprus

In Cyprus, conflict between Greek Cypriots and Turkish Cypriots emerged in the era of British colonialism. It peaked in the 1974 coup of the Greek junta against the Cypriot government, which led to the Turkish invasion of Cyprus. In 1983, Turkish Cypriots' declared the north part of Cyprus an independent state, which to this day is only recognized by Turkey. Cyprus has neither a governmental nor a private system of integrated schools, but since the 2003 partial lifting of restrictions in movements between the boundaries that divide Cyprus, a few international private schools have accepted Turkish Cypriot students so that Greek Cypriots and Turkish Cypriots could learn together.[127]

A study conducted on one of these schools suggested that the co-existence of the opposing groups in the same school (echoing the contact hypothesis)

---

121 McGlynn and Bekerman, *supra* note 81, 702–703.

122 *Id.*, 701.

123 *Id.*, 703

124 *Id.*, 697–698, 700.

125 *Id.*, 701.

126 *Id.*

127 Zembylas, *supra* note 81, 439.

is not a sufficient condition to change the divisive discourses and practices regarding national identity and ethnic conflict in Cyprus.[128] Because the study discovered that the co-existence of the groups failed to socialize the pupils, it suggested that a critical multiculturalism approach be applied:[129] "[S]uch educational practices and policies...leave room for competing narratives and different identities."[130] The study criticized the school project for functioning in isolation, neglecting any reference to the social and political aspects outside it; yet these surrounding, structural inequalities and political structures that the school embodies, undoubtedly influence issues of identity and social relations being worked out in the school.[131] The study, therefore, supports engaging teachers, students, and parents in critical dialogue that would free of identity so as to make it a topic of reflection, thus enabling the participants to cast off the limitations of representing members of a specific nation or ethnicity.[132]

Israel

The case of Israel with regard to multicultural education is the most fraught of those I examine here, as it encompasses both a national conflict issue and a language barrier. The strained relations between the two nationalities, deriving also from a religious conflict, are rooted in centuries-old conflict. In terms of modern history, the conflict is anchored in the establishment of a Jewish state after the ending of the British mandate in 1947, which left the Arab inhabitants of Palestine with no national state of their own.[133] As the tension is between two nationalities, and because Arabic is not compulsory in the Israeli educational system, language also becomes an issue in integrated education in Israel. Multicultural education in Israel is thus accompanied by a "two-way" bilingual education, described above.

Today there are five Jewish-Arab bilingual schools in Israel. The first was established already in 1980 as a private initiative of the village called Neve Shalom/Wahat al-Salam.[134] In 1997, the Center for Bilingual Education in Israel

128 *Id.* 448.
129 *Id.*, 449, 450.
130 *Id.*, 450.
131 *Id.*
132 *Id.*, 451.
133 This conflict is discussed in depth in the next chapter.
134 This village, whose name's meaning in both Hebrew and Arabic is "oasis of peace," is a village of Jewish and Palestinian Arab citizens of Israel. They established the village as a venture of common life of Jewish and Arabs, advancing peace and equality between the two peoples.

established two similar schools in the north of the country and in Jerusalem. Two others—one in the Arab Triangle region and one in the city of Beer Sheva—were the outcome of independent initiatives to which the Center for Bilingual education joined later.[135] It is important to note that these schools are very unique in the Israeli education system, which generally advocates a complete separation between Jewish and Arab education systems.[136]

The bilingualism of the schools raises several issues that are incorporated within the power relations between the groups of Israeli and Palestinian-Arabs in Israel. Studies on the methods of the schools raised the importance of "language awareness" in the schools, revealing asymmetry between Arabic and Hebrew in Israeli society (Hebrew being the dominant language and Arabic being almost unknown to Jews).[137] It also exemplified the inequalities between the status of Hebrew and Arabic in both societies. While Arab pupils and their parents appreciate the importance of learning Hebrew, Jewish parents generally hope that their children learn Arabic; but they do not emphasize their success in these studies, since they are not accompanied by any practical need.[138]

With regard to multicultural education, the bilingual schools generally use a pluralist approach. The curriculum in these schools is the standard curriculum of the state's non-religious school system, with the only difference being the fact that the studies are conducted both in Arabic and in Hebrew.[139] Thus, knowledge is not reconstructed and content is not integrated in ways that reflect the narratives of both communities. Yet, the schools' pluralist character is expressed in special ceremonies held in the holidays, which in some cases reinterpret traditional meanings of symbols and legacies of both Jewish and Arab (Muslim and Christian) populations.[140] The pluralist approach is also reflected in the policy of mutual recognition and respect, which at the same time emphasizes cultural difference and strengthens traditional identities.[141] However, while researchers found that in some cases children were not strongly oriented toward a specific ethnic identity in their everyday interactions, they

135 Robert, *supra* note 81, 38.

136 See the discussion of the education system for Jewish and Arab populations in Israel in the following chapter.

137 Robert, *supra* note 81, 39.

138 *Id.*, 40.

139 McGlynn and Bekerman, *supra* note 81, 692.

140 See, for example, the discussion of a unique ceremony of three religious holidays: *Hanukkha, Id'l Fitter* and Christmas in Bekerman, *supra* note 79.

141 McGlynn and Bekerman, *supra* note 81, 698, 699; Robert, *supra* note 81, 41–42.

also discovered that avoiding the prominence of identity is not an easy task for the teachers and the parents in terms of policy and practice.[142]

The pluralist approach of these schools has faced recent criticism for failing to recognize power relations and inequalities between Jews and Arabs, which creates an essentialist concept of identity. Yet, two factors make changing the schools' educational method a difficult mission. First, as Bekerman discovered, both Arab and Jewish parents are content with the schools' policy of strengthening the children's original national identity. Second, the schools' policy is in line with the Ministry of Education's policy, which financially supports the schools[143] and which would likely object to historical narratives that deviate from the official curriculum and from those prevalent in the Jewish society.[144] Indeed, the official and prevalent historical/cultural narratives in Israeli society exclusively reflect those of the Jewish majority, as we shall see in the following chapter. I suggest that this is a major problem for Israel's multinational society, and I look for ways to overcome it using the proposed civic nationalism-plus-citizenship model.

142 McGlynn and Bekerman, *supra* note 81, 700.

143 Except for the *Neve Shalom/Wahat al-Salam* School, which asked the Ministry of Education to downgrade its level of recognition in order to be freed from much of the ministry's supervision. See, Robert, *supra* note 81, 42, note 5.

144 *Id.*, at 41–42.

CHAPTER 7

Case Study: The Jewish–Palestinian National Conflict in Israel

In this chapter I examine the applicability of the civic-nationalism-plus model to Israel, whose society is divided in terms of nationality between Palestinian-Arabs and Jews. I analyze the cultural division between Jews and Palestinians in Israel, researching both its historical roots and its current implications for the integration between those groups. I base my discussion on the conclusion from the above chapters: that is, that internal self-determination and territorial or personal autonomy are not sufficient to foster feelings of allegiance to the state among the members of its minority groups, and hence a different model is required.

Before delving into the discussion, however, I will clarify that, for reasons I will explore henceforth, the political circumstances that prevail in Israel and that underlie the conflict between Jews and Palestinians make the application of the civic-nationalism-plus model currently impractical. Therefore, my examination and conclusions with regard to future possible implications will be of a more speculative nature.

The Zionist Project: Israel as the Homeland of the Jews

The national conflict between the two major national communities residing in Israel—Jews and Palestinian-Arabs—is described in two ways: as either a *Jewish*-Arab/Palestinian conflict or an *Israeli*-Arab/Palestinian conflict. This difference is significant to the question of what a national identity in Israel means. The more prevalent description is the latter, with "Israeli" referring to the Jews alone, excluding the Palestinian-Arabs.[1] This definition of the conflict implies, either intentionally or inadvertently, that the state of Israel, and hence its national identity, belongs exclusively to the Jews. The Palestinian-Arabs are, at best, a protected minority whose individual rights should be secured; in the

1 Alexander Yacobson and Amnon Rubinstein, ISRAEL AND THE FAMILY OF NATIONS 166–167, 183–184 (2010). I will henceforth use the term "Palestinian-Arabs" to refer to the Arab citizens of Israel. The term "Palestinians" will be used to refer to both the Palestinian-Arabs in Israel and the Palestinians living in the occupied territories.

 | DOI 10.1163/9789004294332_009

worst case, the members of this minority may be legally discriminated against because they do not bear the same duties as the Jews in Israel do.[2]

I do not subscribe to this prevalent definition of the conflict and I will relate to its deficiencies later in this chapter. For now it is sufficient to say that I use the definition "Jewish-Palestinian conflict" when referring to the conflict between the Jews and the Palestinians both in Israel and in the occupied territories, and "Jewish- Palestinian/Arab" conflict when referring only to the conflict within the borders of Israel. This definition suggests that the a priori assumption that the Israeli national identity is in fact Jewish is wrong. Truly, this point of departure gives rise to another more fundamental question: Can Zionist perceptions of Israel as the homeland of the Jews co-exist with such a perception of an Israeli national identity? Later in this chapter I will answer this question in the affirmative. However, I will now turn to a brief historical review of the conflict and suggest that the more prevalent designation of this conflict, that is, an Israeli-Arab conflict, has historical roots.

For the purposes of the discussion of the Israeli national identity, the Jewish-Palestinian conflict can be traced back to the establishment of the state of Israel in 1948.[3] After the rejection of the United Nations partition plan for Palestine[4] by the Palestinian population in Israel and near the end of the 1947–1949 war, the Palestinian-Arabs became a small minority of about 12.5 percent of the population of the state of Israel.[5] Israeli citizenship was granted at first to about 60,000 Palestinians according to the Israeli Citizenship Law of 1952.[6] Yet, until 1966, those citizens were constrained to a military administration that restricted many of their civil rights, such as freedom of movement, employment, and property rights.[7] After the abolition of the

2 Gershon Shafir, Yoav Peled, BEING ISRAELI: THE DYNAMICS OF MULTIPLE CITIZENSHIP 126 (2002); Ayelet Shachar, *Whose Republic? Citizenship and Membership in the Israeli Polity*, 13 GEO. IMMIGR. L.J. 233, 260–261 (1999).

3 The conflict can be traced back to the religious conflict between Muslims and Jews and to the ruptures between Jews and Arabs during the British Mandate rule in Palestine; however, discussion of these roots is beyond the scope of this chapter. For general sources on the history of the conflict, see, Meron Benvenisti, CITY OF STONE: THE HIDDEN HISTORY OF JERUSALEM (1998); Josh Brooman, COFLICT IN PALESTINE: JEWS, ARABS AND THE MIDDLE EAST SINCE 1900 (1989); Marcella Simoni, AT THE MARGINS OF CONFLICT: SOCIAL PERSPECTIVES ON ARABS AND JEWS IN BRITISH PALESTINE (2010).

4 "Palestine" was Israel's name during the British Mandatory rule and before Israel gained its independence.

5 Yoav Peled, THE CHALLENGE OF ETHNIC DEMOCRACY 96 (2014).

6 *Id.*

7 Shafir & Peled, *supra* note 2, 112.

military administration and with the amendment of the citizenship law in 1980, more Palestinians were entitled to receive Israeli citizenship.[8] Currently, the Palestinian-Arabs citizens make up about 17 percent of the Israeli citizen population.[9]

However, granting the Palestinian-Arabs in Israel rights of citizenship[10] did not mean that the Zionist Jews who were and still are the majority in Israel intended to turn Israel into a bi-national state. On the contrary, the Zionist project's goal was, generally speaking, to create an ethnocratic Jewish state, albeit one moderated by the formal conferring of civil and political individual rights to all its citizens, including the Palestinian-Arabs.[11] The mission of the Zionist movement was to establish Israel as the homeland of the Jews.[12]

Various efforts have been made to achieve the above-described mission during the establishment of the state and even earlier through activities of Zionist organizations (i.e., the Jewish Agency for Israel and the Zionist Congress). Starting with means to strengthen the hegemony of the Jewish collectivity (such as land redemption[13] and setting immigration quotas for the benefit of Jews[14]) and continuing with legal and bureaucratic mechanisms that preserved Jewish predominance in almost every personal right from economics through labor and education,[15] the Zionist project was successful in shaping Israel as a state whose "ethno-republican discourse of citizenship [is based on]

8 Peled, *supra* note 5, 97.

9 *Id.*

10 This move is in direct contrast to Israel's first Prime Minister's (David Ben-Gurion) opposition to granting the Palestinian-Arabs a right of citizenship for fear that such move would subvert the idea of Israel as a homeland for the Jews. See, *id.*

11 Shafir & Peled, *supra* note 2, 125.

12 Chaim Gans, A Just Zionism 53–55 (2008).

13 For an extensive discussion of the efforts made for land redemption see, Shafir & Peled, *supra* note 2, 112–116; Peled, *supra* note 5, 98–100.

14 These demands were fulfilled by the legislation of several statutes that set favorable conditions for Jews to become citizens of Israel: Khok Hashvut (Law of Return), 5710–1950, 4 LSI 114 (1949–50) (Isr.) [hereinafter *the Law of Return*] and Khok Haezrahut (the Citizenship Law), 5712–1952, 6 LSI 50 (1951–52) (Isr.).

15 There is extensive literature on the official and unofficial discrimination of the Palestinian citizens in Israel: for example, Shafir & Peled, *supra* note 2, 112–125; Peled, *supra* note 5, 110–118; Gad Barzilai, Communities and the Law: Politics and Cultures of Legal Identities (2003); Yousef T. Jabareen, *Constitution Building and Equality in Deeply-Divided Societies: The Case of the Palestinian-Arab Minority in Israel*, 26 Wis. Int'l L.J. 345 (2008); Ilan Saban, *Minority Rights in Deeply Divided Societies: A Framework for Analysis and the Case of the Arab-Palestinian Minority in Israel*, 36 N.Y.U. J. Int'l L. & Pol. 885, 924–982 (2004).

Jewish ethnicity [as] a necessary condition for membership in the political community."[16]

The above-described ethnic Jewish character of the state of Israel is reinforced in Israel's constitutional framework, which, it has been claimed, "invests Israel's Jewish identity with a quasi- axiomatic status."[17] Several laws—among them, a Basic Law, which in the absence of a formal constitution serves as a component of Israel's constitutional infrastructure—determine, with a perpetual intent, Israel's character as a "Jewish-democratic state." The "Basic Law: The Knesset"[18] prohibits any list of candidates or any individual candidate for the parliament elections to deny the existence of the state of Israel as a *Jewish* and democratic state.[19] The Parties Law[20] prohibits the registration of a party if among its goals or deeds, implicitly or explicitly, is a denial of the existence of the State of Israel as a Jewish and democratic state.[21] The Knesset Regulations[22] stipulate that the chairperson of the Knesset and the deputies will not approve a bill that, in their opinion, denies the existence of the State of Israel as the state of the Jewish people.[23]

It should be emphasized that the characterization of Israel as "Jewish" is not intended to reflect a religious sense but rather a civic one. That is, this definition does not suggest that Israel is a religious state;[24] but it rather sustains

---

16 Shafir & Peled, *supra* note 2, 125.

17 Saban, *supra* note 15, 985.

18 Khok Yesod: Ha-Knesset [Basic Law: The Knesset], 1958, 12 L.S.I. 85.

19 *Id.*, Section 7A. The importance of Section 7A of the Knesset Basic Law, *id.*, for Israel's constitutional foundations is described in Sharon Weintal, "The Inherent Authority of Judges in a Three-Track Democracy to Recognise Unenumerated Constitutional Rights: The Israeli Story of a Judicial Mission with No Ammunition," *in* ISRAELI CONSTITUTIONAL LAW IN THE MAKING 292 (Gideon Sapir, Daphne Barak-Erez, and Aharon Barak eds., 2013). I thank Dr. Ynaiv Roznai for this reference.

20 Khok Ha-Miflagot [Parties Law], 1992, S.H. 190.

21 *Id.*, Section 5.

22 Hakhlatat Ha-Knesset Bidvar Takanot Ha-Knesset [Knesset Rules of Procedure], 30 May 2012, Section 75 e available at: The Knesset, <http://www.knesset.gov.il/rules/eng/contents.htm>.

23 *Id.*

24 There is a deep controversy in Israel regarding the question of what the term "Jewish" should include and to what extent religious Jewish norms should be incorporated in the characterization of the state. See, for example, ISRAEL: A DEMOCRATIC JEWISH SOCIETY TOWARDS THE 21ST CENTURY: CONVERSATIONS WITH THE FOUNDING FATHERS (Yair Auron ed., 1986); ISRAEL AS A JEWISH AND DEMOCRATIC STATE (Asher Maoz ed., 2011); Election Confirmation 11280/02, *Central Elections Committee v. Ahmed Tibi*, Election Confirmation 50/03, *Central Elections Committee v. Azmi Bishara* (published in

Israel's national character, so that "Jewish" refers to ethnic origin.[25] This concept is expressed by the law of the Population Registry,[26] which authorizes the Minister of Interior to determine the details of identity cards for Israeli:[27] when these ministers came to include "nationality" among the details to be identified on the card, they used the terms "Jewish" as a nationality for Jews and "Arab" for the Palestinian-Arabs.

The characterization of Israel as a Jewish (and democratic) state is thus considered a legal fundamental principle of the Israeli state. But this definition is indirectly extrapolated from laws that regulate different matters, as there are no laws that directly and positively define the character of the state. Since 2011, a number of bills have been proposed intended to stipulate Israel as a Jewish and democratic state.[28] These bills pursue the goal attributed to the Zionist project in its advent: that is, determining the Jewishness of the state and excluding the Palestinian-Arabs from participating in the process of the formation of the state's character.[29]

Therefore, while the Jewish nationality is assimilated within the overall nationalistic characterization of Israel as a Jewish state, the Palestinian-Arabs experience a split of nationality. They are Israeli citizens according to the Israeli citizenship law,[30] but Israel does not intend to incorporate Arab nationality in the definition of the state's character in any legal or other formal or informal way.[31] This point is crucial and I will return to it later. I will now turn to

---

Nevo, 15.5.2003) [hereinafter *Central Election Committee v. Tibi and Bishara*]. An English abstract of the decision is available at: <http://adalah.org/eng/Articles/594/Elections-Disqualifications-Cases>. In this case, the former president of the Israeli Supreme Court, Chief Justice Barak, preferred a narrow definition of the term "Jewish." *Cf* the deceased Justice Menachem Elon's definition of Israel as Jewish in the first place, in Menachem Elon, New Horizons in Medical Ethics : decision of the Supreme Court of Israel in the Shefer case, civil appeal 88/506, Yael Shefer v. the State of Israel 48 (1) P.D. 87 (1997). Nevertheless, the primary meaning of the term "Jewish" is a national characteristic.

25 On the interchangeability of the terms "Jewish" and "Hebrew" see H.C. 11286/03 Ornan et al. v. the Ministry of Interior (published in Nevo, 20.9.2004) (Hebrew).

26 Khok Mirsham Ha'uchlusin [Population Registry Law], 5725–1965, 19 LSI 288 (1964–65) (Isr.).

27 *Id.*

28 See, for example, Draft Basic Law: Israel—the Nation-State of the Jewish People, P/3541/18, *available at*: <http://www.acri.org.il/en/wp-content/uploads/2011/10/Jewish-state-bill-ENG.pdf>.

29 Shafir & Peled, *supra* note 2, 125.

30 Citizenship Law, *supra* note 14.

31 There is also no official legitimacy for an "Israeli" nationality, and the Israeli Supreme Court has on several occasions rejected applications of Israeli citizens to be registered as

a discussion of the type of rights and privileges that have nevertheless been conferred upon the Palestinian-Arabs as individuals and as a group, most of which are not national rights.

The Jewish ruling establishment has granted and continues to grant the Palestinian-Arab minority some group-differentiated rights, mainly accommodation rights and, to a far lesser extent, self-government rights and rights of special representation and allocation of state resources.[32] Even more so, Saban notes,

> since the 1990's there was a constant improvement in representation and allocation rights that the Palestinian-Arab minority was granted and which resulted in legislation, adjudication, and in practices that shaped the composition of special regulatory institutions, all of them stipulated a principle of minority participation in certain societal institutions, namely, the civil service and the directorates of the government corporations.[33]

Nevertheless, the mitigation of the institutional discrimination of Palestinian-Arab citizens focused mainly on the field of individual rights. While Palestinian-Arabs were individually gradually being granted more equality[34] and better civil and political status,[35] the state of Israel refused to recognize them as an autonomous national minority and as a result granted them almost

Israeli instead of Jewish or Arab. See, H.C 8573/08 Ornan v. the Ministry of Interior (published in Nevo, 2.10.2013) (Hebrew); H.C. 630/70 Tamarin v. State of Israel, 26(i) P.D. 197. I will discuss the concept of an Israeli nationality *infra*.

32 Saban, *supra* note 15, 977.

33 *Id.*

34 See, for example, Khok Shivyon Hizdamnuyot Ba'avoda [Equality of Opportunities at Work Law], 5748–1988, which prohibits setting discriminating racial criteria for hiring and firing; Khok Ha-Khavarot Ha-Memshaltiyot (Tikun Mispar 7) [Government Corporations Law (Amendment No. 7)], 2000, S.H. 207, and Khok Sheirut Ha-Medina (Minuyim) [State Service (Appointments) Law], 1959, 13 L.S.I. 87, which set affirmative action practices for the benefit of the Arabs, Druze, and Circassians in the civil service and in the directorates of government corporations; and the Cooperative Society Ordinance (Amendment 8), which prohibits setting discriminating racial criteria by admission committees of small community villages.

35 H.C. 6698/95, Kaadan v. Minhal Mekarke'ey Yisra-el [Israel Land Administration], 54 (1) P.D. 258 [hereinafter *Kaadan case*] A formal English translation is available at: <http://elyon1.court.gov.il/files_eng/95/980/066/a14/95066980.a14.pdf>.

no national group rights.[36] The only exceptions were the status of the Arabic language as a semi-official language and a limited autonomy for the Palestinian-Arabs in the public education system.[37] Yet, even these rights were limited in their scope. Even though Arabic was given an official status by Israeli law, which incorporated British Mandatory law that determined English, Arabic, and Hebrew as the formal languages of Palestine,[38] Israeli law did not grant Arabic language the full and comprehensive status of an official language.[39] State authorities are in some cases obliged to use Arabic in public, but this obligation "has eroded over the years,"[40] and "while Palestinian-Arabs were in fact forced to become bilingual, the Jewish public was not."[41] With regard to education, the Palestinian-Arabs were given the right to operate a segregated education system from the early days of the state of Israel, enabling them to educate their children in Arabic and to learn Arab history and culture.[42] Yet, the system is not autonomous, but controlled by the state.[43] First, the state of Israel monitors the contents of the curricula in the Arab education system,[44] a supervision that, up to the late 1990s, aimed to dull the Palestinian's national consciousness and remove their national narrative from the history and literary studies.[45] Furthermore, this monitoring compels the Palestinian-Arab education system to include Jewish studies in its curricula, such as Hebrew language and literature, Jewish history, and even Bible study.[46] By contrast, Jewish pupils are

---

36 Barzilai, *supra* note 15, 110–115. In comparison, broad group rights pertaining to freedom of religion are granted to religious communities in Israel, including Palestinian-Arab Muslims, Christians, Druze, and Circassians. For a thorough discussion of Israel's accommodation of religious group rights of the Palestinian-Arab community, see, Michael M. Karayanni, *The Separate Nature of the Religious Accommodations for the Palestinian-Arab Minority in Israel*, 5 (1) NORTHWESTERN JOURNAL OF INTERNATIONAL HUMAN RIGHTS 41 (2007). See also, Sammy Smooha, AUTONOMY FOR ARABS IN ISRAEL? 59 (1999) (Hebrew) [hereinafter *Smooha, Autonomy*].

37 Saban, *supra* note 15, 940; Peled, *supra* note 5, 105–106.

38 Palestine Order-in-Council, art. 82, in 3 LAWS OF PALESTINE 2569, 2588 (Robert Harry Drayton ed., rev. ed. 1934).

39 Saban, *supra* note 15, 929. For a comprehensive discussion of the status of the Arabic language in Israel see *id.*, 929–937; See also Barzilai, *supra* note 15, 110–114.

40 Saban, *supra* note 15, 931.

41 *Id.*, 030

42 Peled, *supra* note 5, 105–106.

43 It is, hence, referred to by scholars as: "controlled segregation." See, *id.*, 105.

44 Saban, *supra* note 15, 940.

45 *Id.*

46 Peled, *supra* note 5, 105; Saban, *supra* note 15, 940.

mandated to learn Arabic for only about three years at primary school,[47] and Arab history and culture are scarcely taught.[48]

As a consequence of Israel's almost complete denial of the Palestinian-Arabs' national rights, the Palestinian-Arabs' legal right to internal self-determination[49] is very limited. Understood as "the right of every citizen to take part in the conduct of public affairs at any level"[50] and as "a peoples [right to pursue] its political, economic, social and cultural development within the framework of an existing state,"[51] the right to internal self-determination is best fulfilled in a state that enables group participation in societal decision-making or special veto powers for minorities.[52] But the Palestinian-Arabs enjoy none of these privileges, and this is due both to Israel's constitutional form of governance and to formal and informal practices of excluding representatives of the Palestinian-Arab minority from government and public institutions.[53]

Israel is not a federal state,[54] and hence it lacks the mechanisms of incorporation of minorities in government that ensure that their interests are respected by the state. Palestinian-Arabs enjoy no form of autonomy—territorial or personal[55]—and hence have no means of self-government.[56] In addition, they are not proportionately and authentically represented in any of the decision-making Israeli institutions, such as those responsible for land allocation

---

47 Smadar Donitsa-Schmidt, Ofra Inbar, Elana Shohamy, *The Effects of Teaching Spoken Arabic on Students' Attitudes and Motivation in Israel*, 88(2) THE MODERN LANGUAGE JOURNAL 217 (2004).

48 Peled, *supra* note 5, 106.

49 The right of internal self-determination of peoples is discussed in the second chapter of this book.

50 General Recommendation 21, The right to self-determination (Forty-eighth session, 1996), U.N. Doc. A/51/18, Annex VIII at 125 (1996), 4.

51 Re Secession of Quebec, [1998] 2 S.C.R 217 (Can.) 130 at 437–438.

52 See the discussion in the third chapter of the special group differentiated rights of participation in the government in Canada, Belgium, and Spain.

53 Saban, *supra* note 15, 974–975.

54 It is even considered as one of the most centralized unitary states. See, *id.*, 974.

55 As explained above, this chapter refers to territorial autonomy. Personal autonomy means that minorities are "allowed to have some control over their institutions, such as schools, media [and other cultural institutions] without creating any territorial base for potential secessionism." See, Will Kymlicka, *Justice and Security*, *in* ETHNICITY, NATIONALISM, AND MINORITY RIGHTS 144, 165 (Stephen May, Tariq Modood, and Judith Squires eds., 2004). Personal autonomy is more suited for minorities that are not concentrated in specific areas in the state.

56 Smooha, Autonomy, *supra* note 36, 62.

or public broadcasting.[57] In fact, those bodies are completely dedicated to preserving Jewish interests,[58] and moreover, there are no parallel formal institutions for the benefit of the Palestinian-Arab population.[59] Informal, popular-voluntary institutions established by the Palestinian-Arab community, such as the Committee for the Protection of Arab Lands, have not been welcomed by state authorities.[60]

In terms of government participation, Palestinian-Arabs' presence in the legislative body, the Israeli parliament, is conditioned upon a legal duty not to deny Israel's essence as a Jewish and democratic state.[61] In addition, as Saban notes, "there is no right, constitutional practice, or even informal practice of including Arab (or binational) parties in the government";[62] on the contrary, these parties were never included in any coalition and only one government so far has depended on the support of an outside Palestinian-Arab party.[63]

In addition to the practical exclusion of Palestinian-Arabs from political public life and public decision-making, and as a consequence of this practice, Palestinian-Arabs are also prohibited from contributing to the shaping of the state's character or influencing the state's symbolic representation. Israel's national character is completely and unequivocally Jewish.[64] The flag presents the Jewish King David's shield; the national anthem echoes the Jews' hope to be redeemed in Israel, their homeland; the names of streets and national monuments reflect Jewish history and culture, as do bank notes, stamps, and coins. Lastly, most of the national broadcasting is in Hebrew and is dedicated to Jewish culture and heritage, with only a small part of it dedicated to Arab culture and language. The symbolic level is then the most conspicuous realization of

---

57 Jabareen, *supra* note 15, 370–371.

58 For example, The World Zionist Organization of the Jewish Agency and the Jewish National Fund, which fulfill government functions and whose activities are solely dedicated for the benefit of the Jewish population. See *id.*, 370–371.

59 *Id.*, 373.

60 *Id.*

61 Basic Law: The Knesset, *supra* note 18.

62 Saban, *supra* note 15, 975.

63 *Id.*; Peled, *supra* note 5, 119.

64 Gans, *supra note* 12, 141. From 2005 to 2006 the Israeli Knesset Constitution, Law and Justice Committee worked on drafts for a constitution for Israel which focused on solving the tensions between religion and state. The Israeli-Arab members of Parliament did not participate in this project, nor were any of the drafts formally published in Arabic. For elaboration on this project see Hana Lerner, Making Constitutions in Deeply Divided Societies 212–225 (2013).

the Zionist project's goal described above—to establish Israel as the homeland of the Jews exclusively.

All of this somewhat clarifies why the Jewish-Palestinian conflict is more commonly referred to as the Israeli-Palestinian or Israeli-Arab conflict. Since both the public and symbolic life of the state are exclusively designed by Jews, the state of Israel is almost intuitively grasped as belonging exclusively to the Jews, and hence, Jews are recognized as "Israelis" while Palestinian-Arabs are not.[65] The latter are more often recognized as Arabs, or at best as Israeli-Arabs. They are rarely referred to as simply Israeli.[66]

The above notwithstanding, two main questions remain. Do the Palestinian-Arabs even want to have an Israeli identity, and, if the answer is positive, what are the prevalent obstacles to forming such an identity (beyond the historical ones described above)? These questions will be dealt with in the following subsection.

The Formation of an Israeli Identity

On the one hand, the Jews and the Palestinian-Arabs in Israel can be described as "rival nationalities,"[67] that is, two national communities that claim for competitive and conflicting rights over the country they identify as their historic homeland. Several incidents turned the Jews and the Palestinian-Arabs into such rival nationalities, among them, the Palestinian-Arabs' rejection of the 1947 UN partition plan for Palestine; the war that followed and ended in Jewish victory, which the Palestinian-Arabs defined as their "*al-nacba*," that is, the grievance over their land dispossession[68]; the establishment of a Jewish ethno-democracy; and the growing development of a Palestinian national movement.[69]

Throughout the years of the military administration, designed to regulate the lives of the Palestinian-Arabs in Israel, the Palestinian-Arabs struggled mainly for their civil rights and did not demand their national rights, as the military administration worked to cut off the Palestinian-Arabs from their

---

65 Yacobson & Rubinstein, *supra* note 1, 166–167, 183–184.

66 *Id.*

67 David Miller, *Nationality in Divided Societies*, *in* MULTINATIONAL DEMOCRACIES 299, 303 (Alain-G. Gagnon, James Tully eds., 2001).

68 Peled, *supra* note 5, 209.

69 *Id.*, 109.

Arab-Palestinian environment.[70] The Palestinian national movement only began after the end of the Six-Days war in 1967, with the abolition of the military administration and the renewal of contacts between Palestinian-Arabs in Israel and the Palestinians in the occupied territories.[71] A number of representative organizations formed by Palestinian-Arab intellectual leaders emerged in that period, such as the Community of Heads of Arab Local Councils, the Supreme Follow-up Committee of Arabs in Israel, and the Committee to Defend the Lands.[72] In addition, new political parties that emphasized both the national rights and the civil rights of the Palestinian-Arab national minority in Israel emerged.[73]

The new Palestinian-Arab political parties and their public organizations transformed the Palestinian-Arab political discourse into a twofold discussion, with emphasis on the national aspect. On the one hand, it focused on the rights of the Palestinian-Arabs in Israel, including their national rights; but it also demanded a solution to the national problem in the context of the general Palestinian question, including the Palestinians living in the occupied territories and not in sovereign Israel.[74] These goals were first publicly expressed in a document in June 6, 1980, considered to be the first political text of the new political Palestinian discourse in Israel.[75] The document declared that Israel was the Palestinian people's one and only homeland and that the Palestinian-Arabs formed a part of this people and, hence, deserved to enjoy this people's rights of self-determination.[76] In addition, the document warned against the national oppression and racial discrimination of the Palestinian-Arabs in Israel in various areas of life.[77]

Following active efforts of the Palestinian leadership to pursue these goals of the Palestinian movement, another major ideological development

70 Muhammad Amara and Mohanad Mostafa, *The Impact of The Occupation of the West Bank and the Gaza Strip on The Political Discourse of the Palestinians in Israel, in* The Impacts of Lasting Occupation 279 (Daniel Bar-Tal and Izhak Schnell eds., 2013).

71 Peled, *supra* note 5, 109.

72 *Id.*

73 *Id.*, at 111; Amara and Mostafa, *supra* note 70, 280. At first, only joint Jewish-Arab political parties ran for election, but since the 1990s, independent Arab lists have also begun to emerge. See, Peled, *supra* note 5, 110–111.

74 Amara and Mostafa, *supra* note 70, 286.

75 *Id.*

76 *Id.*

77 *Id.*, 286–287.

occurred in 2007 when a series of "future vision documents"[78] was adopted by several civic organizations in the Arab community and endorsed by the Palestinian-Arab political parties in parliament.[79] These documents presented Israel as a bi-national democracy instead of a Jewish and democratic state and demanded the establishment of bureaucratic mechanisms that would ensure the Palestinian-Arabs' influence over the decision-making process in the Israeli government.[80] Hence, despite the awakening of a national Palestinian-Arab movement and some of the Palestinian organizations' pan-Arab inclinations,[81] the Palestinian-Arab leadership and public seem to support neither a disengagement from Israel nor unification with the Palestinians in the occupied territories. They rather, as Smooha identified, went through "a historical process of the Israelization of their identity and politics."[82]

Truly, the Palestinian-Arabs demand self-determination. Yet, this demand is for internal self-determination, that is, non-territorial institutional autonomy that includes control over educational system and state recognition of Arab national organizations and a proportional share of national resources.[83] On the other hand, with regard to demands for dissociation, in 1989 Smooha discovered that "80 percent of the Palestinian-Arabs would feel better as Israeli citizens if a Palestinian state were to be established in the West Bank and Gaza Strip. Yet, only 8 percent of them…are willing to consider a move to such a state."[84] Moreover, in later years nearly 80 percent of Palestinian citizens, including young people eligible for civil service, supported this kind of

78 The National Committee for the Heads of the Arab Local Authorities in Israel, *The Future Vision of the Palestinian-Arabs in Israel* (2006), available at: <http://adalah.org/newsletter/eng/dec06/tasawor-mostaqbali.pdf>. [hereinafter *The Future Vision Documents*].

79 Yacobson & Rubinstein, *supra* note 1, 150.

80 *Id.* On the future vision documents see also, Peled, *supra* note 5, 142–146.

81 *Id.*, 120.

82 Shafir & Peled, *supra* note 2, 129, citing Smooha.

83 *Id.*, 135, citing Smooha, and see also Jabareen, *supra* note 15, 392–397, and The Future Vision Documents, *supra* note 78. These documents were written by a group of intellectual leaders of the Palestinian-Arabs in Israel with an intent to "self-defin[e] [their] entity, relation with the rest of the Palestinians and [their] relation with the State and to connect them to create a firm integral homogeneous vision [that]… includes all the political, cultural, economic, educational and social aspects."

84 Shafir & Peled, *supra* note 2, 128, citing Smooha. *Cf.* Yacobson and Rubinstein's claim that the Jews and the Arabs have two distinct and separate national identities and that Israeli-Arab citizens do not consider their national identity as a sub-division of an Israeli one. Therefore, there can be no definition of a national identity common to all of Israel's citizens. See, Yacobson & Rubinstein, *supra* note 1, 166–167.

service, from which Palestinian citizens are currently exempted.[85] The reasons that were given for such support emphasized the service's contribution to enhancing integration of Palestinians in Israeli society and their equality within the state.[86]

The question is, therefore: What impedes the integration of a Palestinian-Arab identity within the Israeli identity? The fundamental platform for this exclusion was presented above as including both the Palestinian-Arabs' personal and national deep discrimination and the emergence of Israel as an ethnocracy, or in other words, the ethno-republican ethos of the state of Israel, a state that is not, in fact, civic nationalistic. Three factors can be added to this platform: the Jewish-Palestinian conflict; Palestinian-Arab public's general support of the Palestinians in the occupied territories and their armed struggle against Israel; and the exclusion of the former from mandatory military service. I look at each of these briefly in the following paragraphs.

Jewish-Palestinian Conflict

The Jewish-Palestinian conflict can be traced back to the question of a national identity in Israel. Currently, the Jews and the Arab-Palestinians live as rival nationalities, and this reality evidently shapes their relations and their mutual unwillingness to incorporate their national identities into a unified Israeli identity.[87] Indeed, in practice we see a deep separation between the Jewish and the Arab public, emanating both from an institutional policy and from societal inclinations.[88] Ninety percent of Palestinian-Arabs live in separated cities and villages, and the rest live in separated neighborhoods in Jewish cities.[89] Institutional separation can be traced to the education systems, where integrated primary and secondary schools for Jews and Palestinian-Arabs are scarce. Only in higher education is integration forced, mainly because there are very few Arab colleges and not a single Palestinian-Arab university.[90] This separation is also expressed in the Palestinian-Arabs' exclusion from mandatory military or civil service, which I will discuss further below. With regard to civil society, voluntary separation between Jews and Palestinian-Arabs is observed in every field of social life. Because the two different societies have

85 Peled, *supra* note 5, 146.

86 *Id.*

87 Gans, *supra* note 12, 78.

88 Smooha, Autonomy, *supra* note 36, 65.

89 *Id.*

90 *Id.*

few occasions to meet and integrate, neighborly relationships between Jews and Palestinian-Arabs are uncommon, as are friendships and integrated social activities, such as sports or youth movements.[91]

Moreover, the rivalry between the Jewish and Arab cultures is not a temporary situation but rather one deeply rooted in the past and therefore here to stay. Long before the establishment of the state of Israel, the Jews and the Arabs lived as two conflicting nationalities, and no meaningful attempt has ever been made to consolidate the two opposing cultures.[92] On the contrary, the Jews have always kept close connections with the Jews in the Diaspora and the Palestinian-Arabs with the Arabs in the neighboring states and in particular with Palestinians in the occupied territories.[93] Furthermore, not only has Palestine never been an autonomous region in Israel (as have the Basque country and Catalonia in Spain and Scotland in Great Britain), but the Palestinian-Arab identity cannot be viewed as a component of Israeli identity.[94] Any attempt to "forge or 'engineer'" such an identity would be completely artificial.[95]

Palestinian-Arab Public Support of Palestinians in the Occupied Territories

The second factor that impedes a consolidated Israeli identity is tied to the Palestinian-Arab public's general support of the Palestinians in the occupied territories and their armed struggle against Israel. This support generates suspicion towards the Palestinian-Arabs among the Jewish public in general and in particular among the Jewish establishment and state authorities.[96] Hence, the question of minority rights is securitized and, as Kymlicka observes, "the space for moral argument and democratic debate drastically shrinks."[97] The Israeli state is less and less willing to enable autonomy for the Palestinian-Arab minority, let alone to involve the Arab minority in the process of shaping the state's symbolic character, due to persistent fear of growing secessionist and irredentist elements.[98]

91 *Id.*, 65–66.

92 Yacobson & Rubinstein, *supra* note 1, 182.

93 *Id.*, 181–182.

94 *Id.*, 182.

95 *Id.*

96 Smooha, Autonomy, *supra* note 36, 62.

97 Kymlicka, Justice and Security, *supra* note 55, 158. See also Smooha, Autonomy, *supra* note 36, 57.

98 Smooha, Autonomy, *supra* note 36, 62.

Exclusion of Palestinians from Mandatory Military Service

One result of the securitization of the minority rights question and the public and institutional fears of Palestinian-Arabs is that Palestinian-Arabs are excluded from mandatory military service, and hence from partaking in the ethos and practice of full citizenship in Israel and from attending to the common good of society.[99] Shachar observes that because of the prevailing republican concept of citizenship in Israel,

> [P]olitical membership in Israel implies a profound connection between having full citizenship and the duty of military service... [Mandatory military service in Israel serves as] the proof of inclusion in the body politic...in which a connection is made between the commitment to make sacrifices for the nation and the right to fair share in governing.[100]

Yet, the Palestinian-Arabs are in practice exempted from this service, mainly because since its inception Israel has been involved in armed conflicts against other Arabs in neighboring states, as well as against the Palestinians in the occupied territories.[101] Considering the emblematic importance of military service to the notion of citizenship in Israel, this exemption not only blocks the Palestinian-Arab citizens from several civil privileges,[102] it also implies that this group cannot fully integrate within Israeli society by equally sharing both the rights and the duties of citizens in the state.[103] Thus,

> military service has become an obvious demarcating tool for distinguishing between different members of the same polity, that is, between those who truly belong to the republic and those who are entitled to the rights of citizenship in the state but are conceived as less than full members of the political community because they do not partake in its most fundamental expressions of self-determination, i.e., military service.[104]

---

99 Shafir & Peled, *supra* note 2, 126; Shachar, *supra* note 2, 260.

100 Shachar, *supra* note 2, 260.

101 In addition, Israel did not offer the Palestinian-Arabs the alternative of a national service instead of a military service. See Shafir & Peled, *supra* note 2, 126.

102 These privileges—such as social benefits including supplementary children allowances, tax credits, and assistance in mortgage payments—are dependent on performing a military service. See, Shachar, *supra* note 2, 261. As the Palestinian-Arabs cannot choose to perform this duty, the dispossession of these privileges amounts to discrimination.

103 *Id.*

104 *Id.*

The above analysis seems to suggest that Israeli identity is and can be nothing but a Jewish identity. In this chapter, however, I refute this presumption and suggest guidelines for future application of the civic-nationalism-plus model I put forward in this book. Before delving into analysis of these guidelines, however, I will tackle the arguments of those who claim that this model is inapplicable in the Jewish-Palestinian Arabs case.

The first argument is that integrating the Palestinian-Arab culture in the Israeli identity will inevitably result in turning Israel into a bi-national state and thus defeat the fundamental justification of establishing the state of Israel in the first place as a homeland for the Jews and a solution for anti-Semitism.[105] According to this view, only an ethnocratic Israel that realizes exclusive national rights for the Jews can maintain Israel as securing the Jews' right to self-determination and prevent future horrific events, such as the massacre of the Jews in the Holocaust.[106]

However, the polarity of this conclusion can be contested. Indeed, the Jewish people has a right to self-determination, like any other people.[107] Since Israel is the only state that can realize this right of the Jewish people, a Jewish majority should be legally secured in the form of preserving built-in discrimination in immigration quotas in favor of the Jews through the Law of Return.[108]

105 Ruth Gavison, *Immigration and the Human Rights Discourse: The Universality of Human Rights and the Relevance of States and Numbers*, 43(1) ISR. L. REV. 7 (2010). See also, Ruth Gavison, *The Jews' Right to Statehood, A Defense*, 15 Azure 70 (2003); Yacobson & Rubinstein, *supra* note 1, 150–156, 180–191. Chaim Gans critically calls the stream of thought that these scholars represent "a statist interpretation of the (Jews') right to self-determination." On this concept and its criticism, see, Gans, *supra* note 12, 53–80. Note that the justifications for the establishment of the state of Israel as the homeland of the Jews are also extrapolated from the 1948 Israel's Proclamation of Independence: "Eretz-Israel [(Hebrew)—the Land of Israel, Palestine] was the birthplace of the Jewish people… The catastrophe which recently befell the Jewish people—the massacre of millions of Jews in Europe—was another clear demonstration of the urgency of solving the problem of its homelessness by re-establishing in Eretz-Israel the Jewish State, which would open the gates of the homeland wide to every Jew and confer upon the Jewish people the status of a fully privileged member of the comity of nations." See, Proclamation of Independence, *Official Gazette*: Number 1; Tel Aviv, 5 Iyar 5708, 14.5.1948 Page 1. An English version is available at the Israeli Parliament website: <http://www.knesset.gov.il/docs/eng/megilat_eng.htm>.

106 Gans, *supra* note 12, 53–80.

107 Among the numerous writings on the right to self-determination of peoples, see for example, *supra*, Chapter 2, note 8 and the sources it cites.

108 Kaadan case, *supra* note 35, 282. See also Gans' "substatist" interpretation of the Jews' right to self-determination, according to which Jewish hegemony in Israel is justified only with

However, in all other material goods allocated by the state, including national rights and the right to participate in the formation of the symbolic space of the state, the state should strive for parity between Jews and Arabs,[109] as was expressed by the Israeli Supreme Court's ruling:

> The Jewish people founded the Jewish state, a point-of-departure from which we shall continue on our journey...but having been established, it [the State] practices equality between its citizens. The State of Israel is a Jewish state within which minorities live, among them the Arab minority. Each member of the minorities that live in Israel enjoys full equality of rights. It is true that a special key to the house was given to the members of the Jewish people (see the Law of Return, 1950). But once a person resides in the house as a citizen by law, he enjoys equal rights like all the other members of the house.[110]

The second argument to retain the hegemony of Jewish culture in Israel's identity accepts that the Palestinian-Arabs should enjoy national rights, but it assumes that these rights should be realized in a Palestinian state and not in Israel.[111] Hence, the Palestinian-Arabs residing in Israel should live in Israel as equal individual citizens, but they should enjoy almost no national rights.[112] The reasoning is that if other solutions are followed, and Israel becomes either a bi-national state or a state that allows space for Palestinian-Arabic culture, then the result will be unfair: the Palestinian-Arabs will have one and a half states and the Jews will be left with half a state.[113] Those who argue against this unfairness affirm, at the same time, that "the state must pursue a policy of civil equality and integration."[114] But this demand seems to be only paying lip service to the fundamental principle of ensuring minority rights in a

---

regard to the Jews' "military power and [to] the maintenance of a demographic majority [and] only until a relationship of trust develops between the parties." Gans, *supra* note 12, 80. Note that even though Gans supports the maintenance of a Jewish demographic majority, he suggests that "nationality-based priorities in immigration do not demand automatically allowing all Jews to immigrate to Israel and acquire Israeli citizenship or barring all non-Jews from doing so." See his analysis at 117–138.

109 Saban, *supra* note 15, 1003; Gans, *supra* note 12, 141–143.

110 Kaadan case, *supra* note 35, 282.

111 Yacobson & Rubinstein, *supra* note 1, 149–151, 191.

112 Except for the preservation of the Arabic language as a formal language in Israel. See, *id.*, 150–151. On this proposal in general, see, *id.*, 133–191.

113 *Id.*, 150.

114 *Id.*, 188.

democracy, rather than providing a practical solution, given the importance (established above) of both the right to internal self-determination and participation in forming national symbols to create loyalty and feelings of belonging to the state on part of minorities. Hence, those who demand that Israel remain an exclusively Jewish state must bear the consequences of putting up with a disintegrated minority group within it. Note, however, that objections to the civic-nationalism-plus model can also stem from the other political polar, i.e., from an anti-Zionist agenda. According to such objections, Israel should not secure a Jewish majority but rather be a democratic state preserving no special privileges for any nation.

The contrasting viewpoint I endorse in this chapter is that the disintegration of the Palestinian-Arabs in Israel is not an unavoidable necessity, and that integration is possible—albeit within a Zionist conception that allows, at least temporarily, for built-in discrimination in immigration quotas in favor of the Jews. Indeed, different groups and political parties in Israel have different visions regarding the character of the state of Israel, some of which I have referred to above. Hence, the model I suggest should be seen as another vision, one that may comply with some of the other visions and not with others. In addition, three fundamental preconditions are required for the realization of the model, that is, for an integration of the Jews and the Palestinian-Arabs and the formation of a consolidated Israeli identity. First, the conflict between the Jews and the Palestinian-Arabs must be resolved, and an independent Palestinian state in which the national rights of Palestinians are fully realized should be established. Second, all forms of individual discrimination between Jews and Palestinian-Arabs should be abolished, so that the Palestinian-Arabs will not feel they are second-rate citizens in terms of civil equality. Third, political mechanisms ensuring that the political interests of the Palestinian-Arabs are secured and respected by the state and providing them with the ability to influence political decisions should be formed.

Such mechanisms can be formed through the various types of politics of recognition discussed in previous chapters, such as deliberative, contestatory, or communicative democracy.[115] However, and as I also suggested, such processes should be accompanied by the politics of reconciliation, a precondition for deliberative democracy, which provides for acknowledgment and remedy of historic wrongs, unjustified hierarchies, and stigmatization.[116] The politics

---

115 Will Kymlicka and Bashir Bashir, *Struggles for Inclusion and Reconciliation in Modern Democracies in* THE POLITICS OF RECONCILIATION IN MULTICULTURAL SOCIETIES 2 (Will Kymlicka and Bashir Bashir eds., 2008).

116 *Id.*, 5, 18.

of reconciliation aims to overcome the tendency of dominant groups in historically divided societies "to avoid an open discussion of the historical process by which they came to be dominant and in particular to avoid listening to [the interpretations of] subordinate national groups [for these processes]."[117] Hence, it is only "an explicit commitment to a politics of reconciliation that involves acknowledging and rectifying past injustices"[118] that enables deliberative democracy in divided societies such as Israel's.[119]

Processes of deliberative democracy were applied in the conflict-resolution in Northern Ireland, a case study with important lessons for the Jewish-Palestinian conflict. The conflict between the two rival nationalities of Irish Catholics and Protestants in Northern Ireland has seen significant progress toward resolution in the last two decades, mainly due to arrangements for multinational or binational societies.[120] Following Ireland's partition in 1920 and the establishment of two states—Northern Ireland, which remained part of the United Kingdom, and independent Southern Ireland—the situation in Northern Ireland became unstable, with friction between the Protestant pro-British majority and a dominant Catholic minority of about 40 percent of the population.[121] After a long period of violent conflict between the rival populations in Northern Ireland, the Belfast agreement of 1998 recognized both communities in the state as intertwined in the area with historic relations to the territory.[122] Hence, the agreement provided the communities with power-sharing arrangements and institutions that gave each community special rights in the government.[123]

The situation in Northern Ireland differs from the situation in Israel in some respects: for example, two kin-states (Britain and Ireland) sponsored the agreement, with Britain still preserving its interests in Northern Ireland; and the arrangement did not render Northern Ireland a completely independent state.[124] The arrangement also did not intend to create a shared Northern-Irish identity,

---

117 *Id.*, 18.

118 *Id.*, 19.

119 For a discussion of the importance of the politics of reconciliation in the Israeli society see, Nadim N. Rouhana, *Reconciling History and Equal Citizenship in Israel: Democracy and the Politics of Historical Denial*, *in* THE POLITICS OF RECONCILIATION IN MULTICULTURAL SOCIETIES 70 93 (Will Kymlicka and Bashir Bashir eds., 2008).

120 Saban, *supra* note 15, 996.

121 Peled, *supra* note 5, 16; Yacobson & Rubinstein, *supra* note 1, 162.

122 Iris M. Young, INCLUSION AND DEMOCRACY 263 (2000).

123 *Id.*; Yacobson & Rubinstein, *supra* note 1, 162.

124 Saban, *supra* note 15, 996.

but rather to preserve the interests of both of the large communities in the area. If the Catholics became a majority in the area and decided to secede from the United Kingdom and join the Irish republic, the Protestant minority in the state would no longer be living in a neutral state, as the Irish flag, the state's national holidays, and its schools' curricula express nothing but Catholic Irish narrative.[125]

Nevertheless, this arrangement still expresses Young's concept of relational autonomy, in which a notion of integration of cultures rather than segregation can be formed where a people stands in interdependent relations with others.[126] This is also what civic-nationalism-plus aims for—and, as shown above, it seems a plausible option for the situation in Israel as well.

Civic-Nationalism-Plus in Israel: Toward a New Israeli Identity

I now turn to discuss broad guidelines for the formation of an overarching identity according to civic-nationalism-plus. As noted above, the application of this model to the Jews-Palestinians conflict in Israel is still speculative; hence, I will not present a detailed model of incorporating the identities of Palestinian-Arabs and Jews for the formation of an Israeli identity, but will rather discuss the general requirements for such a project to be realized.

The civic-nationalism-plus model incorporates the tenets of civic nationalism—that is, territorialism, participation, citizenship, and civic education—with a commitment to establish an infrastructure of common national symbols that motivate the development of feelings of belonging and loyalty to the nation. I will discuss three means that can be used to inculcate the goals of this model: education, civil service, and shared national symbols.

Multicultural Education

I illustrated the significance of civic education in inculcating the norms and values through which a nation-state attempts to identify and define itself[127] in the previous chapter's discussion of multicultural education. Indeed, multicultural education in Israel can greatly contribute to eradicating trends of separation between Jews and Palestinian-Arabs, which, until very recently, were

125 Yacobson & Rubinstein, *supra* note 1, 163.

126 Young, *supra* note 122, 259.

127 See, discussion in Chapter 5.

encouraged by Israel's formal education system.[128] We have seen that the bilingual Jewish-Arab schools that apply multicultural education are a first step in that direction. Despite the challenges these schools face, described in the previous chapter, their aim for equal status through the use of both languages, that is, Hebrew and Arabic, and the policy of mutual recognition and respect for the different cultural traditional identities[129] is an important part of civic education.

Yet, a major deficiency in the overall educational system in Israel, including the bilingual schools, is the curriculum, which is constructed according to the Jewish-Zionist narrative (i.e., the majority) and fails to take into account the values, history, and culture of the minority. A further step towards civic education would be to incorporate within the curricula the teaching of democratic, liberal, and civic values, such as human rights, basic freedoms, and toleration for other individuals' and groups' cultures. Such a curriculum would also emphasize the common public values in Israel upon which civic nationalism is based, as well as love for the homeland and the common sense of belonging.[130]

In fact, a step in this direction has already been taken by the Israeli legislature, which amended the State Education Law in 2000[131] to reflect a change in the goals of public education.[132] The original version of Article 2 of the law determined:

> The object of state education is to base elementary education in the State on the values of Jewish culture and the achievements of science, on love of the homeland and loyalty to the State and the Jewish people, on practice in agricultural work and handicraft, on *chalutzic* [i.e., pioneer] training, and on striving for a society built on freedom, equality, tolerance, mutual assistance and love of mankind.[133]

---

128 See the above discussion of the education system for the Palestinian-Arab public and the domination of Jewish culture over this system.

129 Claire McGlynn, Zvi Bekerman, *The Management of Pupil Difference in Catholic-Protestant and Palestinian-Jewish Integrated Education in Northern Ireland and Israel*, 37(5) COMPARE 689, 698, 899 (2007); Mark Robert, The Construction of Culture in Multicultural Education: Classroom Participation and Teacher-student Interaction in a Jewish-Arab School, Thesis submitted for the degree of Doctor of Philosophy, April 2013, at 41–42.

130 See, Khok Khinukh Mamlakhti (Tikun Mispar 5) [State Education Law (Amendment No. 5)], 2000, S.H. 122 [hereinafter *State Education Law (2000)*].

131 *Id.*

132 Saban, *supra* note 15, 940.

133 Khok Khinukh Mamlakhti [State Education Law], 7 L.S.I. 113, art. 2 (1952–1953) [hereinafter *State Education Law*].

In contrast, the new version of that article determines the following goals of state education:

> (1) To educate a person to love humanity, love his people and love his land, and to be a loyal citizen of the State of Israel, who honors his parents and his family, his heritage, his cultural identity, and his language;
>
> (2) To impart the principles of the Declaration of Independence of the State of Israel and the values of the State of Israel as a Jewish and democratic state and to develop an attitude of respect for human rights, basic freedoms, democratic values, upholding the law, and the culture and viewpoints of others, and also to educate towards the aspiration for peace and tolerance in relations between individuals and between peoples; ...
>
> (11) To recognize the special language, culture, history, heritage, and tradition of the Arab population and of other population groups in the State of Israel, and to recognize the equal rights of all citizens of Israel.[134]

The new version of the law emphasizes democratic and civil values. It does not demand that non-Jewish Israelis be loyal to the "Jewish and democratic state of Israel" but rather that they love the land, which is also their own. In addition, while the former version of the law accepted the hegemony of the Jewish-Zionist narrative and stressed Jewish values and *chalutzic* training, this version emphasizes the importance of recognizing the language, culture, and history of the Arab population and other groups, and of educating towards the aspiration for peace and tolerance in relations between individuals and peoples.[135]

Equal Access to Civil Service

Feelings of belonging and allegiance to the state could also be fostered by encouraging civil service within the Palestinian-Arab public. This suggestion is predicated upon the assumption that mandatory military service is still considered a civic virtue in the eyes of the general public in Israel—a questionable point given the decline of republicanism and increasingly liberal image of Israeli society over the last decade.[136] Nevertheless, military service is still a precondition for the entitlement to numerous social privileges,[137] and hence serves as a "membership card" in Israeli society. Given these conditions, an

134 State Education Law (2000), *supra* note 130, art. 2.

135 *Id.*

136 Peled, *supra* note 5, 117.

137 See, *supra* note 102 and accompanying text.

alternative for the Palestinian-Arabs, in the form of a mandatory civil service, is a fundamental condition for this group's integration within Israeli society.

Uniting National Symbols

Lastly, and in combination with civic education and civil service, ways must be found to create a common symbolic space in civil society for Jews and Arabs. Indeed, the role of national symbols in facilitating and strengthening emotional identification of the citizens with its state cannot be overstated. While exploring the full range of options of recreating the symbolic space of the state is beyond the scope of this book; I will put forward some proposals that have been made.

Hizky Shoham, in his book on the role of festivals in civic culture in Israel, suggests that social integration can be facilitated in two stages through a process of naturalization of Jewish culture in Israel.[138] First, Jewish culture should be seen as a civic culture rather than a religious culture, and its pervasiveness in Israeli (i.e., the majority) society should be increased to encompass all citizens and contribute to social integration.[139] This could be done, for example, by transforming Jewish festivals into civic festivals in which all people can participate—without, of course, being forced to relinquish their own cultural heritage and customs. Such processes are common in other states, such as the US or Canada, which have civic holidays that all minorities celebrate.[140] Thus, "the fifteenth of Shvat"[141] could be treated as an ecological festival, like the national tree day in other states, and so could Yom Kippur.[142] Second, this Jewish civic culture should be infused with elements of the Arabic-Muslim culture, including not only "tokenist" aspects, such as food and music (which are already penetrating Jewish-Israeli culture), but the culture's deeper legacy and historical narratives.[143] In this way, the two cultures will influence each other in a rich dialogue that is encouraged and supported by public institutions and figures of the Israeli state, making the new integrated culture into an official civic one.[144]

---

138 Hizky Shoham, Let's Celebrate! Festivals and Civic Culture in Israel 185 (2014). [Hebrew].

139 *Id.*, 191.

140 *Id.*, 207.

141 The Hebrew month of *Shvat* falls in January or February in the Gregorian calendar.

142 *Yom Kippur* is a religious festival during which, due to the original religious custom of fasting, all businesses are shut down and the roads are free of vehicles.

143 Shoham, *supra* note 138, 207.

144 *Id.*, 207–208.

Such a process is being tested by the bilingual schools in Israel schools, in which festival ceremonies incorporate the heritage of all three major religions in Israel (Judaism, Islam and Christianity) using symbols that exemplify both the distinctiveness and commonality of Jews and Arabs.[145] These ceremonies also challenge the Zionist master narrative, "explor[ing] possibilities outside the present conflict" and searching for both new and familiar expressions of meaning and identity.[146]

Finally, the dialogue between cultures should engender and incorporate Jewish and Palestinian-Arab national symbols. The symbolic spaces of the state range from the spiritual and less concrete (national narratives in history, civic studies and literature in state schools, public broadcasting, national museum exhibits) to more concrete and tangible symbols (the national flag, street names, state monuments, the national anthem). There are, thus, various ways that the state can create shared national symbols. For example, while the current Israeli calendar officially marks only Jewish festivals, it could be modified into a common calendar that includes the festivals of all major three religions in Israel, either turning them into official days of rest or choosing other ways to publicly recognize them.[147] Another more challenging change to consider is the state symbol, currently the Jewish King David's shield. A more common national symbol might be the olive tree, an endemic tree of Israel with a central place in both Jewish and Palestinian-Arab mythologies—despite its serving also as a symbol of conflicting Jewish and Palestinian nationalistic claims of authentic connection to the land.[148] Echoing the Canadian maple tree, whose story of "climbing" onto the Canadian flag was discussed in a previous chapter, the olive tree can symbolize the physical and spiritual connection of both Jews and Palestinians-Arabs to the land of Israel, and in this way serve as a symbol of peace and mutual recognition of the inevitable reality of these nations living together in Israel.[149]

To conclude, the process of forming an Israeli identity according to the civic-nationalism-plus citizenship model might be a long and difficult one; however,

---

145 Zvi Bekerman, *Reshaping Conflict Through Schooll Ceremonial Events in Israeli Palestinians-Jewish Coeducation*, 34(2) ANTHROPOLOGY & EDUCATION QUARTERLY 205, 217 (2003).

146 *Id.*, 218. Indeed, currently such processes are still accompanied by tensions and difficulties emerging from the pervasiveness of the national conflict between Jews and Arabs. Therefore, Memorial Day and *Al-Nacba* were presented as "two…separate commemorative procedures wrapped in multiple thorny tensions." See *id.*, 219.

147 Shoham, *supra* note 138, 211–212.

148 Bekerman, *supra* note 145, 219.

149 Shoham, *supra* note 138, 216.

to my mind, it is not completely impossible. Current political developments have brought this issue into public awareness. The 2014 Israeli-Palestinian negotiations towards a peace process have sparked public discussion of what defines the national character of a state in general, and the state of Israel in particular. Israel has demanded that the Palestinians recognize Israel as a Jewish state.[150] Public opinion in Israel is divided on this issue. Some claim that such formal recognition is crucial for practical reasons (as it will prove that the Palestinians are willing to end the conflict in a two-nation-state solution) as well as theoretical reasons (as Israel will formally be recognized as the homeland for Jews).[151] Others claim that Israel does not need such formal and outside recognition.[152] Yet, these conflicting attitudes expose a pervasive concept in Israeli society: that Israel is nothing but a Jewish (and democratic) state. I suggest that the solution is not complete dichotomy and that Israeli identity can be formed in different ways. The question of whether such an option can ever be realized can only be answered in the days to come.

---

150 Michael Wilner, *Kerry: Netanyahu Wrong to Insist Palestinians Recognize Israel as Jewish state*, The Jerusalem Post, March 3 2014 <http://www.jpost.com/Diplomacy-and-Politics/Kerry-says-Netanyahu-wrong-to-insist-Palestinians-recognize-Israel-as-Jewish-state-345341>.

151 Chuck Freilich, *Why Palestine Must Recognize Israel as a Jewish State*, The National Interest, April 3 2014, <http://nationalinterest.org/commentary/why-palestine-must-recognize-israel-jewish-state-10174>.

152 Elad Benari, *Galon Accuses Netanyahu of "Rewriting History,"* Arutz Sheva, 21 March 2014, <http://www.israelnationalnews.com/News/News.aspx/178731#.UoEgiJvNt9A>.

Conclusion

> If I am me because I am me, and you are you because you are you, then I am me and you are you. But if I am me because you are you and you are you because I am me, then I am not me and you are not you![1]

The saying attributed to the Kotzker Rebbe cited above implies that identity is formed through a process of inward looking and not through negation with the other. The analogy suggested in this book is that in searching for a common identity, societies need not characterize themselves in the course of confrontation with "the other"; instead, they can look for what unites the different groups that compose them. The search for ties that bind must include discussion and a search for a common endeavor. In this way, instead of focusing on a legal discourse that creates a set of rights and responsibilities, the multinational society should engage in dialogue to clarify the meaning of the membership in the political community and to create a strengthened civic identity.

Since the mid-20th century, the discussion of the rights of minorities, including national rights, has increased in complexity, continuously shifting focus with the political developments in the international community. One of most conspicuous of these developments can be seen in the flexible status of the concept of the nation-state. Nevertheless, it seems that political theories of nationalism—which differ in some respects but are similar in adhering to the political force of the nation-state—remain relevant for questions that arise about the cohesion of multinational states.

In this book I accounted for the cohesion of multinational states by suggesting a model of citizenship that rests on the concepts of nationalism, multiculturalism, and liberalism, but also claiming that these theories cannot serve independently as the basis for such a model. Pure liberalism misses the aspect that nationalist theories grasp according to which community is a vital force in sustaining people's need to share civic ends in a political community. Pluralist or radical multicultural views fail to ensure the common goals of a large civic community; according to such views, these goals do not even exist, and we end up only with a commitment to the narrow interests of the group.

The common ends of the large political community are emphasized by elements of nationalistic theories that serve to explain why nationalism sustains the cohesiveness of societies, referring to compatriots' allegiance to a state and sense of belonging to a community. I hence claimed these theories apply not only

1 Menachem Mendel Morgensztern of Kotzk, known as the Kotzker Rebbe (1787–1859).

 | DOI 10.1163/9789004294332_010

to societies composed of a single national group, but also to multinational societies. I rested this applicability on two pillars: (i) the right to self-determination of peoples, and (ii) the strengthening of the ethos of civic nationalism by enabling identification with shared national symbols in a multinational state.

Having revisited the right of self-determination of peoples and focusing on its internal aspect, I argued that this right is central in the legal discourse of human and peoples' rights, and hence that one cannot overestimate its ability to entrench the national group's identity within a multinational state. In practical terms, this right is best realized in the political regime of federalism, whose strengths and deficiencies I analyzed according to three case studies: Canada, Belgium, and Spain.

However, the right to internal self-determination is less effective in enabling the minority's integration within the overall society of a multinational state. In order to achieve this goal, I suggested a model of integration that I refer to as "civic-nationalism-plus." This model assumes an infrastructure of civic nationalism in which the overarching national identity is based on a shared civic narrative of rights and duties, and it is best accomplished when this discourse is a democratic one that stresses the values of equality, human dignity, and toleration.

Nevertheless, civic nationalism lacks a concrete element crucial to the development of feelings of belonging and allegiance to a state, which is best achieved through identification with national symbols. I claimed that the psychological and cultural force of national symbols throughout history in forming and maintaining cohesive societies suggests that shared national symbols are also fundamental in forming and preserving multinational societies. I argued that the dynamic character of the process of creating national symbols could sometimes benefit national minorities, supporting their ability to partake in designing the society's cultural "code" or "alphabet." I referred to the case of the renewed Canadian flag to exemplify this claim.

As I suggested that the cultural "code" or "alphabet" of multinational states should be a multicultural one, I presented multicultural and civic education as supplying the fundamental substance for achieving such a shared code. I presented both the achievements of and the obstacles still faced by multicultural education by referring to case studies in societies torn apart by a national or a religious conflict, such as Northern Ireland, Cyprus, and Israel. Indeed, as I suggested in the final chapter, multicultural education is the infrastructure for applying the civic-nationalism-plus model to the formation of a shared Israeli identity of both Jews and Palestinian-Arabs. In order to assess the applicability of this model to the Israeli society, I examined the roots of the Jewish-Palestinian conflict, the prevailing theories and viewpoints on the national identity of the state of Israel, and the relationship between Israel's two major communities: the Jews and the Palestinian-Arabs.

I rejected the view that ensuring the right of self-determination to the Jewish people in Israel demands an exclusively Jewish national character and a negation of the national rights of the Palestinian-Arab minority.[2] I suggested as an alternative that—with the exception of preserving the Law of Return to ensure privileges for Jews in immigration quotas—we can achieve equality between Jews and Palestinian-Arabs in terms of both individual and national rights through the civic-nationalism-plus model. I conditioned the applicability of the model on several preconditions, the most noted of which is ending the conflict between Jews and Palestinians outside Israel and diminishing hostile feelings between the two communities. While these preconditions may not appear achievable in the near future, I suggested that we remain open to the feasibility of the formation of an Israeli identity inclusive of both Jews and Palestinian-Arabs.

The formation of an inclusive Israeli identity requires sorting out binding ties in a society that does not yet share a common story. As a first step, multicultural education provides the option for both societies in Israel—i.e., the Jews and the Palestinian-Arabs—to become familiar with and respect each other's narratives. However, we should acknowledge the possibility that a construction of a shared story may not be feasible. In such a case, the only choice will be secession.

Yet, the Israeli case, which presents the society of a relatively young state, may strengthen the claim that the civic-nationalism-plus model, in which minorities receive a right to influence the character of the state by participating in forming shared national symbols and narratives, can apply to either newly established states or to homeland communities in long-established states such as Belgium, Spain or Canada. However, the model cannot allow for newcomers to shape the character of the state they immigrated to. On the one hand, the justification of this claim rests on the concept of self-determination of peoples. As was shown in the second chapter, the right to self-determination of peoples justifies some nation-based priorities,[3] such as the right to self-rule and to equal representation in the public sphere. While members of homeland communities in a state are entitled to self-rule and self-representation rights, other groups, such as ethnic groups or immigrants, are entitled only

2 Supporters of this view, nevertheless, accept the prevailing legal reality that Arabic has a formal status in Israeli law. See, Alexander Yacobson and Amnon Rubinstein, Israel and the Family of Nations 150–151 (2010).

3 Chaim Gans, A Just Zionism 122 (2008).

to self-representation rights.[4] On the other hand, the question remains of whether the character of the state should be shaped exclusively by the groups holding the right to self-determination or also by groups who are entitled to self-representation rights. Indeed, allowing such a prerogative for immigrants adversely affects the stability of state's identity. It may also intensify trends of seclusion among the majority community in long established nation-states, as it might feel threatened by what it sees as the newcomers' attempt to dominate. Lastly, it can be claimed that the act of immigration itself implies that people knowingly leaving an old culture and legacy behind in order to join a new one.

Nevertheless, the relationship between immigrants and homeland communities is not a static one, and we may see unpredictable changes in the future of nation-states. The historical processes and the changes in the concept of nation-state referred to in this book definitely support such assumption, as does the concept of fluid identities explored in the fourth chapter, according to which groups develop a new hybrid code of their own. Therefore, the reconfiguration of national identities, such as the one suggested by civic-nationalism-plus, depends on a dynamic process. While such a process will more likely begin in relatively newly established states, it is not unimaginable that it could be the experience of long-established societies as well.

---

4 Will Kymlicka, Multicultural Citizenship: A Liberal Theory of Minority Rights 27–33 (1995).

APPENDIX 1

Reference Re Secession of Quebec, [1998] 2 S.C.R. 217[1]

IN THE MATTER OF Section 53 of the *Supreme Court Act*, R.S.C., 1985, c. S-26;
AND IN THE MATTER OF a Reference by the Governor in Council concerning certain questions relating to the secession of Quebec from Canada, as set out in Order in Council P.C. 1996–1497, dated the 30th day of September, 1996
Indexed as: Reference re Secession of Quebec
File No.: 25506.
1998: February 16, 17, 18, 19; 1998: August 20.
Present: Lamer C.J. and L'Heureux-Dubé, Gonthier, Cory, McLachlin, Iacobucci, Major, Bastarache and Binnie JJ.
reference by governor in council

Constitutional law—Supreme Court of Canada—Reference jurisdiction—Whether Supreme Court's reference jurisdiction constitutional—Constitution Act, 1867, s. 101—Supreme Court Act, R.S.C., 1985, c. S-26, s. 53.

Courts—Supreme Court of Canada—Reference jurisdiction—Governor in Council referring to Supreme Court three questions relating to secession of Quebec from Canada—Whether questions submitted fall outside scope of reference provision of Supreme Court Act—Whether questions submitted justiciable—Supreme Court Act, R.S.C., 1985, c. S-26, s. 53.

Constitutional law—Secession of province—Unilateral secession—Whether Quebec can secede unilaterally from Canada under Constitution.

International law—Secession of province of Canadian federation—Right of self-determination—Effectivity principle—Whether international law gives Quebec right to secede unilaterally from Canada.

Pursuant to s. 53 of the *Supreme Court Act*, the Governor in Council referred the following questions to this Court:

1. Under the Constitution of Canada, can the National Assembly, legislature or government of Quebec effect the secession of Quebec from Canada unilaterally?
2. Does international law give the National Assembly, legislature or government of Quebec the right to effect the secession of Quebec from Canada unilaterally? In this regard, is there a right to self-determination under international law that

1 Judgements of the Supreme Court of Canada, http://scc-csc.lexum.com/scc-csc/scc-csc/en/item/1643/index.do.

 | DOI 10.1163/9789004294332_011

would give the National Assembly, legislature or government of Quebec the right to effect the secession of Quebec from Canada unilaterally?

3. In the event of a conflict between domestic and international law on the right of the National Assembly, legislature or government of Quebec to effect the secession of Quebec from Canada unilaterally, which would take precedence in Canada?

Issues regarding the Court's reference jurisdiction were raised by the *amicus curiae*. He argued that s. 53 of the *Supreme Court Act* was unconstitutional; that, even if the Court's reference jurisdiction was constitutionally valid, the questions submitted were outside the scope of s. 53; and, finally, that these questions were not justiciable.

Held: Section 53 of the *Supreme Court Act* is constitutional and the Court should answer the reference questions.

(1) *Supreme Court's Reference Jurisdiction*

Section 101 of the *Constitution Act, 1867* gives Parliament the authority to grant this Court the reference jurisdiction provided for in s. 53 of the *Supreme Court Act*. The words "general court of appeal" in s. 101 denote the status of the Court within the national court structure and should not be taken as a restrictive definition of the Court's functions. While, in most instances, this Court acts as the exclusive ultimate appellate court in the country, an appellate court can receive, on an exceptional basis, original jurisdiction not incompatible with its appellate jurisdiction. Even if there were any conflict between this Court's reference jurisdiction and the original jurisdiction of the provincial superior courts, any such conflict must be resolved in favour of Parliament's exercise of its plenary power to establish a "general court of appeal." A "general court of appeal" may also properly undertake other legal functions, such as the rendering of advisory opinions. There is no constitutional bar to this Court's receipt of jurisdiction to undertake an advisory role.

The reference questions are within the scope of s. 53 of the *Supreme Court Act*. Question 1 is directed, at least in part, to the interpretation of the *Constitution Acts*, which are referred to in s. 53(1) (*a*). Both Questions 1 and 2 fall within s. 53(1) (*d*), since they relate to the powers of the legislature or government of a Canadian province. Finally, all three questions are "important questions of law or fact concerning any matter" and thus come within s. 53(2). In answering Question 2, the Court is not exceeding its jurisdiction by purporting to act as an international tribunal. The Court is providing an advisory opinion to the Governor in Council in its capacity as a national court on legal questions touching and concerning the future of the Canadian federation. Further, Question 2 is not beyond the competence of this Court, as a domestic court, because it requires the Court to look at international law rather than domestic law. More importantly, Question 2 does not ask an abstract question of "pure" international law but seeks to determine the legal rights and obligations of the legislature or government of Quebec, institutions that exist as part of the Canadian legal order. International law must be addressed since it has been invoked as a consideration in the context of this Reference.

The reference questions are justiciable and should be answered. They do not ask the Court to usurp any democratic decision that the people of Quebec may be called upon to make. The questions, as interpreted by the Court, are strictly limited to aspects of the legal framework in which that democratic decision is to be taken. Since the reference questions may clearly be interpreted as directed to legal issues, the Court is in a position to answer them. The Court cannot exercise its discretion to refuse to answer the questions on a pragmatic basis. The questions raise issues of fundamental public importance and they are not too imprecise or ambiguous to permit a proper legal answer. Nor has the Court been provided with insufficient information regarding the present context in which the questions arise. Finally, the Court may deal on a reference with issues that might otherwise be considered not yet "ripe" for decision.

(2) *Question 1*

The Constitution is more than a written text. It embraces the entire global system of rules and principles which govern the exercise of constitutional authority. A superficial reading of selected provisions of the written constitutional enactment, without more, may be misleading. It is necessary to make a more profound investigation of the underlying principles animating the whole of the Constitution, including the principles of federalism, democracy, constitutionalism and the rule of law, and respect for minorities. Those principles must inform our overall appreciation of the constitutional rights and obligations that would come into play in the event that a clear majority of Quebecers votes on a clear question in favour of secession.

The Court in this Reference is required to consider whether Quebec has a right to unilateral secession. Arguments in support of the existence of such a right were primarily based on the principle of democracy. Democracy, however, means more than simple majority rule. Constitutional jurisprudence shows that democracy exists in the larger context of other constitutional values. Since Confederation, the people of the provinces and territories have created close ties of interdependence (economic, social, political and cultural) based on shared values that include federalism, democracy, constitutionalism and the rule of law, and respect for minorities. A democratic decision of Quebecers in favour of secession would put those relationships at risk. The Constitution vouchsafes order and stability, and accordingly secession of a province "under the Constitution" could not be achieved unilaterally, that is, without principled negotiation with other participants in Confederation within the existing constitutional framework.

Our democratic institutions necessarily accommodate a continuous process of discussion and evolution, which is reflected in the constitutional right of each participant in the federation to initiate constitutional change. This right implies a reciprocal duty on the other participants to engage in discussions to address any legitimate initiative to change the constitutional order. A clear majority vote in Quebec on a clear question in favour of secession would confer democratic legitimacy on the secession initiative which all of the other participants in Confederation would have to recognize.

Quebec could not, despite a clear referendum result, purport to invoke a right of self-determination to dictate the terms of a proposed secession to the other parties to the federation. The democratic vote, by however strong a majority, would have no legal effect on its own and could not push aside the principles of federalism and the rule of law, the rights of individuals and minorities, or the operation of democracy in the other provinces or in Canada as a whole. Democratic rights under the Constitution cannot be divorced from constitutional obligations. Nor, however, can the reverse proposition be accepted: the continued existence and operation of the Canadian constitutional order could not be indifferent to a clear expression of a clear majority of Quebecers that they no longer wish to remain in Canada. The other provinces and the federal government would have no basis to deny the right of the government of Quebec to pursue secession should a clear majority of the people of Quebec choose that goal, so long as in doing so, Quebec respects the rights of others. The negotiations that followed such a vote would address the potential act of secession as well as its possible terms should in fact secession proceed. There would be no conclusions predetermined by law on any issue. Negotiations would need to address the interests of the other provinces, the federal government and Quebec and indeed the rights of all Canadians both within and outside Quebec, and specifically the rights of minorities.

The negotiation process would require the reconciliation of various rights and obligations by negotiation between two legitimate majorities, namely, the majority of the population of Quebec, and that of Canada as a whole. A political majority at either level that does not act in accordance with the underlying constitutional principles puts at risk the legitimacy of its exercise of its rights, and the ultimate acceptance of the result by the international community.

The task of the Court has been to clarify the legal framework within which political decisions are to be taken "under the Constitution" and not to usurp the prerogatives of the political forces that operate within that framework. The obligations identified by the Court are binding obligations under the Constitution. However, it will be for the political actors to determine what constitutes "a clear majority on a clear question" in the circumstances under which a future referendum vote may be taken. Equally, in the event of demonstrated majority support for Quebec secession, the content and process of the negotiations will be for the political actors to settle. The reconciliation of the various legitimate constitutional interests is necessarily committed to the political rather than the judicial realm precisely because that reconciliation can only be achieved through the give and take of political negotiations. To the extent issues addressed in the course of negotiation are political, the courts, appreciating their proper role in the constitutional scheme, would have no supervisory role.

(3) *Question 2*

The Court was also required to consider whether a right to unilateral secession exists under international law. Some supporting an affirmative answer did so on the basis of the recognized right to self-determination that belongs to all "peoples." Although much of the Quebec population certainly shares many of the characteristics of a people, it is not necessary to decide the "people" issue because, whatever may be the correct determination of this issue in the context of Quebec, a right to secession only arises under the principle of self-determination of people at international law where "a people" is governed as part of a colonial empire; where "a people" is subject to alien subjugation, domination or exploitation; and possibly where "a people" is denied any meaningful exercise of its right to self-determination within the state of which it forms a part. In other circumstances, peoples are expected to achieve self-determination within the framework of their existing state. A state whose government represents the whole of the people or peoples resident within its territory, on a basis of equality and without discrimination, and respects the principles of self-determination in its internal arrangements, is entitled to maintain its territorial integrity under international law and to have that territorial integrity recognized by other states. Quebec does not meet the threshold of a colonial people or an oppressed people, nor can it be suggested that Quebecers have been denied meaningful access to government to pursue their political, economic, cultural and social development. In the circumstances, the "National Assembly, the legislature or the government of Quebec" do not enjoy a right at international law to effect the secession of Quebec from Canada unilaterally.

Although there is no right, under the Constitution or at international law, to unilateral secession, the possibility of an unconstitutional declaration of secession leading to a *de facto* secession is not ruled out. The ultimate success of such a secession would be dependent on recognition by the international community, which is likely to consider the legality and legitimacy of secession having regard to, amongst other facts, the conduct of Quebec and Canada, in determining whether to grant or withhold recognition. Even if granted, such recognition would not, however, provide any retroactive justification for the act of secession, either under the Constitution of Canada or at international law.

(4) *Question 3*

In view of the answers to Questions 1 and 2, there is no conflict between domestic and international law to be addressed in the context of this Reference.

Cases Cited

Referred to: *Reference re Manitoba Language Rights*, [1985] 1 S.C.R. 721; *Re References by Governor-General in Council* (1910), 43 S.C.R. 536, aff'd [1912] A.C. 571; *Quebec North Shore Paper Co. v. Canadian Pacific Ltd.*, [1977] 2 S.C.R. 1054; *De Demko v. Home Secretary*, [1959] A.C. 654; *Re Forest and Registrar of Court of Appeal of Manitoba* (1977), 77 D.L.R. (3d) 445; *Attorney-General for Ontario v. Attorney-General for Canada*, [1947] A.C. 127; *Muskrat v. United States*, 219 U.S. 346 (1911); *Reference re Powers to Levy Rates on Foreign Legations and High Commissioners' Residences*, [1943] S.C.R. 208; *Reference re Ownership of Offshore Mineral Rights of British Columbia*, [1967] S.C.R. 792; *Reference re Newfoundland Continental Shelf*, [1984] 1 S.C.R. 86; *Reference re Canada Assistance Plan (B.C.)*, [1991] 2 S.C.R. 525; *McEvoy v. Attorney General for New Brunswick*, [1983] 1 S.C.R. 704; *Reference re Waters and Water-Powers*, [1929] S.C.R. 200; *Reference re Goods and Services Tax*, [1992] 2 S.C.R. 445; *Reference re Remuneration of Judges of the Provincial Court of Prince Edward Island*, [1997] 3 S.C.R. 3; *Reference re Education System in Island of Montreal*, [1926] S.C.R. 246; *Reference re Authority of Parliament in relation to the Upper House*, [1980] 1 S.C.R. 54; *Reference re Resolution to amend the Constitution*, [1981] 1 S.C.R. 753; *Reference re Objection by Quebec to a Resolution to Amend the Constitution*, [1982] 2 S.C.R. 793; *OPSEU v. Ontario (Attorney General)*, [1987] 2 S.C.R. 2; *Edwards v. Attorney-General for Canada*, [1930] A.C. 124; *New Brunswick Broadcasting Co. v. Nova Scotia (Speaker of the House of Assembly)*, [1993] 1 S.C.R. 319; *Fraser v. Public Service Staff Relations Board*, [1985] 2 S.C.R. 455; *Liquidators of the Maritime Bank of Canada v. Receiver-General of New Brunswick*, [1892] A.C. 437; *Northern Telecom Canada Ltd. v. Communication Workers of Canada*, [1983] 1 S.C.R. 733; *Re the Initiative and Referendum Act*, [1919] A.C. 935; *Haig v. Canada*, [1993] 2 S.C.R. 995; *R.v.S. (S.)*, [1990] 2 S.C.R. 254; *Switzman v. Elbling*, [1957] S.C.R. 285; *Saumur v. City of Quebec*, [1953] 2 S.C.R. 299; *Boucher v. The King*, [1951] S.C.R. 265; *Reference re Alberta Statutes*, [1938] S.C.R. 100; *Reference re Provincial Electoral Boundaries (Sask.)*, [1991] 2 S.C.R. 158; *R.v. Oakes*, [1986] 1 S.C.R. 103; *Harvey v. New Brunswick (Attorney General)*, [1996] 2 S.C.R. 876; *Roncarelli v. Duplessis*, [1959] S.C.R. 121; *Operation Dismantle Inc. v. The Queen*, [1985] 1 S.C.R. 441; *Reference re Bill 30, An Act to amend the Education Act (Ont.)*, [1987] 1 S.C.R. 1148; *Reference re Education Act (Que.)*, [1993] 2 S.C.R. 511; *Greater Montreal Protestant School Board v. Quebec (Attorney General)*, [1989] 1 S.C.R. 377; *Adler v. Ontario*, [1996] 3 S.C.R. 609; *Société des Acadiens du Nouveau-Brunswick Inc. v. Association of Parents for Fairness in Education*, [1986] 1 S.C.R. 549; *Reference re Public Schools Act (Man.), s. 79(3), (4) and (7)*, [1993] 1 S.C.R. 839; *Mahe v. Alberta*, [1990] 1 S.C.R. 342; *R.v. Sparrow*, [1990] 1 S.C.R. 1075; *Canada (Auditor General) v. Canada (Minister of Energy, Mines and Resources)*, [1989] 2 S.C.R. 49.

Statutes and Regulations Cited

Ala. Code 1975 § 12-2-10.
Bill of Rights of 1689 (Eng.), 1 Will. & Mar. sess. 2, c. 2.
Canadian Charter of Rights and Freedoms, ss. 2, 3, 4, 7 to 14, 15, 25, 33.
Charter of the United Nations, Can. T.S. 1945 No. 7, Arts. 1(2), 55.
Constitution Act, 1867, preamble, ss. 91, 92(14), 96, 101.
Constitution Act, 1982, ss. 25, 35, 52(1), (2).
Convention for the Protection of Human Rights and Fundamental Freedoms, Protocol No. 2, Europ. T.S. No. 5, p. 36.
Del. Code Ann. tit. 10, § 141 (1996 Supp.).
International Covenant on Civil and Political Rights, 999 U.N.T.S. 171, Art. 1.
International Covenant on Economic, Social and Cultural Rights, 993 U.N.T.S. 3, Art. 1.
Magna Carta (1215).
Statute of the Inter-American Court of Human Rights (1979), Art. 2.
Statute of Westminster, 1931 (U.K.), 22 & 23 Geo. 5, c. 4 [reprinted in R.S.C., 1985, App. II, No. 27].
Supreme Court Act, R.S.C., 1985, c. S-26, ss. 3, 53(1) (*a*), (*d*), (2).
Treaty establishing the European Community, Art. 228(6).
Union Act, 1840 (U.K.), 3–4 Vict., c. 35 [reprinted in R.S.C., 1985, App. II, No. 4].
United States Constitution, art. III, § 2.

Authors Cited

Canada. Legislature. *Parliamentary Debates on the subject of the Confederation of the British North American Provinces*, 3rd Sess., 8th Provincial Parliament of Canada. Quebec: Hunter, Rose & Co., 1865.
Cassese, Antonio. *Self-determination of peoples: A legal reappraisal*. Cambridge: Cambridge University Press, 1995.
Conference on Security and Co-operation in Europe. *Concluding Document of the Vienna Meeting 1986*, Vienna 1989. Ottawa: Department of External Affairs, 1989.
Conference on Security and Co-operation in Europe. *Final Act*, 14 I.L.M. 1292 (1975).
de Smith, S.A. "Constitutional Lawyers in Revolutionary Situations" (1968), 7 *West. Ont. L. Rev.* 93.
Doehring, Karl. "Self-Determination." In Bruno Simma, ed., *The Charter of the United Nations: A Commentary*. Oxford: Oxford University Press, 1994.
European Community. Declaration. *Guidelines on the Recognition of New States in Eastern Europe and in the Soviet Union*, December 16, 1991, 31 I.L.M. 1486 (1992).

Favoreu, Louis. "American and European Models of Constitutional Justice." In David S. Clark, ed., *Comparative and Private International Law: Essays in Honor of John Henry Merryman on his Seventieth Birthday*. Berlin: Duncker & Humblot, 1990, 105.

Hogg, Peter W. *Constitutional Law of Canada*, 4th ed. Scarborough, Ont.: Carswell, 1997.

Jennings, Robert Yewdall. *The Acquisition of Territory in International Law*. Manchester: Manchester University Press, 1963.

MacLauchlan, H. Wade. "Accounting for Democracy and the Rule of Law in the Quebec Secession Reference" (1997), 76 *Can. Bar Rev.* 155.

Pope, Joseph, ed. *Confederation: Being a Series of Hitherto Unpublished Documents Bearing on the British North America Act*. Toronto: Carswell, 1895.

United Nations. General Assembly. *Declaration on Principles of International Law concerning Friendly Relations and Co-operation among States in accordance with the Charter of the United Nations*, GA Res. 2625 (XXV), 24 October 1970.

United Nations. General Assembly. *Declaration on the Occasion of the Fiftieth Anniversary of the United Nations*, GA Res. 50/6, 9 November 1995.

United Nations. World Conference on Human Rights. *Vienna Declaration and Programme of Action*, A/CONF.157/24 (Part 1), 25 June 1993, Chapter 3.

Wade, H.W.R. "The Basis of Legal Sovereignty," [1955] *Camb. L.J.* 172.

Wheare, Kenneth Clinton. *Federal Government*, 4th ed. London: Oxford University Press, 1963.

REFERENCE by the Governor in Council, pursuant to s. 53 of the Supreme Court Act, concerning the secession of Quebec from Canada.

L. Yves Fortier, Q.C., Pierre Bienvenu, Warren J. Newman, Jean-Marc Aubry, Q.C., and *Mary Dawson, Q.C.*, for the Attorney General of Canada.

André Joli-C{oe}ur, Michel Paradis, Louis Masson, André Binette, Clément Samson, Martin Bédard and *Martin St-Amant*, for the *amicus curiae*.

Donna J. Miller, Q.C., and *Deborah L. Carlson*, for the intervener the Attorney General of Manitoba.

Graeme G. Mitchell and *John D. Whyte, Q.C.*, for the intervener the Attorney General for Saskatchewan.

Bernard W. Funston, for the intervener the Minister of Justice of the Northwest Territories.

Stuart J. Whitley, Q.C., and *Howard L. Kushner*, for the intervener the Minister of Justice for the Government of the Yukon Territory.

Agnès Laporte and *Richard Gaudreau*, for the intervener Kitigan Zibi Anishinabeg.

Claude-Armand Sheppard, Paul Joffe and *Andrew Orkin*, for the intervener the Grand Council of the Crees (Eeyou Estchee).

Peter W. Hutchins and *Carol Hilling*, for the intervener the Makivik Corporation.

Michael Sherry, for the intervener the Chiefs of Ontario.

Raj Anand and *M. Kate Stephenson*, for the intervener the Minority Advocacy and Rights Council.

Mary Eberts and *Anne Bayefsky*, for the intervener the *Ad Hoc* Committee of Canadian Women on the Constitution.

Guy Bertrand and *Patrick Monahan*, for the intervener Guy Bertrand.

Stephen A. Scott, for the interveners Roopnarine Singh, Keith Owen Henderson, Claude Leclerc, Kenneth O'Donnell and Van Hoven Petteway.

Vincent Pouliot, on his own behalf.

//The Court//

The following is the judgment delivered by
THE COURT—

I Introduction

1 This Reference requires us to consider momentous questions that go to the heart of our system of constitutional government. The observation we made more than a decade ago in *Reference re Manitoba Language Rights*, [1985] 1 S.C.R. 721 (*Manitoba Language Rights Reference*), at p. 728, applies with equal force here: as in that case, the present one "combines legal and constitutional questions of the utmost subtlety and complexity with political questions of great sensitivity." In our view, it is not possible to answer the questions that have been put to us without a consideration of a number of underlying principles. An exploration of the meaning and nature of these underlying principles is not merely of academic interest. On the contrary, such an exploration is of immense practical utility. Only once those underlying principles have been examined and delineated may a considered response to the questions we are required to answer emerge.

2 The questions posed by the Governor in Council by way of Order in Council P.C. 1996–1497, dated September 30, 1996, read as follows:

1. Under the Constitution of Canada, can the National Assembly, legislature or government of Quebec effect the secession of Quebec from Canada unilaterally?
2. Does international law give the National Assembly, legislature or government of Quebec the right to effect the secession of Quebec from Canada unilaterally? In this regard, is there a right to self-determination under international law that would give the National Assembly, legislature or government of Quebec the right to effect the secession of Quebec from Canada unilaterally?
3. In the event of a conflict between domestic and international law on the right of the National Assembly, legislature or government of Quebec to effect the secession of Quebec from Canada unilaterally, which would take precedence in Canada?

3 Before turning to Question 1, as a preliminary matter, it is necessary to deal with the issues raised with regard to this Court's reference jurisdiction.

II The Preliminary Objections to the Court's Reference Jurisdiction

4 The *amicus curiae* argued that s. 101 of the *Constitution Act, 1867* does not give Parliament the authority to grant this Court the jurisdiction provided for in s. 53 of the *Supreme Court Act*, R.S.C., 1985, c. S-26. Alternatively, it is submitted that even if Parliament were entitled to enact s. 53 of the *Supreme Court Act*, the scope of that section should be interpreted to exclude the kinds of questions the Governor in Council has submitted in this Reference. In particular, it is contended that this Court cannot answer Question 2, since it is a question of "pure" international law over which this Court has no jurisdiction. Finally, even if this Court's reference jurisdiction is constitutionally valid, and even if the questions are within the purview of s. 53 of the *Supreme Court Act*, it is argued that the three questions referred to the Court are speculative, of a political nature, and, in any event, are not ripe for judicial decision, and therefore are not justiciable.

5 Notwithstanding certain formal objections by the Attorney General of Canada, it is our view that the *amicus curiae* was within his rights to make the preliminary objections, and that we should deal with them.

A *The Constitutional Validity of Section 53 of the Supreme Court Act*

6 In *Re References by Governor-General in Council* (1910), 43 S.C.R. 536, affirmed on appeal to the Privy Council, [1912] A.C. 571 (*sub nom. Attorney-General for Ontario v. Attorney-General for Canada*), the constitutionality of this Court's special jurisdiction was twice upheld. The Court is asked to revisit these decisions. In light of the significant changes in the role of this Court since 1912, and the very important issues raised in this Reference, it is appropriate to reconsider briefly the constitutional validity of the Court's reference jurisdiction.

7 Section 3 of the *Supreme Court Act* establishes this Court both as a "general court of appeal" for Canada and as an "additional court for the better administration of the laws of Canada." These two roles reflect the two heads of power enumerated in s. 101 of the *Constitution Act, 1867*. However, the "laws of Canada" referred to in s. 101 consist only of federal law and statute: see *Quebec North Shore Paper Co. v. Canadian Pacific Ltd.*, [1977] 2 S.C.R. 1054, at pp. 1065–1066. As a result, the phrase "additional courts" contained in s. 101 is an insufficient basis upon which to ground the special jurisdiction established in s. 53 of the *Supreme Court Act*, which clearly exceeds a consideration of federal law alone (see, e.g., s. 53(2)). Section 53 must therefore be taken as enacted pursuant to Parliament's power to create a "general court of appeal" for Canada.

8 Section 53 of the *Supreme Court Act* is *intra vires* Parliament's power under s. 101 if, in "pith and substance," it is legislation in relation to the constitution or organization of a "general court of appeal." Section 53 is defined by two leading characteristics—it establishes an original jurisdiction in this Court and imposes a duty on the Court to render advisory opinions. Section 53 is therefore constitutionally valid only if (1) a "general court of appeal" may properly exercise an original jurisdiction; and (2) a "general court of appeal" may properly undertake other legal functions, such as the rendering of advisory opinions.

(1) May a Court of Appeal Exercise an Original Jurisdiction?

9 The words "general court of appeal" in s. 101 denote the status of the Court within the national court structure and should not be taken as a restrictive definition of the Court's functions. In most instances, this Court acts as the exclusive ultimate appellate court in the country, and, as such, is properly constituted as the "general court of appeal" for Canada. Moreover, it is clear that an appellate court can receive, on an exceptional basis, original jurisdiction not incompatible with its appellate jurisdiction.

10 The English Court of Appeal, the U.S. Supreme Court and certain courts of appeal in Canada exercise an original jurisdiction in addition to their appellate functions. See *De Demko v. Home Secretary*, [1959] A.C. 654 (H.L.), at p. 660; *Re Forest and Registrar of Court of Appeal of Manitoba* (1977), 77 D.L.R. (3d) 445 (Man. C.A.), at p. 453; United States Constitution, art. III, § 2. Although these courts are not constituted under a head of power similar to s. 101, they certainly provide examples which suggest that there is nothing inherently self-contradictory about an appellate court exercising original jurisdiction on an exceptional basis.

11 It is also argued that this Court's original jurisdiction is unconstitutional because it conflicts with the original jurisdiction of the provincial superior courts and usurps the normal appellate process. However, Parliament's power to establish a general court of appeal pursuant to s. 101 is plenary, and takes priority over the province's power to control the administration of justice in s. 92(14). See *Attorney-General for Ontario v. Attorney-General for Canada*, [1947] A.C. 127 (P.C.). Thus, even if it could be said that there is any conflict between this Court's reference jurisdiction and the original jurisdiction of the provincial superior courts, any such conflict must be resolved in favour of Parliament's exercise of its plenary power to establish a "general court of appeal" provided, as discussed below, advisory functions are not to be considered inconsistent with the functions of a general court of appeal.

(2) May a Court of Appeal Undertake Advisory Functions?

12 The *amicus curiae* submits that

> [TRANSLATION] [e]ither this constitutional power [to give the highest court in the federation jurisdiction to give advisory opinions] is expressly provided for by

> the Constitution, as is the case in India (*Constitution of India*, art. 143), or it is not provided for therein and so it simply does not exist. This is what the Supreme Court of the United States has held. [Emphasis added.]

13 However, the U.S. Supreme Court did not conclude that it was unable to render advisory opinions because no such express power was included in the United States Constitution. Quite the contrary, it based this conclusion on the express limitation in art. III, § 2 restricting federal court jurisdiction to actual "cases" or "controversies." See, e.g., *Muskrat v. United States*, 219 U.S. 346 (1911), at p. 362. This section reflects the strict separation of powers in the American federal constitutional arrangement. Where the "case or controversy" limitation is missing from their respective state constitutions, some American state courts do undertake advisory functions (e.g., in at least two states—Alabama and Delaware—advisory opinions are authorized, in certain circumstances, by statute: see Ala. Code 1975 § 12-2-10; Del. Code Ann. tit. 10, § 141 (1996 Supp.)).

14 In addition, the judicial systems in several European countries (such as Germany, France, Italy, Spain, Portugal and Belgium) include courts dedicated to the review of constitutional claims; these tribunals do not require a concrete dispute involving individual rights to examine the constitutionality of a new law—an "abstract or objective question" is sufficient. See L. Favoreu, "American and European Models of Constitutional Justice," in D.S. Clark, ed., *Comparative and Private International Law* (1990), 105, at p. 113. The European Court of Justice, the European Court of Human Rights, and the Inter-American Court of Human Rights also all enjoy explicit grants of jurisdiction to render advisory opinions. See *Treaty establishing the European Community*, Art. 228(6); Protocol No. 2 of the *Convention for the Protection of Human Rights and Fundamental Freedoms*, Europ. T.S. No. 5, p. 36; *Statute of the Inter-American Court of Human Rights*, Art. 2. There is no plausible basis on which to conclude that a court is, by its nature, inherently precluded from undertaking another legal function in tandem with its judicial duties.

15 Moreover, the Canadian Constitution does not insist on a strict separation of powers. Parliament and the provincial legislatures may properly confer other legal functions on the courts, and may confer certain judicial functions on bodies that are not courts. The exception to this rule relates only to s. 96 courts. Thus, even though the rendering of advisory opinions is quite clearly done outside the framework of adversarial litigation, and such opinions are traditionally obtained by the executive from the law officers of the Crown, there is no constitutional bar to this Court's receipt of jurisdiction to undertake such an advisory role. The legislative grant of reference jurisdiction found in s. 53 of the *Supreme Court Act* is therefore constitutionally valid.

B The Court's Jurisdiction under Section 53

16 Section 53 provides in its relevant parts as follows:

> 53. (1) The Governor in Council may refer to the Court for hearing and consideration important questions of law or fact concerning
>
> (*a*) the interpretation of the *Constitution Acts*;
>
> ...
>
> (*d*) the powers of the Parliament of Canada, or of the legislatures of the provinces, or of the respective governments thereof, whether or not the particular power in question has been or is proposed to be exercised.
>
> (2) The Governor in Council may refer to the Court for hearing and consideration important questions of law or fact concerning any matter, whether or not in the opinion of the Court *ejusdem generis* with the enumerations contained in subsection (1), with reference to which the Governor in Council sees fit to submit any such question.
>
> (3) Any question concerning any of the matters mentioned in subsections (1) and (2), and referred to the Court by the Governor in Council, shall be conclusively deemed to be an important question.

17 It is argued that even if Parliament were entitled to enact s. 53 of the *Supreme Court Act*, the questions submitted by the Governor in Council fall outside the scope of that section.

18 This submission cannot be accepted. Question 1 is directed, at least in part, to the interpretation of the *Constitution Acts*, which are referred to in s. 53(1) (*a*). Both Question 1 and Question 2 fall within s. 53(1) (*d*), since they relate to the powers of the legislature or government of a Canadian province. Finally, all three questions are clearly "important questions of law or fact concerning any matter" so that they must come within s. 53(2).

19 However, the *amicus curiae* has also raised some specific concerns regarding this Court's jurisdiction to answer Question 2. The question, on its face, falls within the scope of s. 53, but the concern is a more general one with respect to the jurisdiction of this Court, as a domestic tribunal, to answer what is described as a question of "pure" international law.

20 The first contention is that in answering Question 2, the Court would be exceeding its jurisdiction by purporting to act as an international tribunal. The simple answer to this submission is that this Court would not, in providing an advisory opinion in the context of a reference, be purporting to "act as" or substitute itself for an international tribunal. In accordance with well accepted principles of international law, this Court's

answer to Question 2 would not purport to bind any other state or international tribunal that might subsequently consider a similar question. The Court nevertheless has jurisdiction to provide an advisory opinion to the Governor in Council in its capacity as a national court on legal questions touching and concerning the future of the Canadian federation.

21 Second, there is a concern that Question 2 is beyond the competence of this Court, as a domestic court, because it requires the Court to look at international law rather than domestic law.

22 This concern is groundless. In a number of previous cases, it has been necessary for this Court to look to international law to determine the rights or obligations of some actor within the Canadian legal system. For example, in *Reference re Powers to Levy Rates on Foreign Legations and High Commissioners' Residences*, [1943] S.C.R. 208, the Court was required to determine whether, taking into account the principles of international law with respect to diplomatic immunity, a municipal council had the power to levy rates on certain properties owned by foreign governments. In two subsequent references, this Court used international law to determine whether the federal government or a province possessed proprietary rights in certain portions of the territorial sea and continental shelf (*Reference re Ownership of Offshore Mineral Rights of British Columbia*, [1967] S.C.R. 792; *Reference re Newfoundland Continental Shelf*, [1984] 1 S.C.R. 86).

23 More importantly, Question 2 of this Reference does not ask an abstract question of "pure" international law but seeks to determine the legal rights and obligations of the National Assembly, legislature or government of Quebec, institutions that clearly exist as part of the Canadian legal order. As will be seen, the *amicus curiae* himself submitted that the success of any initiative on the part of Quebec to secede from the Canadian federation would be governed by international law. In these circumstances, a consideration of international law in the context of this Reference about the legal aspects of the unilateral secession of Quebec is not only permissible but unavoidable.

C *Justiciability*

24 It is submitted that even if the Court has jurisdiction over the questions referred, the questions themselves are not justiciable. Three main arguments are raised in this regard:

(1) the questions are not justiciable because they are too "theoretical" or speculative;
(2) the questions are not justiciable because they are political in nature;
(3) the questions are not yet ripe for judicial consideration.

25 In the context of a reference, the Court, rather than acting in its traditional adjudicative function, is acting in an advisory capacity. The very fact that the Court may be

asked hypothetical questions in a reference, such as the constitutionality of proposed legislation, engages the Court in an exercise it would never entertain in the context of litigation. No matter how closely the procedure on a reference may mirror the litigation process, a reference does not engage the Court in a disposition of rights. For the same reason, the Court may deal on a reference with issues that might otherwise be considered not yet "ripe" for decision.

26 Though a reference differs from the Court's usual adjudicative function, the Court should not, even in the context of a reference, entertain questions that would be inappropriate to answer. However, given the very different nature of a reference, the question of the appropriateness of answering a question should not focus on whether the dispute is formally adversarial or whether it disposes of cognizable rights. Rather, it should consider whether the dispute is appropriately addressed by a court of law. As we stated in *Reference re Canada Assistance Plan* (B.C.), [1991] 2 S.C.R. 525, at p. 545:

> While there may be many reasons why a question is non-justiciable, in this appeal the Attorney General of Canada submitted that to answer the questions would draw the Court into a political controversy and involve it in the legislative process. In exercising its discretion whether to determine a matter that is alleged to be non-justiciable, the Court's primary concern is to retain its proper role within the constitutional framework of our democratic form of government.... In considering its appropriate role the Court must determine whether the question is purely political in nature and should, therefore, be determined in another forum or whether it has a sufficient legal component to warrant the intervention of the judicial branch. [Emphasis added.]

Thus the circumstances in which the Court may decline to answer a reference question on the basis of "non-justiciability" include:

(i) if to do so would take the Court beyond its own assessment of its proper role in the constitutional framework of our democratic form of government or

(ii) if the Court could not give an answer that lies within its area of expertise: the interpretation of law.

27 As to the "proper role" of the Court, it is important to underline, contrary to the submission of the *amicus curiae*, that the questions posed in this Reference do not ask the Court to usurp any democratic decision that the people of Quebec may be called upon to make. The questions posed by the Governor in Council, as we interpret them, are strictly limited to aspects of the legal framework in which that democratic decision is to be taken. The attempted analogy to the U.S. "political questions" doctrine

therefore has no application. The legal framework having been clarified, it will be for the population of Quebec, acting through the political process, to decide whether or not to pursue secession. As will be seen, the legal framework involves the rights and obligations of Canadians who live outside the province of Quebec, as well as those who live within Quebec.

28 As to the "legal" nature of the questions posed, if the Court is of the opinion that it is being asked a question with a significant extralegal component, it may interpret the question so as to answer only its legal aspects; if this is not possible, the Court may decline to answer the question. In the present Reference the questions may clearly be interpreted as directed to legal issues, and, so interpreted, the Court is in a position to answer them.

29 Finally, we turn to the proposition that even though the questions referred to us are justiciable in the "reference" sense, the Court must still determine whether it should exercise its discretion to refuse to answer the questions on a pragmatic basis.

30 Generally, the instances in which the Court has exercised its discretion to refuse to answer a reference question that is otherwise justiciable can be broadly divided into two categories. First, where the question is too imprecise or ambiguous to permit a complete or accurate answer: see, e.g., *McEvoy v. Attorney General for New Brunswick*, [1983] 1 S.C.R. 704; *Reference re Waters and Water-Powers*, [1929] S.C.R. 200; *Reference re Goods and Services Tax*, [1992] 2 S.C.R. 445; *Reference re Remuneration of Judges of the Provincial Court of Prince Edward Island*, [1997] 3 S.C.R. 3 (*Provincial Judges Reference*), at para. 256. Second, where the parties have not provided sufficient information to allow the Court to provide a complete or accurate answer: see, e.g., *Reference re Education System in Island of Montreal*, [1926] S.C.R. 246; *Reference re Authority of Parliament in relation to the Upper House*, [1980] 1 S.C.R. 54 (*Senate Reference*); *Provincial Judges Reference*, at para. 257.

31 There is no doubt that the questions posed in this Reference raise difficult issues and are susceptible to varying interpretations. However, rather than refusing to answer at all, the Court is guided by the approach advocated by the majority on the "conventions" issue in *Reference re Resolution to Amend the Constitution*, [1981] 1 S.C.R. 753 (*Patriation Reference*), at pp. 875–876:

> If the questions are thought to be ambiguous, this Court should not, in a constitutional reference, be in a worse position than that of a witness in a trial and feel compelled simply to answer yes or no. Should it find that a question might be misleading, or should it simply avoid the risk of misunderstanding, the Court is free either to interpret the question…or it may qualify both the question and the answer.…

The Reference questions raise issues of fundamental public importance. It cannot be said that the questions are too imprecise or ambiguous to permit a proper legal answer. Nor can it be said that the Court has been provided with insufficient information regarding the present context in which the questions arise. Thus, the Court is duty bound in the circumstances to provide its answers.

III Reference Questions

A *Question 1*

Under the Constitution of Canada, can the National Assembly, legislature or government of Quebec effect the secession of Quebec from Canada unilaterally?

(1) Introduction

32 As we confirmed in *Reference re Objection by Quebec to a Resolution to amend the Constitution*, [1982] 2 S.C.R. 793, at p. 806, "The *Constitution Act, 1982* is now in force. Its legality is neither challenged nor assailable." The "Constitution of Canada" certainly includes the constitutional texts enumerated in s. 52(2) of the *Constitution Act, 1982*. Although these texts have a primary place in determining constitutional rules, they are not exhaustive. The Constitution also "embraces unwritten, as well as written rules," as we recently observed in the *Provincial Judges Reference, supra*, at para. 92. Finally, as was said in the *Patriation Reference, supra*, at p. 874, the Constitution of Canada includes

> the global system of rules and principles which govern the exercise of constitutional authority in the whole and in every part of the Canadian state.

These supporting principles and rules, which include constitutional conventions and the workings of Parliament, are a necessary part of our Constitution because problems or situations may arise which are not expressly dealt with by the text of the Constitution. In order to endure over time, a constitution must contain a comprehensive set of rules and principles which are capable of providing an exhaustive legal framework for our system of government. Such principles and rules emerge from an understanding of the constitutional text itself, the historical context, and previous judicial interpretations of constitutional meaning. In our view, there are four fundamental and organizing principles of the Constitution which are relevant to addressing the question before us (although this enumeration is by no means exhaustive): federalism; democracy; constitutionalism and the rule of law; and respect for minorities. The foundation and substance of these principles are addressed in the following paragraphs. We will then turn to their specific application to the first reference question before us.

(2) Historical Context: The Significance of Confederation

33 In our constitutional tradition, legality and legitimacy are linked. The precise nature of this link will be discussed below. However, at this stage, we wish to emphasize only that our constitutional history demonstrates that our governing institutions have adapted and changed to reflect changing social and political values. This has generally been accomplished by methods that have ensured continuity, stability and legal order.

34 Because this Reference deals with questions fundamental to the nature of Canada, it should not be surprising that it is necessary to review the context in which the Canadian union has evolved. To this end, we will briefly describe the legal evolution of the Constitution and the foundational principles governing constitutional amendments. Our purpose is not to be exhaustive, but to highlight the features most relevant in the context of this Reference.

35 Confederation was an initiative of elected representatives of the people then living in the colonies scattered across part of what is now Canada. It was not initiated by Imperial *fiat*. In March 1864, a select committee of the Legislative Assembly of the Province of Canada, chaired by George Brown, began to explore prospects for constitutional reform. The committee's report, released in June 1864, recommended that a federal union encompassing Canada East and Canada West, and perhaps the other British North American colonies, be pursued. A group of Reformers from Canada West, led by Brown, joined with Étienne P. Taché and John A. Macdonald in a coalition government for the purpose of engaging in constitutional reform along the lines of the federal model proposed by the committee's report.

36 An opening to pursue federal union soon arose. The leaders of the maritime colonies had planned to meet at Charlottetown in the fall to discuss the perennial topic of maritime union. The Province of Canada secured invitations to send a Canadian delegation. On September 1, 1864, 23 delegates (five from New Brunswick, five from Nova Scotia, five from Prince Edward Island, and eight from the Province of Canada) met in Charlottetown. After five days of discussion, the delegates reached agreement on a plan for federal union.

37 The salient aspects of the agreement may be briefly outlined. There was to be a federal union featuring a bicameral central legislature. Representation in the Lower House was to be based on population, whereas in the Upper House it was to be based on regional equality, the regions comprising Canada East, Canada West and the Maritimes. The significance of the adoption of a federal form of government cannot be exaggerated. Without it, neither the agreement of the delegates from Canada East nor that of the delegates from the maritime colonies could have been obtained.

38 Several matters remained to be resolved, and so the Charlottetown delegates agreed to meet again at Quebec in October, and to invite Newfoundland to send a delegation to join them. The Quebec Conference began on October 10, 1864. Thirty-three delegates (two from Newfoundland, seven from New Brunswick, five from Nova Scotia, seven from Prince Edward Island, and twelve from the Province of Canada) met over a two and a half week period. Precise consideration of each aspect of the federal structure preoccupied the political agenda. The delegates approved 72 resolutions, addressing almost all of what subsequently made its way into the final text of the *Constitution Act, 1867*. These included guarantees to protect French language and culture, both directly (by making French an official language in Quebec and Canada as a whole) and indirectly (by allocating jurisdiction over education and "Property and Civil Rights in the Province" to the provinces). The protection of minorities was thus reaffirmed.

39 Legally, there remained only the requirement to have the Quebec Resolutions put into proper form and passed by the Imperial Parliament in London. However, politically, it was thought that more was required. Indeed, Resolution 70 provided that "The Sanction of the Imperial and Local Parliaments shall be sought for the Union of the Provinces, on the principles adopted by the Conference." (Cited in J. Pope, ed., *Confederation: Being a Series of Hitherto Unpublished Documents Bearing on the British North America Act* (1895), at p. 52 (emphasis added).)

40 Confirmation of the Quebec Resolutions was achieved more smoothly in central Canada than in the Maritimes. In February and March 1865, the Quebec Resolutions were the subject of almost six weeks of sustained debate in both houses of the Canadian legislature. The Canadian Legislative Assembly approved the Quebec Resolutions in March 1865 with the support of a majority of members from both Canada East and Canada West. The governments of both Prince Edward Island and Newfoundland chose, in accordance with popular sentiment in both colonies, not to accede to the Quebec Resolutions. In New Brunswick, a general election was required before Premier Tilley's pro-Confederation party prevailed. In Nova Scotia, Premier Tupper ultimately obtained a resolution from the House of Assembly favouring Confederation.

41 Sixteen delegates (five from New Brunswick, five from Nova Scotia, and six from the Province of Canada) met in London in December 1866 to finalize the plan for Confederation. To this end, they agreed to some slight modifications and additions to the Quebec Resolutions. Minor changes were made to the distribution of powers, provision was made for the appointment of extra senators in the event of a deadlock between the House of Commons and the Senate, and certain religious minorities were given the right to appeal to the federal government where their denominational school rights were adversely affected by provincial legislation. The British North America Bill was drafted after the London Conference with the assistance of the Colonial Office, and was introduced into the House of Lords in February 1867. The Act

passed third reading in the House of Commons on March 8, received royal assent on March 29, and was proclaimed on July 1, 1867. The Dominion of Canada thus became a reality.

42 There was an early attempt at secession. In the first Dominion election in September 1867, Premier Tupper's forces were decimated: members opposed to Confederation won 18 of Nova Scotia's 19 federal seats, and in the simultaneous provincial election, 36 of the 38 seats in the provincial legislature. Newly-elected Premier Joseph Howe led a delegation to the Imperial Parliament in London in an effort to undo the new constitutional arrangements, but it was too late. The Colonial Office rejected Premier Howe's plea to permit Nova Scotia to withdraw from Confederation. As the Colonial Secretary wrote in 1868:

> The neighbouring province of New Brunswick has entered into the union in reliance on having with it the sister province of Nova Scotia; and vast obligations, political and commercial, have already been contracted on the faith of a measure so long discussed and so solemnly adopted.... I trust that the Assembly and the people of Nova Scotia will not be surprised that the Queen's government feel that they would not be warranted in advising the reversal of a great measure of state, attended by so many extensive consequences already in operation....
>
> Quoted in H. WADE MACLAUCHLAN, "Accounting for Democracy and the Rule of Law in the Quebec Secession Reference" (1997), 76 *Can. Bar Rev.* 155, at p. 168.

The interdependence characterized by "vast obligations, political and commercial," referred to by the Colonial Secretary in 1868, has, of course, multiplied immeasurably in the last 130 years.

43 Federalism was a legal response to the underlying political and cultural realities that existed at Confederation and continue to exist today. At Confederation, political leaders told their respective communities that the Canadian union would be able to reconcile diversity with unity. It is pertinent, in the context of the present Reference, to mention the words of George-Étienne Cartier (cited in the *Parliamentary Debates on the subject of the Confederation* (1865), at p. 60):

> Now, when we [are] united together, if union [is] attained, we [shall] form a political nationality with which neither the national origin, nor the religion of any individual, [will] interfere. It was lamented by some that we had this diversity of races, and hopes were expressed that this distinctive feature would cease. The idea of unity of races [is] utopian—it [is] impossible. Distinctions of this kind [will] always exist. Dissimilarity, in fact, appear[s] to be the order of the physical world and of the moral world, as well as in the political world. But with regard to the objection based on this fact, to the effect that a great nation [can]not be

> formed because Lower Canada [is] in great part French and Catholic, and Upper Canada [is] British and Protestant, and the Lower Provinces [are] mixed, it [is] futile and worthless in the extreme.... In our own Federation we [will] have Catholic and Protestant, English, French, Irish and Scotch, and each by his efforts and his success [will] increase the prosperity and glory of the new Confederacy.... [W]e [are] of different races, not for the purpose of warring against each other, but in order to compete and emulate for the general welfare.

The federal-provincial division of powers was a legal recognition of the diversity that existed among the initial members of Confederation, and manifested a concern to accommodate that diversity within a single nation by granting significant powers to provincial governments. The *Constitution Act, 1867* was an act of nation-building. It was the first step in the transition from colonies separately dependent on the Imperial Parliament for their governance to a unified and independent political state in which different peoples could resolve their disagreements and work together toward common goals and a common interest. Federalism was the political mechanism by which diversity could be reconciled with unity.

44 A federal-provincial division of powers necessitated a written constitution which circumscribed the powers of the new Dominion and Provinces of Canada. Despite its federal structure, the new Dominion was to have "a Constitution similar in Principle to that of the United Kingdom" (*Constitution Act, 1867*, preamble). Allowing for the obvious differences between the governance of Canada and the United Kingdom, it was nevertheless thought important to thus emphasize the continuity of constitutional principles, including democratic institutions and the rule of law; and the continuity of the exercise of sovereign power transferred from Westminster to the federal and provincial capitals of Canada.

45 After 1867, the Canadian federation continued to evolve both territorially and politically. New territories were admitted to the union and new provinces were formed. In 1870, Rupert's Land and the Northwest Territories were admitted and Manitoba was formed as a province. British Columbia was admitted in 1871, Prince Edward Island in 1873, and the Arctic Islands were added in 1880. In 1898, the Yukon Territory and in 1905, the provinces of Alberta and Saskatchewan were formed from the Northwest Territories. Newfoundland was admitted in 1949 by an amendment to the *Constitution Act, 1867*. The new territory of Nunavut was carved out of the Northwest Territories in 1993 with the partition to become effective in April 1999.

46 Canada's evolution from colony to fully independent state was gradual. The Imperial Parliament's passage of the *Statute of Westminster, 1931* (U.K.), 22 & 23 Geo. 5, c. 4, confirmed in law what had earlier been confirmed in fact by the Balfour Declaration of 1926, namely, that Canada was an independent country. Thereafter, Canadian law alone governed in Canada, except where Canada expressly consented to the

continued application of Imperial legislation. Canada's independence from Britain was achieved through legal and political evolution with an adherence to the rule of law and stability. The proclamation of the *Constitution Act, 1982* removed the last vestige of British authority over the Canadian Constitution and re-affirmed Canada's commitment to the protection of its minority, aboriginal, equality, legal and language rights, and fundamental freedoms as set out in the *Canadian Charter of Rights and Freedoms*.

47 Legal continuity, which requires an orderly transfer of authority, necessitated that the 1982 amendments be made by the Westminster Parliament, but the legitimacy as distinguished from the formal legality of the amendments derived from political decisions taken in Canada within a legal framework which this Court, in the *Patriation Reference*, had ruled was in accordance with our Constitution. It should be noted, parenthetically, that the 1982 amendments did not alter the basic division of powers in ss. 91 and 92 of the *Constitution Act, 1867*, which is the primary textual expression of the principle of federalism in our Constitution, agreed upon at Confederation. It did, however, have the important effect that, despite the refusal of the government of Quebec to join in its adoption, Quebec has become bound to the terms of a Constitution that is different from that which prevailed previously, particularly as regards provisions governing its amendment, and the *Canadian Charter of Rights and Freedoms*. As to the latter, to the extent that the scope of legislative powers was thereafter to be constrained by the *Charter*, the constraint operated as much against federal legislative powers as against provincial legislative powers. Moreover, it is to be remembered that s. 33, the "notwithstanding clause," gives Parliament and the provincial legislatures authority to legislate on matters within their jurisdiction in derogation of the fundamental freedoms (s. 2), legal rights (ss. 7 to 14) and equality rights (s. 15) provisions of the *Charter*.

48 We think it apparent from even this brief historical review that the evolution of our constitutional arrangements has been characterized by adherence to the rule of law, respect for democratic institutions, the accommodation of minorities, insistence that governments adhere to constitutional conduct and a desire for continuity and stability. We now turn to a discussion of the general constitutional principles that bear on the present Reference.

(3) Analysis of the Constitutional Principles

(a) *Nature of the Principles*

49 What are those underlying principles? Our Constitution is primarily a written one, the product of 131 years of evolution. Behind the written word is an historical lineage stretching back through the ages, which aids in the consideration of the underlying constitutional principles. These principles inform and sustain the constitutional text: they are the vital unstated assumptions upon which the text is based. The following discussion addresses the four foundational constitutional principles that are most

germane for resolution of this Reference: federalism, democracy, constitutionalism and the rule of law, and respect for minority rights. These defining principles function in symbiosis. No single principle can be defined in isolation from the others, nor does any one principle trump or exclude the operation of any other.

50 Our Constitution has an internal architecture, or what the majority of this Court in *OPSEU v. Ontario (Attorney General)*, [1987] 2 S.C.R. 2, at p. 57, called a "basic constitutional structure." The individual elements of the Constitution are linked to the others, and must be interpreted by reference to the structure of the Constitution as a whole. As we recently emphasized in the *Provincial Judges Reference*, certain underlying principles infuse our Constitution and breathe life into it. Speaking of the rule of law principle in the *Manitoba Language Rights Reference, supra*, at p. 750, we held that "the principle is clearly implicit in the very nature of a Constitution." The same may be said of the other three constitutional principles we underscore today.

51 Although these underlying principles are not explicitly made part of the Constitution by any written provision, other than in some respects by the oblique reference in the preamble to the *Constitution Act, 1867*, it would be impossible to conceive of our constitutional structure without them. The principles dictate major elements of the architecture of the Constitution itself and are as such its lifeblood.

52 The principles assist in the interpretation of the text and the delineation of spheres of jurisdiction, the scope of rights and obligations, and the role of our political institutions. Equally important, observance of and respect for these principles is essential to the ongoing process of constitutional development and evolution of our Constitution as a "living tree," to invoke the famous description in *Edwards v. Attorney-General for Canada*, [1930] A.C. 124 (P.C.), at p. 136. As this Court indicated in *New Brunswick Broadcasting Co. v. Nova Scotia (Speaker of the House of Assembly)*, [1993] 1 S.C.R. 319, Canadians have long recognized the existence and importance of unwritten constitutional principles in our system of government.

53 Given the existence of these underlying constitutional principles, what use may the Court make of them? In the *Provincial Judges Reference, supra*, at paras. 93 and 104, we cautioned that the recognition of these constitutional principles (the majority opinion referred to them as "organizing principles" and described one of them, judicial independence, as an "unwritten norm") could not be taken as an invitation to dispense with the written text of the Constitution. On the contrary, we confirmed that there are compelling reasons to insist upon the primacy of our written constitution. A written constitution promotes legal certainty and predictability, and it provides a foundation and a touchstone for the exercise of constitutional judicial review. However, we also observed in the *Provincial Judges Reference* that the effect of the preamble to the *Constitution Act, 1867* was to incorporate certain constitutional principles by reference, a point made earlier in *Fraser v. Public Service Staff Relations Board*, [1985] 2 S.C.R. 455, at pp. 462–463. In the *Provincial Judges Reference*, at para. 104, we determined that the preamble "invites

the courts to turn those principles into the premises of a constitutional argument that culminates in the filling of gaps in the express terms of the constitutional text."

54 Underlying constitutional principles may in certain circumstances give rise to substantive legal obligations (have "full legal force," as we described it in the *Patriation Reference*, *supra*, at p. 845), which constitute substantive limitations upon government action. These principles may give rise to very abstract and general obligations, or they may be more specific and precise in nature. The principles are not merely descriptive, but are also invested with a powerful normative force, and are binding upon both courts and governments. "In other words," as this Court confirmed in the *Manitoba Language Rights Reference*, *supra*, at p. 752, "in the process of Constitutional adjudication, the Court may have regard to unwritten postulates which form the very foundation of the Constitution of Canada." It is to a discussion of those underlying constitutional principles that we now turn.

(b) *Federalism*

55 It is undisputed that Canada is a federal state. Yet many commentators have observed that, according to the precise terms of the *Constitution Act, 1867*, the federal system was only partial. See, e.g., K.C. Wheare, *Federal Government* (4th ed. 1963), at pp. 18–20. This was so because, on paper, the federal government retained sweeping powers which threatened to undermine the autonomy of the provinces. Here again, however, a review of the written provisions of the Constitution does not provide the entire picture. Our political and constitutional practice has adhered to an underlying principle of federalism, and has interpreted the written provisions of the Constitution in this light. For example, although the federal power of disallowance was included in the *Constitution Act, 1867*, the underlying principle of federalism triumphed early. Many constitutional scholars contend that the federal power of disallowance has been abandoned (e.g., P.W. Hogg, *Constitutional Law of Canada* (4th ed. 1997), at p. 120).

56 In a federal system of government such as ours, political power is shared by two orders of government: the federal government on the one hand, and the provinces on the other. Each is assigned respective spheres of jurisdiction by the *Constitution Act, 1867*. See, e.g., *Liquidators of the Maritime Bank of Canada v. Receiver-General of New Brunswick*, [1892] A.C. 437 (P.C.), at pp. 441–442. It is up to the courts "to control the limits of the respective sovereignties": *Northern Telecom Canada Ltd. v. Communication Workers of Canada*, [1983] 1 S.C.R. 733, at p. 741. In interpreting our Constitution, the courts have always been concerned with the federalism principle, inherent in the structure of our constitutional arrangements, which has from the beginning been the lodestar by which the courts have been guided.

57 This underlying principle of federalism, then, has exercised a role of considerable importance in the interpretation of the written provisions of our Constitution.

In the *Patriation Reference, supra*, at pp. 905–909, we confirmed that the principle of federalism runs through the political and legal systems of Canada. Indeed, Martland and Ritchie JJ., dissenting in the *Patriation Reference*, at p. 821, considered federalism to be "the dominant principle of Canadian constitutional law." With the enactment of the *Charter*, that proposition may have less force than it once did, but there can be little doubt that the principle of federalism remains a central organizational theme of our Constitution. Less obviously, perhaps, but certainly of equal importance, federalism is a political and legal response to underlying social and political realities.

58 The principle of federalism recognizes the diversity of the component parts of Confederation, and the autonomy of provincial governments to develop their societies within their respective spheres of jurisdiction. The federal structure of our country also facilitates democratic participation by distributing power to the government thought to be most suited to achieving the particular societal objective having regard to this diversity. The scheme of the *Constitution Act, 1867*, it was said in *Re the Initiative and Referendum Act*, [1919] A.C. 935 (P.C.), at p. 942, was

> not to weld the Provinces into one, nor to subordinate Provincial Governments to a central authority, but to establish a central government in which these Provinces should be represented, entrusted with exclusive authority only in affairs in which they had a common interest. Subject to this each Province was to retain its independence and autonomy and to be directly under the Crown as its head.

More recently, in *Haig v. Canada*, [1993] 2 S.C.R. 995, at p. 1047, the majority of this Court held that differences between provinces "are a rational part of the political reality in the federal process." It was referring to the differential application of federal law in individual provinces, but the point applies more generally. A unanimous Court expressed similar views in *R. v. S. (S.)*, [1990] 2 S.C.R. 254, at pp. 287–288.

59 The principle of federalism facilitates the pursuit of collective goals by cultural and linguistic minorities which form the majority within a particular province. This is the case in Quebec, where the majority of the population is French-speaking, and which possesses a distinct culture. This is not merely the result of chance. The social and demographic reality of Quebec explains the existence of the province of Quebec as a political unit and indeed, was one of the essential reasons for establishing a federal structure for the Canadian union in 1867. The experience of both Canada East and Canada West under the *Union Act, 1840* (U.K.), 3–4 Vict., c. 35, had not been satisfactory. The federal structure adopted at Confederation enabled French-speaking Canadians to form a numerical majority in the province of Quebec, and so exercise the considerable provincial powers conferred by the *Constitution Act, 1867* in such a way as to promote their language and culture. It also made provision for certain guaranteed representation within the federal Parliament itself.

60 Federalism was also welcomed by Nova Scotia and New Brunswick, both of which also affirmed their will to protect their individual cultures and their autonomy over local matters. All new provinces joining the federation sought to achieve similar objectives, which are no less vigorously pursued by the provinces and territories as we approach the new millennium.

(c) *Democracy*

61 Democracy is a fundamental value in our constitutional law and political culture. While it has both an institutional and an individual aspect, the democratic principle was also argued before us in the sense of the supremacy of the sovereign will of a people, in this case potentially to be expressed by Quebecers in support of unilateral secession. It is useful to explore in a summary way these different aspects of the democratic principle.

62 The principle of democracy has always informed the design of our constitutional structure, and continues to act as an essential interpretive consideration to this day. A majority of this Court in *OPSEU v. Ontario*, *supra*, at p. 57, confirmed that "the basic structure of our Constitution, as established by the Constitution Act, 1867, contemplates the existence of certain political institutions, including freely elected legislative bodies at the federal and provincial levels." As is apparent from an earlier line of decisions emanating from this Court, including *Switzman v. Elbling*, [1957] S.C.R. 285, *Saumur v. City of Quebec*, [1953] 2 S.C.R. 299, *Boucher v. The King*, [1951] S.C.R. 265, and *Reference re Alberta Statutes*, [1938] S.C.R. 100, the democracy principle can best be understood as a sort of baseline against which the framers of our Constitution, and subsequently, our elected representatives under it, have always operated. It is perhaps for this reason that the principle was not explicitly identified in the text of the Constitution Act, 1867 itself. To have done so might have appeared redundant, even silly, to the framers. As explained in the *Provincial Judges Reference*, *supra*, at para. 100, it is evident that our Constitution contemplates that Canada shall be a constitutional democracy. Yet this merely demonstrates the importance of underlying constitutional principles that are nowhere explicitly described in our constitutional texts. The representative and democratic nature of our political institutions was simply assumed.

63 Democracy is commonly understood as being a political system of majority rule. It is essential to be clear what this means. The evolution of our democratic tradition can be traced back to the *Magna Carta* (1215) and before, through the long struggle for Parliamentary supremacy which culminated in the English *Bill of Rights* of 1689, the emergence of representative political institutions in the colonial era, the development of responsible government in the 19th century, and eventually, the achievement of Confederation itself in 1867. "[T]he Canadian tradition," the majority of this Court held in *Reference re Provincial Electoral Boundaries (Sask.)*, [1991] 2 S.C.R. 158, at p. 186, is "one of evolutionary democracy moving in uneven steps toward the goal of universal

suffrage and more effective representation." Since Confederation, efforts to extend the franchise to those unjustly excluded from participation in our political system—such as women, minorities, and aboriginal peoples—have continued, with some success, to the present day.

64 Democracy is not simply concerned with the process of government. On the contrary, as suggested in *Switzman v. Elbling, supra*, at p. 306, democracy is fundamentally connected to substantive goals, most importantly, the promotion of self-government. Democracy accommodates cultural and group identities: *Reference re Provincial Electoral Boundaries*, at p. 188. Put another way, a sovereign people exercises its right to self-government through the democratic process. In considering the scope and purpose of the Charter, the Court in *R.v. Oakes*, [1986] 1 S.C.R. 103, articulated some of the values inherent in the notion of democracy (at p. 136):

> The Court must be guided by the values and principles essential to a free and democratic society which I believe to embody, to name but a few, respect for the inherent dignity of the human person, commitment to social justice and equality, accommodation of a wide variety of beliefs, respect for cultural and group identity, and faith in social and political institutions which enhance the participation of individuals and groups in society.

65 In institutional terms, democracy means that each of the provincial legislatures and the federal Parliament is elected by popular franchise. These legislatures, we have said, are "at the core of the system of representative government": *New Brunswick Broadcasting, supra*, at p. 387. In individual terms, the right to vote in elections to the House of Commons and the provincial legislatures, and to be candidates in those elections, is guaranteed to "Every citizen of Canada" by virtue of s. 3 of the Charter. Historically, this Court has interpreted democracy to mean the process of representative and responsible government and the right of citizens to participate in the political process as voters (*Reference re Provincial Electoral Boundaries, supra*) and as candidates (*Harvey v. New Brunswick (Attorney General)*, [1996] 2 S.C.R. 876). In addition, the effect of s. 4 of the Charter is to oblige the House of Commons and the provincial legislatures to hold regular elections and to permit citizens to elect representatives to their political institutions. The democratic principle is affirmed with particular clarity in that s. 4 is not subject to the notwithstanding power contained in s. 33.

66 It is, of course, true that democracy expresses the sovereign will of the people. Yet this expression, too, must be taken in the context of the other institutional values we have identified as pertinent to this Reference. The relationship between democracy and federalism means, for example, that in Canada there may be different and equally legitimate majorities in different provinces and territories and at the federal level. No one majority is more or less "legitimate" than the others as an expression of

democratic opinion, although, of course, the consequences will vary with the subject matter. A federal system of government enables different provinces to pursue policies responsive to the particular concerns and interests of people in that province. At the same time, Canada as a whole is also a democratic community in which citizens construct and achieve goals on a national scale through a federal government acting within the limits of its jurisdiction. The function of federalism is to enable citizens to participate concurrently in different collectivities and to pursue goals at both a provincial and a federal level.

67 The consent of the governed is a value that is basic to our understanding of a free and democratic society. Yet democracy in any real sense of the word cannot exist without the rule of law. It is the law that creates the framework within which the "sovereign will" is to be ascertained and implemented. To be accorded legitimacy, democratic institutions must rest, ultimately, on a legal foundation. That is, they must allow for the participation of, and accountability to, the people, through public institutions created under the Constitution. Equally, however, a system of government cannot survive through adherence to the law alone. A political system must also possess legitimacy, and in our political culture, that requires an interaction between the rule of law and the democratic principle. The system must be capable of reflecting the aspirations of the people. But there is more. Our law's claim to legitimacy also rests on an appeal to moral values, many of which are imbedded in our constitutional structure. It would be a grave mistake to equate legitimacy with the "sovereign will" or majority rule alone, to the exclusion of other constitutional values.

68 Finally, we highlight that a functioning democracy requires a continuous process of discussion. The Constitution mandates government by democratic legislatures, and an executive accountable to them, "resting ultimately on public opinion reached by discussion and the interplay of ideas" (*Saumur v. City of Quebec*, *supra*, at p. 330). At both the federal and provincial level, by its very nature, the need to build majorities necessitates compromise, negotiation, and deliberation. No one has a monopoly on truth, and our system is predicated on the faith that in the marketplace of ideas, the best solutions to public problems will rise to the top. Inevitably, there will be dissenting voices. A democratic system of government is committed to considering those dissenting voices, and seeking to acknowledge and address those voices in the laws by which all in the community must live.

69 The *Constitution Act, 1982* gives expression to this principle, by conferring a right to initiate constitutional change on each participant in Confederation. In our view, the existence of this right imposes a corresponding duty on the participants in Confederation to engage in constitutional discussions in order to acknowledge and address democratic expressions of a desire for change in other provinces. This duty is inherent in the democratic principle which is a fundamental predicate of our system of governance.

(d) *Constitutionalism and the Rule of Law*

70 The principles of constitutionalism and the rule of law lie at the root of our system of government. The rule of law, as observed in *Roncarelli v. Duplessis*, [1959] S.C.R. 121, at p. 142, is "a fundamental postulate of our constitutional structure." As we noted in the *Patriation Reference*, *supra*, at pp. 805–806, "[t]he 'rule of law' is a highly textured expression, importing many things which are beyond the need of these reasons to explore but conveying, for example, a sense of orderliness, of subjection to known legal rules and of executive accountability to legal authority." At its most basic level, the rule of law vouchsafes to the citizens and residents of the country a stable, predictable and ordered society in which to conduct their affairs. It provides a shield for individuals from arbitrary state action.

71 In the *Manitoba Language Rights Reference*, *supra*, at pp. 747–752, this Court outlined the elements of the rule of law. We emphasized, first, that the rule of law provides that the law is supreme over the acts of both government and private persons. There is, in short, one law for all. Second, we explained, at p. 749, that "the rule of law requires the creation and maintenance of an actual order of positive laws which preserves and embodies the more general principle of normative order." It was this second aspect of the rule of law that was primarily at issue in the *Manitoba Language Rights Reference* itself. A third aspect of the rule of law is, as recently confirmed in the *Provincial Judges Reference*, *supra*, at para. 10, that "the exercise of all public power must find its ultimate source in a legal rule." Put another way, the relationship between the state and the individual must be regulated by law. Taken together, these three considerations make up a principle of profound constitutional and political significance.

72 The constitutionalism principle bears considerable similarity to the rule of law, although they are not identical. The essence of constitutionalism in Canada is embodied in s. 52(1) of the *Constitution Act, 1982*, which provides that "[t]he Constitution of Canada is the supreme law of Canada, and any law that is inconsistent with the provisions of the Constitution is, to the extent of the inconsistency, of no force or effect." Simply put, the constitutionalism principle requires that all government action comply with the Constitution. The rule of law principle requires that all government action must comply with the law, including the Constitution. This Court has noted on several occasions that with the adoption of the *Charter*, the Canadian system of government was transformed to a significant extent from a system of Parliamentary supremacy to one of constitutional supremacy. The Constitution binds all governments, both federal and provincial, including the executive branch (*Operation Dismantle Inc. v. The Queen*, [1985] 1 S.C.R. 441, at p. 455). They may not transgress its provisions: indeed, their sole claim to exercise lawful authority rests in the powers allocated to them under the Constitution, and can come from no other source.

73 An understanding of the scope and importance of the principles of the rule of law and constitutionalism is aided by acknowledging explicitly why a constitution is entrenched beyond the reach of simple majority rule. There are three overlapping reasons.

74 First, a constitution may provide an added safeguard for fundamental human rights and individual freedoms which might otherwise be susceptible to government interference. Although democratic government is generally solicitous of those rights, there are occasions when the majority will be tempted to ignore fundamental rights in order to accomplish collective goals more easily or effectively. Constitutional entrenchment ensures that those rights will be given due regard and protection. Second, a constitution may seek to ensure that vulnerable minority groups are endowed with the institutions and rights necessary to maintain and promote their identities against the assimilative pressures of the majority. And third, a constitution may provide for a division of political power that allocates political power amongst different levels of government. That purpose would be defeated if one of those democratically elected levels of government could usurp the powers of the other simply by exercising its legislative power to allocate additional political power to itself unilaterally.

75 The argument that the Constitution may be legitimately circumvented by resort to a majority vote in a province-wide referendum is superficially persuasive, in large measure because it seems to appeal to some of the same principles that underlie the legitimacy of the Constitution itself, namely, democracy and self-government. In short, it is suggested that as the notion of popular sovereignty underlies the legitimacy of our existing constitutional arrangements, so the same popular sovereignty that originally led to the present Constitution must (it is argued) also permit "the people" in their exercise of popular sovereignty to secede by majority vote alone. However, closer analysis reveals that this argument is unsound, because it misunderstands the meaning of popular sovereignty and the essence of a constitutional democracy.

76 Canadians have never accepted that ours is a system of simple majority rule. Our principle of democracy, taken in conjunction with the other constitutional principles discussed here, is richer. Constitutional government is necessarily predicated on the idea that the political representatives of the people of a province have the capacity and the power to commit the province to be bound into the future by the constitutional rules being adopted. These rules are "binding" not in the sense of frustrating the will of a majority of a province, but as defining the majority which must be consulted in order to alter the fundamental balances of political power (including the spheres of autonomy guaranteed by the principle of federalism), individual rights, and minority rights in our society. Of course, those constitutional rules are themselves amenable to amendment, but only through a process of negotiation which ensures that there is an opportunity for the constitutionally defined rights of all the parties to be respected and reconciled.

77 In this way, our belief in democracy may be harmonized with our belief in constitutionalism. Constitutional amendment often requires some form of substantial

consensus precisely because the content of the underlying principles of our Constitution demand it. By requiring broad support in the form of an "enhanced majority" to achieve constitutional change, the Constitution ensures that minority interests must be addressed before proposed changes which would affect them may be enacted.

78 It might be objected, then, that constitutionalism is therefore incompatible with democratic government. This would be an erroneous view. Constitutionalism facilitates—indeed, makes possible—a democratic political system by creating an orderly framework within which people may make political decisions. Viewed correctly, constitutionalism and the rule of law are not in conflict with democracy; rather, they are essential to it. Without that relationship, the political will upon which democratic decisions are taken would itself be undermined.

(e) *Protection of Minorities*

79 The fourth underlying constitutional principle we address here concerns the protection of minorities. There are a number of specific constitutional provisions protecting minority language, religion and education rights. Some of those provisions are, as we have recognized on a number of occasions, the product of historical compromises. As this Court observed in *Reference re Bill 30, An Act to amend the Education Act (Ont.)*, [1987] 1 S.C.R. 1148, at p. 1173, and in *Reference re Education Act (Que.)*, [1993] 2 S.C.R. 511, at pp. 529–530, the protection of minority religious education rights was a central consideration in the negotiations leading to Confederation. In the absence of such protection, it was felt that the minorities in what was then Canada East and Canada West would be submerged and assimilated. See also *Greater Montreal Protestant School Board v. Quebec (Attorney General)*, [1989] 1 S.C.R. 377, at pp. 401–402, and *Adler v. Ontario*, [1996] 3 S.C.R. 609. Similar concerns animated the provisions protecting minority language rights, as noted in *Société des Acadiens du Nouveau-Brunswick Inc. v. Association of Parents for Fairness in Education*, [1986] 1 S.C.R. 549, at p. 564.

80 However, we highlight that even though those provisions were the product of negotiation and political compromise, that does not render them unprincipled. Rather, such a concern reflects a broader principle related to the protection of minority rights. Undoubtedly, the three other constitutional principles inform the scope and operation of the specific provisions that protect the rights of minorities. We emphasize that the protection of minority rights is itself an independent principle underlying our constitutional order. The principle is clearly reflected in the *Charter*'s provisions for the protection of minority rights. See, e.g., *Reference re Public Schools Act (Man.), s. 79(3), (4) and (7)*, [1993] 1 S.C.R. 839, and *Mahe v. Alberta*, [1990] 1 S.C.R. 342.

81 The concern of our courts and governments to protect minorities has been prominent in recent years, particularly following the enactment of the *Charter*. Undoubtedly, one of the key considerations motivating the enactment of the *Charter*, and the process of constitutional judicial review that it entails, is the protection of minorities.

However, it should not be forgotten that the protection of minority rights had a long history before the enactment of the *Charter*. Indeed, the protection of minority rights was clearly an essential consideration in the design of our constitutional structure even at the time of Confederation: *Senate Reference, supra*, at p. 71. Although Canada's record of upholding the rights of minorities is not a spotless one, that goal is one towards which Canadians have been striving since Confederation, and the process has not been without successes. The principle of protecting minority rights continues to exercise influence in the operation and interpretation of our Constitution.

82 Consistent with this long tradition of respect for minorities, which is at least as old as Canada itself, the framers of the *Constitution Act, 1982* included in s. 35 explicit protection for existing aboriginal and treaty rights, and in s. 25, a non-derogation clause in favour of the rights of aboriginal peoples. The "promise" of s. 35, as it was termed in *R.v. Sparrow*, [1990] 1 S.C.R. 1075, at p. 1083, recognized not only the ancient occupation of land by aboriginal peoples, but their contribution to the building of Canada, and the special commitments made to them by successive governments. The protection of these rights, so recently and arduously achieved, whether looked at in their own right or as part of the larger concern with minorities, reflects an important underlying constitutional value.

(4) The Operation of the Constitutional Principles in the Secession Context

83 Secession is the effort of a group or section of a state to withdraw itself from the political and constitutional authority of that state, with a view to achieving statehood for a new territorial unit on the international plane. In a federal state, secession typically takes the form of a territorial unit seeking to withdraw from the federation. Secession is a legal act as much as a political one. By the terms of Question 1 of this Reference, we are asked to rule on the legality of unilateral secession "[u]nder the Constitution of Canada." This is an appropriate question, as the legality of unilateral secession must be evaluated, at least in the first instance, from the perspective of the domestic legal order of the state from which the unit seeks to withdraw. As we shall see below, it is also argued that international law is a relevant standard by which the legality of a purported act of secession may be measured.

84 The secession of a province from Canada must be considered, in legal terms, to require an amendment to the Constitution, which perforce requires negotiation. The amendments necessary to achieve a secession could be radical and extensive. Some commentators have suggested that secession could be a change of such a magnitude that it could not be considered to be merely an amendment to the Constitution. We are not persuaded by this contention. It is of course true that the Constitution is silent as to the ability of a province to secede from Confederation but, although the Constitution

neither expressly authorizes nor prohibits secession, an act of secession would purport to alter the governance of Canadian territory in a manner which undoubtedly is inconsistent with our current constitutional arrangements. The fact that those changes would be profound, or that they would purport to have a significance with respect to international law, does not negate their nature as amendments to the Constitution of Canada.

85 The Constitution is the expression of the sovereignty of the people of Canada. It lies within the power of the people of Canada, acting through their various governments duly elected and recognized under the Constitution, to effect whatever constitutional arrangements are desired within Canadian territory, including, should it be so desired, the secession of Quebec from Canada. As this Court held in the *Manitoba Language Rights Reference, supra*, at p. 745, "[t]he Constitution of a country is a statement of the will of the people to be governed in accordance with certain principles held as fundamental and certain prescriptions restrictive of the powers of the legislature and government." The manner in which such a political will could be formed and mobilized is a somewhat speculative exercise, though we are asked to assume the existence of such a political will for the purpose of answering the question before us. By the terms of this Reference, we have been asked to consider whether it would be constitutional in such a circumstance for the National Assembly, legislature or government of Quebec to effect the secession of Quebec from Canada unilaterally.

86 The "unilateral" nature of the act is of cardinal importance and we must be clear as to what is understood by this term. In one sense, any step towards a constitutional amendment initiated by a single actor on the constitutional stage is "unilateral." We do not believe that this is the meaning contemplated by Question 1, nor is this the sense in which the term has been used in argument before us. Rather, what is claimed by a right to secede "unilaterally" is the right to effectuate secession without prior negotiations with the other provinces and the federal government. At issue is not the legality of the first step but the legality of the final act of purported unilateral secession. The supposed juridical basis for such an act is said to be a clear expression of democratic will in a referendum in the province of Quebec. This claim requires us to examine the possible juridical impact, if any, of such a referendum on the functioning of our Constitution, and on the claimed legality of a unilateral act of secession.

87 Although the Constitution does not itself address the use of a referendum procedure, and the results of a referendum have no direct role or legal effect in our constitutional scheme, a referendum undoubtedly may provide a democratic method of ascertaining the views of the electorate on important political questions on a particular occasion. The democratic principle identified above would demand that considerable weight be given to a clear expression by the people of Quebec of their will to secede from Canada, even though a referendum, in itself and without more, has no direct legal effect, and could not in itself bring about unilateral secession. Our political institutions are premised on the democratic principle, and so an expression of the democratic will

of the people of a province carries weight, in that it would confer legitimacy on the efforts of the government of Quebec to initiate the Constitution's amendment process in order to secede by constitutional means. In this context, we refer to a "clear" majority as a qualitative evaluation. The referendum result, if it is to be taken as an expression of the democratic will, must be free of ambiguity both in terms of the question asked and in terms of the support it achieves.

88 The federalism principle, in conjunction with the democratic principle, dictates that the clear repudiation of the existing constitutional order and the clear expression of the desire to pursue secession by the population of a province would give rise to a reciprocal obligation on all parties to Confederation to negotiate constitutional changes to respond to that desire. The amendment of the Constitution begins with a political process undertaken pursuant to the Constitution itself. In Canada, the initiative for constitutional amendment is the responsibility of democratically elected representatives of the participants in Confederation. Those representatives may, of course, take their cue from a referendum, but in legal terms, constitution-making in Canada, as in many countries, is undertaken by the democratically elected representatives of the people. The corollary of a legitimate attempt by one participant in Confederation to seek an amendment to the Constitution is an obligation on all parties to come to the negotiating table. The clear repudiation by the people of Quebec of the existing constitutional order would confer legitimacy on demands for secession, and place an obligation on the other provinces and the federal government to acknowledge and respect that expression of democratic will by entering into negotiations and conducting them in accordance with the underlying constitutional principles already discussed.

89 What is the content of this obligation to negotiate? At this juncture, we confront the difficult inter-relationship between substantive obligations flowing from the Constitution and questions of judicial competence and restraint in supervising or enforcing those obligations. This is mirrored by the distinction between the legality and the legitimacy of actions taken under the Constitution. We propose to focus first on the substantive obligations flowing from this obligation to negotiate; once the nature of those obligations has been described, it is easier to assess the appropriate means of enforcement of those obligations, and to comment on the distinction between legality and legitimacy.

90 The conduct of the parties in such negotiations would be governed by the same constitutional principles which give rise to the duty to negotiate: federalism, democracy, constitutionalism and the rule of law, and the protection of minorities. Those principles lead us to reject two absolutist propositions. One of those propositions is that there would be a legal obligation on the other provinces and federal government to accede to the secession of a province, subject only to negotiation of the logistical details of secession. This proposition is attributed either to the supposed implications

of the democratic principle of the Constitution, or to the international law principle of self-determination of peoples.

91 For both theoretical and practical reasons, we cannot accept this view. We hold that Quebec could not purport to invoke a right of self-determination such as to dictate the terms of a proposed secession to the other parties: that would not be a negotiation at all. As well, it would be naive to expect that the substantive goal of secession could readily be distinguished from the practical details of secession. The devil would be in the details. The democracy principle, as we have emphasized, cannot be invoked to trump the principles of federalism and rule of law, the rights of individuals and minorities, or the operation of democracy in the other provinces or in Canada as a whole. No negotiations could be effective if their ultimate outcome, secession, is cast as an absolute legal entitlement based upon an obligation to give effect to that act of secession in the Constitution. Such a foregone conclusion would actually undermine the obligation to negotiate and render it hollow.

92 However, we are equally unable to accept the reverse proposition, that a clear expression of self-determination by the people of Quebec would impose no obligations upon the other provinces or the federal government. The continued existence and operation of the Canadian constitutional order cannot remain indifferent to the clear expression of a clear majority of Quebecers that they no longer wish to remain in Canada. This would amount to the assertion that other constitutionally recognized principles necessarily trump the clearly expressed democratic will of the people of Quebec. Such a proposition fails to give sufficient weight to the underlying constitutional principles that must inform the amendment process, including the principles of democracy and federalism. The rights of other provinces and the federal government cannot deny the right of the government of Quebec to pursue secession, should a clear majority of the people of Quebec choose that goal, so long as in doing so, Quebec respects the rights of others. Negotiations would be necessary to address the interests of the federal government, of Quebec and the other provinces, and other participants, as well as the rights of all Canadians both within and outside Quebec.

93 Is the rejection of both of these propositions reconcilable? Yes, once it is realized that none of the rights or principles under discussion is absolute to the exclusion of the others. This observation suggests that other parties cannot exercise their rights in such a way as to amount to an absolute denial of Quebec's rights, and similarly, that so long as Quebec exercises its rights while respecting the rights of others, it may propose secession and seek to achieve it through negotiation. The negotiation process precipitated by a decision of a clear majority of the population of Quebec on a clear question to pursue secession would require the reconciliation of various rights and obligations by the representatives of two legitimate majorities, namely, the clear majority of the population of Quebec, and the clear majority of Canada as a whole, whatever that may be. There can be no suggestion that either of these majorities "trumps"

the other. A political majority that does not act in accordance with the underlying constitutional principles we have identified puts at risk the legitimacy of the exercise of its rights.

94 In such circumstances, the conduct of the parties assumes primary constitutional significance. The negotiation process must be conducted with an eye to the constitutional principles we have outlined, which must inform the actions of all the participants in the negotiation process.

95 Refusal of a party to conduct negotiations in a manner consistent with constitutional principles and values would seriously put at risk the legitimacy of that party's assertion of its rights, and perhaps the negotiation process as a whole. Those who quite legitimately insist upon the importance of upholding the rule of law cannot at the same time be oblivious to the need to act in conformity with constitutional principles and values, and so do their part to contribute to the maintenance and promotion of an environment in which the rule of law may flourish.

96 No one can predict the course that such negotiations might take. The possibility that they might not lead to an agreement amongst the parties must be recognized. Negotiations following a referendum vote in favour of seeking secession would inevitably address a wide range of issues, many of great import. After 131 years of Confederation, there exists, inevitably, a high level of integration in economic, political and social institutions across Canada. The vision of those who brought about Confederation was to create a unified country, not a loose alliance of autonomous provinces. Accordingly, while there are regional economic interests, which sometimes coincide with provincial boundaries, there are also national interests and enterprises (both public and private) that would face potential dismemberment. There is a national economy and a national debt. Arguments were raised before us regarding boundary issues. There are linguistic and cultural minorities, including aboriginal peoples, unevenly distributed across the country who look to the Constitution of Canada for the protection of their rights. Of course, secession would give rise to many issues of great complexity and difficulty. These would have to be resolved within the overall framework of the rule of law, thereby assuring Canadians resident in Quebec and elsewhere a measure of stability in what would likely be a period of considerable upheaval and uncertainty. Nobody seriously suggests that our national existence, seamless in so many aspects, could be effortlessly separated along what are now the provincial boundaries of Quebec. As the Attorney General of Saskatchewan put it in his oral submission:

> A nation is built when the communities that comprise it make commitments to it, when they forego choices and opportunities on behalf of a nation,...when the communities that comprise it make compromises, when they offer each other guarantees, when they make transfers and perhaps most pointedly, when they

> receive from others the benefits of national solidarity. The threads of a thousand acts of accommodation are the fabric of a nation....

97 In the circumstances, negotiations following such a referendum would undoubtedly be difficult. While the negotiators would have to contemplate the possibility of secession, there would be no absolute legal entitlement to it and no assumption that an agreement reconciling all relevant rights and obligations would actually be reached. It is foreseeable that even negotiations carried out in conformity with the underlying constitutional principles could reach an impasse. We need not speculate here as to what would then transpire. Under the Constitution, secession requires that an amendment be negotiated.

98 The respective roles of the courts and political actors in discharging the constitutional obligations we have identified follows ineluctably from the foregoing observations. In the *Patriation Reference*, a distinction was drawn between the law of the Constitution, which, generally speaking, will be enforced by the courts, and other constitutional rules, such as the conventions of the Constitution, which carry only political sanctions. It is also the case, however, that judicial intervention, even in relation to the law of the Constitution, is subject to the Court's appreciation of its proper role in the constitutional scheme.

99 The notion of justiciability is, as we earlier pointed out in dealing with the preliminary objection, linked to the notion of appropriate judicial restraint. We earlier made reference to the discussion of justiciability in *Reference re Canada Assistance Plan, supra*, at p. 545:

> In exercising its discretion whether to determine a matter that is alleged to be non-justiciable, the Court's primary concern is to retain its proper role within the constitutional framework of our democratic form of government.

In *Operation Dismantle, supra*, at p. 459, it was pointed out that justiciability is a "doctrine...founded upon a concern with the appropriate role of the courts as the forum for the resolution of different types of disputes." An analogous doctrine of judicial restraint operates here. Also, as observed in *Canada (Auditor General) v. Canada (Minister of Energy, Mines and Resources)*, [1989] 2 S.C.R. 49 (the *Auditor General*'s case), at p. 91:

> There is an array of issues which calls for the exercise of judicial judgment on whether the questions are properly cognizable by the courts. Ultimately, such judgment depends on the appreciation by the judiciary of its own position in the constitutional scheme.

100 The role of the Court in this Reference is limited to the identification of the relevant aspects of the Constitution in their broadest sense. We have interpreted the questions as relating to the constitutional framework within which political decisions may ultimately be made. Within that framework, the workings of the political process are complex and can only be resolved by means of political judgments and evaluations. The Court has no supervisory role over the political aspects of constitutional negotiations. Equally, the initial impetus for negotiation, namely a clear majority on a clear question in favour of secession, is subject only to political evaluation, and properly so. A right and a corresponding duty to negotiate secession cannot be built on an alleged expression of democratic will if the expression of democratic will is itself fraught with ambiguities. Only the political actors would have the information and expertise to make the appropriate judgment as to the point at which, and the circumstances in which, those ambiguities are resolved one way or the other.

101 If the circumstances giving rise to the duty to negotiate were to arise, the distinction between the strong defence of legitimate interests and the taking of positions which, in fact, ignore the legitimate interests of others is one that also defies legal analysis. The Court would not have access to all of the information available to the political actors, and the methods appropriate for the search for truth in a court of law are ill-suited to getting to the bottom of constitutional negotiations. To the extent that the questions are political in nature, it is not the role of the judiciary to interpose its own views on the different negotiating positions of the parties, even were it invited to do so. Rather, it is the obligation of the elected representatives to give concrete form to the discharge of their constitutional obligations which only they and their electors can ultimately assess. The reconciliation of the various legitimate constitutional interests outlined above is necessarily committed to the political rather than the judicial realm, precisely because that reconciliation can only be achieved through the give and take of the negotiation process. Having established the legal framework, it would be for the democratically elected leadership of the various participants to resolve their differences.

102 The non-justiciability of political issues that lack a legal component does not deprive the surrounding constitutional framework of its binding status, nor does this mean that constitutional obligations could be breached without incurring serious legal repercussions. Where there are legal rights there are remedies, but as we explained in the *Auditor General*'s case, *supra*, at p. 90, and *New Brunswick Broadcasting*, *supra*, the appropriate recourse in some circumstances lies through the workings of the political process rather than the courts.

103 To the extent that a breach of the constitutional duty to negotiate in accordance with the principles described above undermines the legitimacy of a party's actions, it may have important ramifications at the international level. Thus, a failure of the duty to undertake negotiations and pursue them according to constitutional principles may undermine that government's claim to legitimacy which is generally a precondition for recognition by the international community. Conversely, violations of those principles

by the federal or other provincial governments responding to the request for secession may undermine their legitimacy. Thus, a Quebec that had negotiated in conformity with constitutional principles and values in the face of unreasonable intransigence on the part of other participants at the federal or provincial level would be more likely to be recognized than a Quebec which did not itself act according to constitutional principles in the negotiation process. Both the legality of the acts of the parties to the negotiation process under Canadian law, and the perceived legitimacy of such action, would be important considerations in the recognition process. In this way, the adherence of the parties to the obligation to negotiate would be evaluated in an indirect manner on the international plane.

104 Accordingly, the secession of Quebec from Canada cannot be accomplished by the National Assembly, the legislature or government of Quebec unilaterally, that is to say, without principled negotiations, and be considered a lawful act. Any attempt to effect the secession of a province from Canada must be undertaken pursuant to the Constitution of Canada, or else violate the Canadian legal order. However, the continued existence and operation of the Canadian constitutional order cannot remain unaffected by the unambiguous expression of a clear majority of Quebecers that they no longer wish to remain in Canada. The primary means by which that expression is given effect is the constitutional duty to negotiate in accordance with the constitutional principles that we have described herein. In the event secession negotiations are initiated, our Constitution, no less than our history, would call on the participants to work to reconcile the rights, obligations and legitimate aspirations of all Canadians within a framework that emphasizes constitutional responsibilities as much as it does constitutional rights.

105 It will be noted that Question 1 does not ask how secession could be achieved in a constitutional manner, but addresses one form of secession only, namely unilateral secession. Although the applicability of various procedures to achieve lawful secession was raised in argument, each option would require us to assume the existence of facts that at this stage are unknown. In accordance with the usual rule of prudence in constitutional cases, we refrain from pronouncing on the applicability of any particular constitutional procedure to effect secession unless and until sufficiently clear facts exist to squarely raise an issue for judicial determination.

(5) Suggested Principle of Effectivity

106 In the foregoing discussion we have not overlooked the principle of effectivity, which was placed at the forefront in argument before us. For the reasons that follow, we do not think that the principle of effectivity has any application to the issues raised by Question 1. A distinction must be drawn between the right of a people to act, and their power to do so. They are not identical. A right is recognized in law: mere physical ability is not necessarily given status as a right. The fact that an individual or group can act in a certain way says nothing at all about the legal status or consequences of the act.

A power may be exercised even in the absence of a right to do so, but if it is, then it is exercised without legal foundation. Our Constitution does not address powers in this sense. On the contrary, the Constitution is concerned only with the rights and obligations of individuals, groups and governments, and the structure of our institutions. It was suggested before us that the National Assembly, legislature or government of Quebec could unilaterally effect the secession of that province from Canada, but it was not suggested that they might do so as a matter of law: rather, it was contended that they simply could do so as a matter of fact. Although under the Constitution there is no right to pursue secession unilaterally, that is secession without principled negotiation, this does not rule out the possibility of an unconstitutional declaration of secession leading to a *de facto* secession. The ultimate success of such a secession would be dependent on effective control of a territory and recognition by the international community. The principles governing secession at international law are discussed in our answer to Question 2.

107 In our view, the alleged principle of effectivity has no constitutional or legal status in the sense that it does not provide an *ex ante* explanation or justification for an act. In essence, acceptance of a principle of effectivity would be tantamount to accepting that the National Assembly, legislature or government of Quebec may act without regard to the law, simply because it asserts the power to do so. So viewed, the suggestion is that the National Assembly, legislature or government of Quebec could purport to secede the province unilaterally from Canada in disregard of Canadian and international law. It is further suggested that if the secession bid was successful, a new legal order would be created in that province, which would then be considered an independent state.

108 Such a proposition is an assertion of fact, not a statement of law. It may or may not be true; in any event it is irrelevant to the questions of law before us. If, on the other hand, it is put forward as an assertion of law, then it simply amounts to the contention that the law may be broken as long as it can be broken successfully. Such a notion is contrary to the rule of law, and must be rejected.

B *Question 2*

> Does international law give the National Assembly, legislature or government of Quebec the right to effect the secession of Quebec from Canada unilaterally? In this regard, is there a right to self-determination under international law that would give the National Assembly, legislature or government of Quebec the right to effect the secession of Quebec from Canada unilaterally?

109 For reasons already discussed, the Court does not accept the contention that Question 2 raises a question of "pure" international law which this Court has no jurisdiction to address. Question 2 is posed in the context of a Reference to address the

existence or non-existence of a right of unilateral secession by a province of Canada. The *amicus curiae* argues that this question ultimately falls to be determined under international law. In addressing this issue, the Court does not purport to act as an arbiter between sovereign states or more generally within the international community. The Court is engaged in rendering an advisory opinion on certain legal aspects of the continued existence of the Canadian federation. International law has been invoked as a consideration and it must therefore be addressed.

110 The argument before the Court on Question 2 has focused largely on determining whether, under international law, a positive legal right to unilateral secession exists in the factual circumstances assumed for the purpose of our response to Question 1. Arguments were also advanced to the effect that, regardless of the existence or non-existence of a positive right to unilateral secession, international law will in the end recognize effective political realities—including the emergence of a new state—as facts. While our response to Question 2 will address considerations raised by this alternative argument of "effectivity," it should first be noted that the existence of a positive legal entitlement is quite different from a prediction that the law will respond after the fact to a then existing political reality. These two concepts examine different points in time. The questions posed to the Court address legal rights in advance of a unilateral act of purported secession. While we touch below on the practice governing the international recognition of emerging states, the Court is as wary of entertaining speculation about the possible future conduct of sovereign states on the international level as it was under Question 1 to speculate about the possible future course of political negotiations among the participants in the Canadian federation. In both cases, the Reference questions are directed only to the legal framework within which the political actors discharge their various mandates.

(1) Secession at International Law

111 It is clear that international law does not specifically grant component parts of sovereign states the legal right to secede unilaterally from their "parent" state. This is acknowledged by the experts who provided their opinions on behalf of both the *amicus curiae* and the Attorney General of Canada. Given the lack of specific authorization for unilateral secession, proponents of the existence of such a right at international law are therefore left to attempt to found their argument (i) on the proposition that unilateral secession is not specifically prohibited and that what is not specifically prohibited is inferentially permitted; or (ii) on the implied duty of states to recognize the legitimacy of secession brought about by the exercise of the well-established international law right of "a people" to self-determination. The *amicus curiae* addressed the right of self-determination, but submitted that it was not applicable to the circumstances of Quebec within the Canadian federation, irrespective of the existence

or non-existence of a referendum result in favour of secession. We agree on this point with the *amicus curiae*, for reasons that we will briefly develop.

(a) *Absence of a Specific Prohibition*

112 International law contains neither a right of unilateral secession nor the explicit denial of such a right, although such a denial is, to some extent, implicit in the exceptional circumstances required for secession to be permitted under the right of a people to self-determination, e.g., the right of secession that arises in the exceptional situation of an oppressed or colonial people, discussed below. As will be seen, international law places great importance on the territorial integrity of nation states and, by and large, leaves the creation of a new state to be determined by the domestic law of the existing state of which the seceding entity presently forms a part (R.Y. Jennings, *The Acquisition of Territory in International Law* (1963), at pp. 8–9). Where, as here, unilateral secession would be incompatible with the domestic Constitution, international law is likely to accept that conclusion subject to the right of peoples to self-determination, a topic to which we now turn.

(b) *The Right of a People to Self-determination*

113 While international law generally regulates the conduct of nation states, it does, in some specific circumstances, also recognize the "rights" of entities other than nation states—such as the right of a people to self-determination.

114 The existence of the right of a people to self-determination is now so widely recognized in international conventions that the principle has acquired a status beyond "convention" and is considered a general principle of international law. (A. Cassese, *Self-determination of peoples: A legal reappraisal* (1995), at pp. 171–172; K. Doehring, "Self-Determination," in B. Simma, ed., *The Charter of the United Nations: A Commentary* (1994), at p. 70.)

115 Article 1 of the *Charter of the United Nations*, Can. T.S. 1945 No. 7, states in part that one of the purposes of the United Nations (U.N.) is:

> *Article 1*
>
> ...
>
> 2. To develop friendly relations among nations based on respect for the principle of equal rights and self-determination of peoples, and to take other appropriate measures to strengthen universal peace;

116 Article 55 of the U.N. Charter further states that the U.N. shall promote goals such as higher standards of living, full employment and human rights "[w]ith a view to the creation of conditions of stability and well-being which are necessary for peaceful

and friendly relations among nations based on respect for the principle of equal rights and self-determination of peoples."

117 This basic principle of self-determination has been carried forward and addressed in so many U.N. conventions and resolutions that, as noted by Doehring, *supra*, at p. 60:

> The sheer number of resolutions concerning the right of self-determination makes their enumeration impossible.

118 For our purposes, reference to the following conventions and resolutions is sufficient. Article 1 of both the U.N.'s *International* Covenant *on Civil and Political Rights*, 999 U.N.T.S. 171, and its *International Covenant on Economic, Social and Cultural Rights*, 993 U.N.T.S. 3, states:

> 1. All peoples have the right of self-determination. By virtue of that right they freely determine their political status and freely pursue their economic, social and cultural development.

119 Similarly, the U.N. General Assembly's *Declaration on Principles of International Law concerning Friendly Relations and Co-operation among States in accordance with the Charter of the United Nations*, GA Res. 2625 (XXV), 24 October 1970 (*Declaration on Friendly Relations*), states:

> By virtue of the principle of equal rights and self-determination of peoples enshrined in the Charter of the United Nations, all peoples have the right freely to determine, without external interference, their political status and to pursue their economic, social and cultural development, and every State has the duty to respect this right in accordance with the provisions of the Charter.

120 In 1993, the U.N. World Conference on Human Rights adopted the *Vienna Declaration and Programme of Action*, A/CONF.157/24, 25 June 1993, that reaffirmed Article 1 of the two above-mentioned covenants. The U.N. General Assembly's *Declaration on the Occasion of the Fiftieth Anniversary of the United Nations*, GA Res. 50/6, 9 November 1995, also emphasizes the right to self-determination by providing that the U.N.'s member states will:

> 1. ...
>
> Continue to reaffirm the right of self-determination of all peoples, taking into account the particular situation of peoples under colonial or other forms of alien

> domination or foreign occupation, and recognize the right of peoples to take legitimate action in accordance with the Charter of the United Nations to realize their inalienable right of self-determination. This shall not be construed as authorizing or encouraging any action that would dismember or impair, totally or in part, the territorial integrity or political unity of sovereign and independent States conducting themselves in compliance with the principle of equal rights and self-determination of peoples and thus possessed of a Government representing the whole people belonging to the territory without distinction of any kind.... [Emphasis added.]

121 The right to self-determination is also recognized in other international legal documents. For example, the *Final Act of the Conference on Security and Co-operation in Europe*, 14 I.L.M. 1292 (1975) (*Helsinki Final Act*), states (in Part VIII):

> The participating States will respect the equal rights of peoples and their right to self-determination, acting at all times in conformity with the purposes and principles of the Charter of the United Nations and with the relevant norms of international law, including those relating to territorial integrity of States.
>
> By virtue of the principle of equal rights and self-determination of peoples, all peoples always have the right, in full freedom, to determine, when and as they wish, their internal and external political status, without external interference, and to pursue as they wish their political, economic, social and cultural development. [Emphasis added.]

122 As will be seen, international law expects that the right to self-determination will be exercised by peoples within the framework of existing sovereign states and consistently with the maintenance of the territorial integrity of those states. Where this is not possible, in the exceptional circumstances discussed below, a right of secession may arise.

(i) Defining "Peoples"

123 International law grants the right to self-determination to "peoples." Accordingly, access to the right requires the threshold step of characterizing as a people the group seeking self-determination. However, as the right to self-determination has developed by virtue of a combination of international agreements and conventions, coupled with state practice, with little formal elaboration of the definition of "peoples," the result has been that the precise meaning of the term "people" remains somewhat uncertain.

124 It is clear that "a people" may include only a portion of the population of an existing state. The right to self-determination has developed largely as a human right, and is generally used in documents that simultaneously contain references to "nation"

and "state." The juxtaposition of these terms is indicative that the reference to "people" does not necessarily mean the entirety of a state's population. To restrict the definition of the term to the population of existing states would render the granting of a right to self-determination largely duplicative, given the parallel emphasis within the majority of the source documents on the need to protect the territorial integrity of existing states, and would frustrate its remedial purpose.

125 While much of the Quebec population certainly shares many of the characteristics (such as a common language and culture) that would be considered in determining whether a specific group is a "people," as do other groups within Quebec and/or Canada, it is not necessary to explore this legal characterization to resolve Question 2 appropriately. Similarly, it is not necessary for the Court to determine whether, should a Quebec people exist within the definition of public international law, such a people encompasses the entirety of the provincial population or just a portion thereof. Nor is it necessary to examine the position of the aboriginal population within Quebec. As the following discussion of the scope of the right to self-determination will make clear, whatever be the correct application of the definition of people(s) in this context, their right of self-determination cannot in the present circumstances be said to ground a right to unilateral secession.

(ii) Scope of the Right to Self-determination

126 The recognized sources of international law establish that the right to self-determination of a people is normally fulfilled through internal self-determination—a people's pursuit of its political, economic, social and cultural development within the framework of an existing state. A right to external self-determination (which in this case potentially takes the form of the assertion of a right to unilateral secession) arises in only the most extreme of cases and, even then, under carefully defined circumstances. External self-determination can be defined as in the following statement from the *Declaration on Friendly Relations* as

> [t]he establishment of a sovereign and independent State, the free association or integration with an independent State or the emergence into any other political status freely determined by a people constitute modes of implementing the right of self-determination by that people. [Emphasis added.]

127 The international law principle of self-determination has evolved within a framework of respect for the territorial integrity of existing states. The various international documents that support the existence of a people's right to self-determination also contain parallel statements supportive of the conclusion that the exercise of such a right must be sufficiently limited to prevent threats to an existing state's territorial integrity or the stability of relations between sovereign states.

128 The *Declaration on Friendly Relations*, the *Vienna Declaration* and the *Declaration on the Occasion of the Fiftieth Anniversary of the United Nations* are specific. They state, immediately after affirming a people's right to determine political, economic, social and cultural issues, that such rights are not to

> be construed as authorizing or encouraging any action that would dismember or impair, totally or in part, the territorial integrity or political unity of sovereign and independent States conducting themselves in compliance with the principle of equal rights and self-determination of peoples and thus possessed of a Government representing the whole people belonging to the territory without distinction.... [Emphasis added.]

129 Similarly, while the concluding document of the Vienna Meeting in 1989 of the Conference on Security and Co-operation in Europe on the follow-up to the *Helsinki Final Act* again refers to peoples having the right to determine "their internal and external political status" (emphasis added), that statement is immediately followed by express recognition that the participating states will at all times act, as stated in the *Helsinki Final Act*, "in conformity with the purposes and principles of the Charter of the United Nations and with the relevant norms of international law, including those relating to territorial integrity of States" (emphasis added). Principle 5 of the concluding document states that the participating states (including Canada):

> ...confirm their commitment strictly and effectively to observe the principle of the territorial integrity of States. They will refrain from any violation of this principle and thus from any action aimed by direct or indirect means, in contravention of the purposes and principles of the Charter of the United Nations, other obligations under international law or the provisions of the [Helsinki] Final Act, at violating the territorial integrity, political independence or the unity of a State. No actions or situations in contravention of this principle will be recognized as legal by the participating States. [Emphasis added.]

Accordingly, the reference in the *Helsinki Final Act* to a people determining its external political status is interpreted to mean the expression of a people's external political status through the government of the existing state, save in the exceptional circumstances discussed below. As noted by Cassese, *supra*, at p. 287, given the history and textual structure of this document, its reference to external self-determination simply means that "no territorial or other change can be brought about by the central authorities of a State that is contrary to the will of the whole people of that State."

130 While the *International Covenant on Economic, Social and Cultural Rights* and the *International Covenant on Civil and Political Rights* do not specifically refer to

the protection of territorial integrity, they both define the ambit of the right to self-determination in terms that are normally attainable within the framework of an existing state. There is no necessary incompatibility between the maintenance of the territorial integrity of existing states, including Canada, and the right of a "people" to achieve a full measure of self-determination. A state whose government represents the whole of the people or peoples resident within its territory, on a basis of equality and without discrimination, and respects the principles of self-determination in its own internal arrangements, is entitled to the protection under international law of its territorial integrity.

(iii) Colonial and Oppressed Peoples

131 Accordingly, the general state of international law with respect to the right to self-determination is that the right operates within the overriding protection granted to the territorial integrity of "parent" states. However, as noted by Cassese, *supra*, at p. 334, there are certain defined contexts within which the right to the self-determination of peoples does allow that right to be exercised "externally," which, in the context of this Reference, would potentially mean secession:

> ...the right to external self-determination, which entails the possibility of choosing (or restoring) independence, has only been bestowed upon two classes of peoples (those under colonial rule or foreign occupation), based upon the assumption that both classes make up entities that are inherently distinct from the colonialist Power and the occupant Power and that their 'territorial integrity', all but destroyed by the colonialist or occupying Power, should be fully restored....

132 The right of colonial peoples to exercise their right to self-determination by breaking away from the "imperial" power is now undisputed, but is irrelevant to this Reference.

133 The other clear case where a right to external self-determination accrues is where a people is subject to alien subjugation, domination or exploitation outside a colonial context. This recognition finds its roots in the *Declaration on Friendly Relations*:

> Every State has the duty to promote, through joint and separate action, realization of the principle of equal rights and self-determination of peoples, in accordance with the provisions of the Charter, and to render assistance to the United Nations in carrying out the responsibilities entrusted to it by the Charter regarding the implementation of the principle, in order:
>
> (*a*) To promote friendly relations and co-operation among States; and

> (*b*) To bring a speedy end to colonialism, having due regard to the freely expressed will of the peoples concerned;
>
> and bearing in mind that subjection of peoples to alien subjugation, domination and exploitation constitutes a violation of the principle, as well as a denial of fundamental human rights, and is contrary to the Charter.

134 A number of commentators have further asserted that the right to self-determination may ground a right to unilateral secession in a third circumstance. Although this third circumstance has been described in several ways, the underlying proposition is that, when a people is blocked from the meaningful exercise of its right to self-determination internally, it is entitled, as a last resort, to exercise it by secession. The *Vienna Declaration* requirement that governments represent "the whole people belonging to the territory without distinction of any kind" adds credence to the assertion that such a complete blockage may potentially give rise to a right of secession.

135 Clearly, such a circumstance parallels the other two recognized situations in that the ability of a people to exercise its right to self-determination internally is somehow being totally frustrated. While it remains unclear whether this third proposition actually reflects an established international law standard, it is unnecessary for present purposes to make that determination. Even assuming that the third circumstance is sufficient to create a right to unilateral secession under international law, the current Quebec context cannot be said to approach such a threshold. As stated by the *amicus curiae*, Addendum to the factum of the *amicus curiae*, at paras. 15–16:

> [TRANSLATION] 15. The Quebec people is not the victim of attacks on its physical existence or integrity, or of a massive violation of its fundamental rights. The Quebec people is manifestly not, in the opinion of the *amicus curiae*, an oppressed people.
>
> 16. For close to 40 of the last 50 years, the Prime Minister of Canada has been a Quebecer. During this period, Quebecers have held from time to time all the most important positions in the federal Cabinet. During the 8 years prior to June 1997, the Prime Minister and the Leader of the Official Opposition in the House of Commons were both Quebecers. At present, the Prime Minister of Canada, the Right Honourable Chief Justice and two other members of the Court, the Chief of Staff of the Canadian Armed Forces and the Canadian ambassador to the United States, not to mention the Deputy Secretary-General of the United Nations, are all Quebecers. The international achievements of Quebecers in most fields of human endeavour are too numerous to list. Since the dynamism of the Quebec people has been directed toward the business sector, it has been clearly successful in Quebec, the rest of Canada and abroad.

136 The population of Quebec cannot plausibly be said to be denied access to government. Quebecers occupy prominent positions within the government of Canada. Residents of the province freely make political choices and pursue economic, social and cultural development within Quebec, across Canada, and throughout the world. The population of Quebec is equitably represented in legislative, executive and judicial institutions. In short, to reflect the phraseology of the international documents that address the right to self-determination of peoples, Canada is a "sovereign and independent state conducting itself in compliance with the principle of equal rights and self-determination of peoples and thus possessed of a government representing the whole people belonging to the territory without distinction."

137 The continuing failure to reach agreement on amendments to the Constitution, while a matter of concern, does not amount to a denial of self-determination. In the absence of amendments to the Canadian Constitution, we must look at the constitutional arrangements presently in effect, and we cannot conclude under current circumstances that those arrangements place Quebecers in a disadvantaged position within the scope of the international law rule.

138 In summary, the international law right to self-determination only generates, at best, a right to external self-determination in situations of former colonies; where a people is oppressed, as for example under foreign military occupation; or where a definable group is denied meaningful access to government to pursue their political, economic, social and cultural development. In all three situations, the people in question are entitled to a right to external self-determination because they have been denied the ability to exert internally their right to self-determination. Such exceptional circumstances are manifestly inapplicable to Quebec under existing conditions. Accordingly, neither the population of the province of Quebec, even if characterized in terms of "people" or "peoples," nor its representative institutions, the National Assembly, the legislature or government of Quebec, possess a right, under international law, to secede unilaterally from Canada.

139 We would not wish to leave this aspect of our answer to Question 2 without acknowledging the importance of the submissions made to us respecting the rights and concerns of aboriginal peoples in the event of a unilateral secession, as well as the appropriate means of defining the boundaries of a seceding Quebec with particular regard to the northern lands occupied largely by aboriginal peoples. However, the concern of aboriginal peoples is precipitated by the asserted right of Quebec to unilateral secession. In light of our finding that there is no such right applicable to the population of Quebec, either under the Constitution of Canada or at international law, but that on the contrary a clear democratic expression of support for secession would lead under the Constitution to negotiations in which aboriginal interests would be taken into account, it becomes unnecessary to explore further the concerns of the aboriginal peoples in this Reference.

(2) Recognition of a Factual/Political Reality: The "Effectivity" Principle

140 As stated, an argument advanced by the *amicus curiae* on this branch of the Reference was that, while international law may not ground a positive right to unilateral secession in the context of Quebec, international law equally does not prohibit secession and, in fact, international recognition would be conferred on such a political reality if it emerged, for example, via effective control of the territory of what is now the province of Quebec.

141 It is true that international law may well, depending on the circumstances, adapt to recognize a political and/or factual reality, regardless of the legality of the steps leading to its creation. However, as mentioned at the outset, effectivity, as such, does not have any real applicability to Question 2, which asks whether a right to unilateral secession exists.

142 No one doubts that legal consequences may flow from political facts, and that "sovereignty is a political fact for which no purely legal authority can be constituted...," H.W.R. Wade, "The Basis of Legal Sovereignty," [1955] *Camb. L.J.* 172, at p. 196. Secession of a province from Canada, if successful in the streets, might well lead to the creation of a new state. Although recognition by other states is not, at least as a matter of theory, necessary to achieve statehood, the viability of a would-be state in the international community depends, as a practical matter, upon recognition by other states. That process of recognition is guided by legal norms. However, international recognition is not alone constitutive of statehood and, critically, does not relate back to the date of secession to serve retroactively as a source of a "legal" right to secede in the first place. Recognition occurs only after a territorial unit has been successful, as a political fact, in achieving secession.

143 As indicated in responding to Question 1, one of the legal norms which may be recognized by states in granting or withholding recognition of emergent states is the legitimacy of the process by which the *de facto* secession is, or was, being pursued. The process of recognition, once considered to be an exercise of pure sovereign discretion, has come to be associated with legal norms. See, e.g., European Community Declaration on the *Guidelines on the Recognition of New States in Eastern Europe and in the Soviet Union*, 31 I.L.M. 1486 (1992), at p. 1487. While national interest and perceived political advantage to the recognizing state obviously play an important role, foreign states may also take into account their view as to the existence of a right to self-determination on the part of the population of the putative state, and a counterpart domestic evaluation, namely, an examination of the legality of the secession according to the law of the state from which the territorial unit purports to have seceded. As we indicated in our answer to Question 1, an emergent state that has disregarded

legitimate obligations arising out of its previous situation can potentially expect to be hindered by that disregard in achieving international recognition, at least with respect to the timing of that recognition. On the other hand, compliance by the seceding province with such legitimate obligations would weigh in favour of international recognition. The notion that what is not explicitly prohibited is implicitly permitted has little relevance where (as here) international law refers the legality of secession to the domestic law of the seceding state and the law of that state holds unilateral secession to be unconstitutional.

144 As a court of law, we are ultimately concerned only with legal claims. If the principle of "effectivity" is no more than that "successful revolution begets its own legality" (S.A. de Smith, "Constitutional Lawyers in Revolutionary Situations" (1968), 7 *West. Ont. L. Rev.* 93, at p. 96), it necessarily means that legality follows and does not precede the successful revolution. *Ex hypothesi*, the successful revolution took place outside the constitutional framework of the predecessor state, otherwise it would not be characterized as "a revolution." It may be that a unilateral secession by Quebec would eventually be accorded legal status by Canada and other states, and thus give rise to legal consequences; but this does not support the more radical contention that subsequent recognition of a state of affairs brought about by a unilateral declaration of independence could be taken to mean that secession was achieved under colour of a legal right.

145 An argument was made to analogize the principle of effectivity with the second aspect of the rule of law identified by this Court in the *Manitoba Language Rights Reference*, *supra*, at p. 753, namely, avoidance of a legal vacuum. In that Reference, it will be recalled, this Court declined to strike down all of Manitoba's legislation for its failure to comply with constitutional dictates, out of concern that this would leave the province in a state of chaos. In so doing, we recognized that the rule of law is a constitutional principle which permits the courts to address the practical consequences of their actions, particularly in constitutional cases. The similarity between that principle and the principle of effectivity, it was argued, is that both attempt to refashion the law to meet social reality. However, nothing of our concern in the *Manitoba Language Rights Reference* about the severe practical consequences of unconstitutionality affected our conclusion that, as a matter of law, all Manitoba legislation at issue in that case was unconstitutional. The Court's declaration of unconstitutionality was clear and unambiguous. The Court's concern with maintenance of the rule of law was directed in its relevant aspect to the appropriate remedy, which in that case was to suspend the declaration of invalidity to permit appropriate rectification to take place.

146 The principle of effectivity operates very differently. It proclaims that an illegal act may eventually acquire legal status if, as a matter of empirical fact, it is recognized on the international plane. Our law has long recognized that through a combination of

acquiescence and prescription, an illegal act may at some later point be accorded some form of legal status. In the law of property, for example, it is well known that a squatter on land may ultimately become the owner if the true owner sleeps on his or her right to repossess the land. In this way, a change in the factual circumstances may subsequently be reflected in a change in legal status. It is, however, quite another matter to suggest that a subsequent condonation of an initially illegal act retroactively creates a legal right to engage in the act in the first place. The broader contention is not supported by the international principle of effectivity or otherwise and must be rejected.

C *Question 3*

> In the event of a conflict between domestic and international law on the right of the National Assembly, legislature or government of Quebec to effect the secession of Quebec from Canada unilaterally, which would take precedence in Canada?

147 In view of our answers to Questions 1 and 2, there is no conflict between domestic and international law to be addressed in the context of this Reference.

IV Summary of Conclusions

148 As stated at the outset, this Reference has required us to consider momentous questions that go to the heart of our system of constitutional government. We have emphasized that the Constitution is more than a written text. It embraces the entire global system of rules and principles which govern the exercise of constitutional authority. A superficial reading of selected provisions of the written constitutional enactment, without more, may be misleading. It is necessary to make a more profound investigation of the underlying principles that animate the whole of our Constitution, including the principles of federalism, democracy, constitutionalism and the rule of law, and respect for minorities. Those principles must inform our overall appreciation of the constitutional rights and obligations that would come into play in the event a clear majority of Quebecers votes on a clear question in favour of secession.

149 The Reference requires us to consider whether Quebec has a right to unilateral secession. Those who support the existence of such a right found their case primarily on the principle of democracy. Democracy, however, means more than simple majority rule. As reflected in our constitutional jurisprudence, democracy exists in the larger context of other constitutional values such as those already mentioned. In the 131 years since Confederation, the people of the provinces and territories have created close ties of interdependence (economically, socially, politically and culturally) based

on shared values that include federalism, democracy, constitutionalism and the rule of law, and respect for minorities. A democratic decision of Quebecers in favour of secession would put those relationships at risk. The Constitution vouchsafes order and stability, and accordingly secession of a province "under the Constitution" could not be achieved unilaterally, that is, without principled negotiation with other participants in Confederation within the existing constitutional framework.

150 The Constitution is not a straitjacket. Even a brief review of our constitutional history demonstrates periods of momentous and dramatic change. Our democratic institutions necessarily accommodate a continuous process of discussion and evolution, which is reflected in the constitutional right of each participant in the federation to initiate constitutional change. This right implies a reciprocal duty on the other participants to engage in discussions to address any legitimate initiative to change the constitutional order. While it is true that some attempts at constitutional amendment in recent years have faltered, a clear majority vote in Quebec on a clear question in favour of secession would confer democratic legitimacy on the secession initiative which all of the other participants in Confederation would have to recognize.

151 Quebec could not, despite a clear referendum result, purport to invoke a right of self-determination to dictate the terms of a proposed secession to the other parties to the federation. The democratic vote, by however strong a majority, would have no legal effect on its own and could not push aside the principles of federalism and the rule of law, the rights of individuals and minorities, or the operation of democracy in the other provinces or in Canada as a whole. Democratic rights under the Constitution cannot be divorced from constitutional obligations. Nor, however, can the reverse proposition be accepted. The continued existence and operation of the Canadian constitutional order could not be indifferent to a clear expression of a clear majority of Quebecers that they no longer wish to remain in Canada. The other provinces and the federal government would have no basis to deny the right of the government of Quebec to pursue secession, should a clear majority of the people of Quebec choose that goal, so long as in doing so, Quebec respects the rights of others. The negotiations that followed such a vote would address the potential act of secession as well as its possible terms should in fact secession proceed. There would be no conclusions predetermined by law on any issue. Negotiations would need to address the interests of the other provinces, the federal government, Quebec and indeed the rights of all Canadians both within and outside Quebec, and specifically the rights of minorities. No one suggests that it would be an easy set of negotiations.

152 The negotiation process would require the reconciliation of various rights and obligations by negotiation between two legitimate majorities, namely, the majority of the population of Quebec, and that of Canada as a whole. A political majority at either level that does not act in accordance with the underlying constitutional principles we

have mentioned puts at risk the legitimacy of its exercise of its rights, and the ultimate acceptance of the result by the international community.

153 The task of the Court has been to clarify the legal framework within which political decisions are to be taken "under the Constitution," not to usurp the prerogatives of the political forces that operate within that framework. The obligations we have identified are binding obligations under the Constitution of Canada. However, it will be for the political actors to determine what constitutes "a clear majority on a clear question" in the circumstances under which a future referendum vote may be taken. Equally, in the event of demonstrated majority support for Quebec secession, the content and process of the negotiations will be for the political actors to settle. The reconciliation of the various legitimate constitutional interests is necessarily committed to the political rather than the judicial realm precisely because that reconciliation can only be achieved through the give and take of political negotiations. To the extent issues addressed in the course of negotiation are political, the courts, appreciating their proper role in the constitutional scheme, would have no supervisory role.

154 We have also considered whether a positive legal entitlement to secession exists under international law in the factual circumstances contemplated by Question 1, i.e., a clear democratic expression of support on a clear question for Quebec secession. Some of those who supported an affirmative answer to this question did so on the basis of the recognized right to self-determination that belongs to all "peoples." Although much of the Quebec population certainly shares many of the characteristics of a people, it is not necessary to decide the "people" issue because, whatever may be the correct determination of this issue in the context of Quebec, a right to secession only arises under the principle of self-determination of peoples at international law where "a people" is governed as part of a colonial empire; where "a people" is subject to alien subjugation, domination or exploitation; and possibly where "a people" is denied any meaningful exercise of its right to self-determination within the state of which it forms a part. In other circumstances, peoples are expected to achieve self-determination within the framework of their existing state. A state whose government represents the whole of the people or peoples resident within its territory, on a basis of equality and without discrimination, and respects the principles of self-determination in its internal arrangements, is entitled to maintain its territorial integrity under international law and to have that territorial integrity recognized by other states. Quebec does not meet the threshold of a colonial people or an oppressed people, nor can it be suggested that Quebecers have been denied meaningful access to government to pursue their political, economic, cultural and social development. In the circumstances, the National Assembly, the legislature or the government of Quebec do not enjoy a right at international law to effect the secession of Quebec from Canada unilaterally.

155 Although there is no right, under the Constitution or at international law, to unilateral secession, that is secession without negotiation on the basis just discussed,

this does not rule out the possibility of an unconstitutional declaration of secession leading to a *de facto* secession. The ultimate success of such a secession would be dependent on recognition by the international community, which is likely to consider the legality and legitimacy of secession having regard to, amongst other facts, the conduct of Quebec and Canada, in determining whether to grant or withhold recognition. Such recognition, even if granted, would not, however, provide any retroactive justification for the act of secession, either under the Constitution of Canada or at international law.

156 The reference questions are answered accordingly.

Judgment accordingly.

Solicitor for the Attorney General of Canada: George Thomson, Ottawa.

Solicitors appointed by the Court as amicus curiae: Joli-C{oe}ur Lacasse Lemieux Simard St-Pierre, Sainte-Foy.

Solicitor for the intervener the Attorney General of Manitoba: The Department of Justice, Winnipeg.

Solicitor for the intervener the Attorney General for Saskatchewan: W. Brent Cotter, Regina.

Solicitor for the intervener the Minister of Justice of the Northwest Territories: Bernard W. Funston, Gloucester.

Solicitor for the intervener the Minister of Justice for the Government of the Yukon Territory: Stuart J. Whitley, Whitehorse.

Solicitor for the intervener Kitigan Zibi Anishinabeg: Agnès Laporte, Hull.

Solicitors for the intervener the Grand Council of the Crees (Eeyou Estchee): Robinson, Sheppard, Shapiro, Montréal.

Solicitors for the intervener the Makivik Corporation: Hutchins, Soroka & Dionne, Montréal.

Solicitor for the intervener the Chiefs of Ontario: Michael Sherry, Toronto.

Solicitors for the intervener the Minority Advocacy and Rights Council: Scott & Aylen, Toronto.

Solicitors for the intervener the Ad Hoc Committee of Canadian Women on the Constitution: Eberts Symes Street & Corbett, Toronto; Centre for Refugee Studies, North York.

Solicitors for the intervener Guy Bertrand: Guy Bertrand & Associés, Québec; Patrick Monahan, North York.

Solicitors for the interveners Roopnarine Singh, Keith Owen Henderson, Claude Leclerc, Kenneth O'Donnell and Van Hoven Petteway: Stephen A. Scott, Montréal.

Solicitors for the intervener Vincent Pouliot: Paquette & Associés, Montréal.

APPENDIX 2

Belgium's National Anthem- "La Brabançonne"[1]

French Lyrics

O Belgique, ô mère chérie,
A toi nos coeurs, à toi nos bras,
A toi notre sang, ô Patrie !
Nous le jurons tous, tu vivras !
Tu vivras toujours grande et belle
Et ton invincible unité
Aura pour devise immortelle:
Le Roi, la Loi, la Liberté !
Aura pour devise immortelle:
Le Roi, la Loi, la Liberté !
Le Roi, la Loi, la Liberté !
Le Roi, la Loi, la Liberté !

Dutch Lyrics

O dierbaar België, O heilig land der vaad'ren
Onze ziel en ons hart zijn u gewijd.
Aanvaard ons hart en het bloed van onze adren,
Wees ons doel in arbeid en in strijd.
Bloei, o land, in eendracht niet te breken;
Wees immer u zelf en ongeknecht,
Het woord getrouw, dat ge onbevreesd moogt spreken:
Voor Vorst, voor Vrijheid en voor Recht.
Het woord getrouw, dat ge onbevreesd moogt spreken:
Voor Vorst, voor Vrijheid en voor Recht.
Voor Vorst, voor Vrijheid en voor Recht.
Voor Vorst, voor Vrijheid en voor Recht.

1 nationalanthems. Info-http://www.nationalanthems.info/be.htm

 | DOI 10.1163/9789004294332_012

German Lyrics

O liebes Land, o Belgiens Erde,
Dir unser Herz, Dir unsere Hand,
Dir unser Blut, o Heimaterde,
wir schwören's Dir, o Vaterland!
So blühe froh in voller Schöne,
zu der die Freiheit Dich erzog,
und fortan singen Deine Söhne:
Gesetz und König und die Freiheit hoch!
und fortan singen Deine Söhne:
Gesetz und König und die Freiheit hoch!
Gesetz und König und die Freiheit hoch!
Gesetz und König und die Freiheit hoch!

English Translation (of French Lyrics)

O Belgium, dear mother,
To you our hearts, to you our arms,
To you our blood, o fatherland!
We all vow: you will live!
You will always live in grandeur and beauty.
And the immortal motto
Of your invincible unity will be:
For King, Right and Liberty!
Of your invincible unity will be:
For King, Right and Liberty!
For King, Right and Liberty!
For King, Right and Liberty!

APPENDIX 3

Canada's National Anthem- O Canada[1]

English Lyrics

O Canada!
Our home and native land!
True patriot love in all thy sons command.
With glowing hearts we see thee rise,
The True North strong and free!
From far and wide,
O Canada, we stand on guard for thee.
God keep our land glorious and free!
O Canada, we stand on guard for thee.
O Canada, we stand on guard for thee.

French Lyrics

O Canada! Terre de nos aïeux,
Ton front est ceint de fleurons glorieux!
Car ton bras sait porter l'épée,
Il sait porter la croix!
Ton histoire est une épopée
Des plus brillants exploits.
Et ta valeur, de foi trempée,
Protégera nos foyers et nos droits.
Protégera nos foyers et nos droits.

1 nationalanthems. Info - http://www.nationalanthems.info/ca.htm

 | DOI 10.1163/9789004294332_013

APPENDIX 4

Canadian Flag

PHOTO COURTESY OF MAOR EVEN KHEN

 | DOI 10.1163/9789004294332_014

APPENDIX 5

Israeli Flag

PHOTO COURTESY OF MAOR EVEN KHEN

 | DOI 10.1163/9789004294332_015

APPENDIX 6

Israel's National Anthem- Hatikva[1]

Hebrew Lyrics (Hebrew Script)

כָּל עוד בלבב פנימה
נפש יהודי הומייה,
ולפאֲתי מזרח קדימה
עין לציון צופייה;

Chorus
עוד לא אבדה תקותנו,
התקווה בת שנות אלפיים,
להיות עם חופשי בארצנו
ארץ ציון וירושלים.
להיות עם חופשי בארצנו
ארץ ציון וירושלים.

English Translation

As long as in the heart within,
The Jewish soul yearns,
And toward the eastern edges, onward,
An eye gazes toward Zion.

Our hope is not yet lost,
The hope that is two-thousand years old,
To be a free nation in our land,
The Land of Zion, Jerusalem.

---

1 nationalanthems. Info http://www.nationalanthems.info/il.htm

 | DOI 10.1163/9789004294332_016

APPENDIX 7

Israel's Proclamation of Independence[1]

Provisional Government of Israel

Official Gazette: Number 1; Tel Aviv, 5 Iyar 5708, 14.5.1948 Page 1

The Declaration of the Establishment of the State of Israel

The Land of Israel was the birthplace of the Jewish people. Here their spiritual, religious and political identity was shaped. Here they first attained to statehood, created cultural values of national and universal significance and gave to the world the eternal Book of Books.

After being forcibly exiled from their land, the people kept faith with it throughout their Dispersion and never ceased to pray and hope for their return to it and for the restoration in it of their political freedom.

Impelled by this historic and traditional attachment, Jews strove in every successive generation to re-establish themselves in their ancient homeland. In recent decades they returned in their masses. Pioneers, defiant returnees, and defenders, they made deserts bloom, revived the Hebrew language, built villages and towns, and created a thriving community controlling its own economy and culture, loving peace but knowing how to defend itself, bringing the blessings of progress to all the country's inhabitants, and aspiring towards independent nationhood.

In the year 5657 (1897), at the summons of the spiritual father of the Jewish State, Theodore Herzl, the First Zionist Congress convened and proclaimed the right of the Jewish people to national rebirth in its own country.

This right was recognized in the Balfour Declaration of the 2nd November, 1917, and re-affirmed in the Mandate of the League of Nations which, in particular, gave international sanction to the historic connection between the Jewish people and Eretz-Israel and to the right of the Jewish people to rebuild its National Home.

The catastrophe which recently befell the Jewish people—the massacre of millions of Jews in Europe—was another clear demonstration of the urgency

1 The Knesset, https://www.knesset.gov.il/docs/eng/megilat_eng.htm

 | DOI 10.1163/9789004294332_017

of solving the problem of its homelessness by re-establishing in Eretz-Israel the Jewish State, which would open the gates of the homeland wide to every Jew and confer upon the Jewish people the status of a fully privileged member of the community of nations.

Survivors of the Nazi holocaust in Europe, as well as Jews from other parts of the world, continued to migrate to Eretz-Israel, undaunted by difficulties, restrictions and dangers, and never ceased to assert their right to a life of dignity, freedom and honest toil in their national homeland.

In the Second World War, the Jewish community of this country contributed its full share to the struggle of the freedom- and peace-loving nations against the forces of Nazi wickedness and, by the blood of its soldiers and its war effort, gained the right to be reckoned among the peoples who founded the United Nations.

On the 29th November, 1947, the United Nations General Assembly passed a resolution calling for the establishment of a Jewish State in Eretz-Israel; the General Assembly required the inhabitants of Eretz-Israel to take such steps as were necessary on their part for the implementation of that resolution. This recognition by the United Nations of the right of the Jewish people to establish their State is irrevocable.

This right is the natural right of the Jewish people to be masters of their own fate, like all other nations, in their own sovereign State.

Accordingly we, members of the People's Council, representatives of the Jewish Community of Eretz-Israel and of the Zionist Movement, are here assembled on the day of the termination of the British Mandate over Eretz-Israel and, by virtue of our natural and historic right and on the strength of the resolution of the United Nations General Assembly, hereby declare the establishment of a Jewish state in Eretz-Israel, to be known as the State of Israel.

We declare that, with effect from the moment of the termination of the Mandate being tonight, the eve of Sabbath, the 6th Iyar, 5708 (15th May, 1948), until the establishment of the elected, regular authorities of the State in accordance with the Constitution which shall be adopted by the Elected Constituent Assembly not later than the 1st October 1948, the People's Council shall act as a Provisional Council of State, and its executive organ, the People's Administration, shall be the Provisional Government of the Jewish State, to be called "Israel."

The State of Israel will be open for Jewish immigration and for the Ingathering of the Exiles; it will foster the development of the country for the benefit of all its inhabitants; it will be based on freedom, justice and peace as envisaged by the prophets of Israel; it will ensure complete equality of social and political rights to all its inhabitants irrespective of religion, race or sex; it will guarantee freedom of religion, conscience, language, education and culture; it will safeguard the Holy Places of all religions; and it will be faithful to the principles of the Charter of the United Nations.

The State of Israel is prepared to cooperate with the agencies and representatives of the United Nations in implementing the resolution of the General Assembly of the 29th November, 1947, and will take steps to bring about the economic union of the whole of Eretz-Israel.

We appeal to the United Nations to assist the Jewish people in the building-up of its State and to receive the State of Israel into the community of nations.

We appeal—in the very midst of the onslaught launched against us now for months—to the Arab inhabitants of the State of Israel to preserve peace and participate in the upbuilding of the State on the basis of full and equal citizenship and due representation in all its provisional and permanent institutions.

We extend our hand to all neighbouring states and their peoples in an offer of peace and good neighbourliness, and appeal to them to establish bonds of cooperation and mutual help with the sovereign Jewish people settled in its own land. The State of Israel is prepared to do its share in a common effort for the advancement of the entire Middle East.

We appeal to the Jewish people throughout the Diaspora to rally round the Jews of Eretz-Israel in the tasks of immigration and upbuilding and to stand by them in the great struggle for the realization of the age-old dream—the redemption of Israel.

Placing our trust in the Almighty, we affix our signatures to this proclamation at this session of the provisional Council of State, on the soil of the Homeland, in the city of Tel-Aviv, on this Sabbath eve, the 5th day of Iyar, 5708 (14th May, 1948).

David Ben-Gurion

Daniel Auster Mordekhai Bentov Yitzchak Ben Zvi Eliyahu Berligne Fritz Bernstein Rabbi Wolf Gold Meir Grabovsky Yitzchak Gruenbaum Dr. Abraham Granovsky Eliyahu Dobkin Meir Wilner-Kovner Zerach Wahrhaftig Herzl Vardi Rachel Cohen Rabbi Kalman Kahana Saadia Kobashi Rabbi Yitzchak Meir Levin Meir David Loewenstein Zvi Luria Golda Myerson Nachum Nir Zvi Segal Rabbi Yehuda Leib Hacohen Fishman David Zvi Pinkas Aharon Zisling Moshe Kolodny Eliezer Kaplan Abraham Katznelson Felix Rosenblueth David Remez Berl Repetur Mordekhai Shattner Ben Zion Sternberg Bekhor Shitreet Moshe Shapira Moshe Shertok.

Bibliography

International Conventions

African [Banjul] Charter on Human and Peoples' Rights, June 27, 1981, OAU Doc. CAB/LEG/67/3 rev. 5, 21 I.L.M. 58 (1982).

International Covenant on Civil and Political Rights, Dec. 16, 1966, 999 U.N.T.S. 171.

International Covenant on Economic, Social and Cultural Rights, Dec. 16, 1966, 993 U.N.T.S. 3.

Council of Europe, Framework Convention for the Protection of National Minorities, 1 February 1995, ETS 157.

Convention on the Rights of the Child, Nov. 20, 1989, 1577 U.N.T.S. 3.

1960 UNESCO Convention Against Discrimination in Education adopted at the thirtieth plenary meeting, 14 December 1960.

Constitutions and Proclamations of Independence

La Constitución Española, Dec. 29, 1978, BOE núm. 311.

Proclamation of Independence, *Official Gazette*: Number 1; Tel Aviv, 5 Iyar 5708, 14.5.1948 Page 1.

The Parliament of Catalonia, Declaration of Sovereignty and of the Right to Decide of the People of Catalonia (22 January 2013).

National Legislation

Belgium

Loi concernant le régime linguistique dans l'enseignement [An Act respecting the language regulations in education], 30 juillet 1963, 22 août 1963, 8210 [Belg.].

Canada

Official Languages Act (R.S.C., c. 31) (4th Supp.) (1985).

Israel

Khok Yesod: Ha-Knesset [Basic Law: The Knesset], 1958, 12 L.S.I. 85.

Khok Haezrahut (the Citizenship Law), 5712–1952, 6 LSI 50 (1951–52) (Isr.).

Khok Ha-Khavarot Ha-Memshaltiyot (Tikun Mispar 7) [Government Corporations Law (Amendment No. 7)], 2000, S.H. 207.

Khok Khinukh Mamlakhti (Tikun Mispar 5) [State Education Law (Amendment No. 5)], 2000, S.H. 122.

Khok Khinukh Mamlakhti [State Education Law], 7 L.S.I. 113, art. 2 (1952–1953).

Khok Ha-Miflagot [Parties Law], 1992, S.H. 190 (Isr.).

Khok Hashvut [Law of Return], 5710–1950, 4 LSI 114 (1949–50) (Isr.).

Khok Mirsham Ha'uchlusin [Population Registry Law], 5725–1965, 19 LSI 288 (1964–65) (Isr.).

Khok Sheirut Ha-Medina (Minuyim) [State Service (Appointments) Law], 1959, 13 L.S.I. 87.

Khok Shivyon Hizdamnuyot Ba'avoda [Equality of Opportunities at Work Law], 5748–1988.

Hakhlatat Ha-Knesset Bidvar Takanot Ha-Knesset [Knesset Rules of Procedure, 30 May 2012], Section 75 e.

Draft Basic Law: Israel – the Nation-State of the Jewish People, P/3541/18.

Spain

The Statute of Autonomy of Catalonia, Organic Act 4/1979, 18 Dec. 1979.

International Courts

Lautsi v. Italy, App. No. 30814/06, Eur. Ct. H.R. (G.C.) (2011).

National Courts

Canada

Re Secession of Quebec, [1998] 2 S.C.R 217 (Can.) 130.

Israel

Election Confirmation 11280/02, *Central Elections Committee v. Ahmed Tibi;* Election Confirmation 50/03, *Central Elections Committee v. Azmi Bishara* (published in Nevo, 15.5.2003).

H.C. 6698/95, Kaadan v. Minhal Mekarke'ey Yisra-el [Israel Land Administration], 54 (1) P.D. 258.

H.C. 11286/03 Ornan et al. v. the Ministry of Interior (published in Nevo, 20.9.2004) (Hebrew).

H.C. 8573/08 Ornan v. the Ministry of Interior (published in Nevo, 2.10.2013) (Hebrew).

H.C. 630/70, Tamarin v. State of Israel, 26 (i) P.D. 197 (Hebrew).

Books

Akzin, Benjamin STATE AND NATION (1969).

Anderson, Benedict IMAGINED COMMUNITIES (Rev. ed., 2006).

Auron, Yair (ed.), ISRAEL: A DEMOCRATIC JEWISH SOCIETY TOWARDS THE 21ST CENTURY: CONVERSATIONS WITH THE FOUNDING FATHERS (1986).

Barzilai, Gad COMMUNITIES AND THE LAW: POLITICS AND CULTURES OF LEGAL IDENTITIES (2003).

Beiner, Ronald LIBERALISM, NATIONALISM, CITIZENSHIP (2003).

Benvenisti, Meron CITY OF STONE: THE HIDDEN HISTORY OF JERUSALEM (1998).

Berlin, Isaiah AGAINST THE CURRENT: ESSAYS IN THE HISTORY OF IDEAS (1981).

Breuilly, John NATIONALISM AND THE STATE (1982).

Brooman, Josh CONFLICT IN PALESTINE: JEWS, ARABS AND THE MIDDLE EAST SINCE 1900 (1989).

Brown, David CONTEMPORARY NATIONALISM: CIVIC, ETHNOCULTURAL AND MULTICULTURAL POLITICS (2000).

Butler, Judith and Spivak Gayatri Chakravorty, WHO SINGS THE NATION-STATE? LANGUAGE, POLITICS, BELONGING (2007).

Cassese, Antonio SELF DETERMINATION OF PEOPLES: A LEGAL REAPPRAISAL (1995).

Cobban, Alfred THE NATION STATE AND NATIONAL SELF-DETERMINATION (Rev. ed., 1969).

Conversi, Daniele THE BASQUES, THE CATALANS AND SPAIN: ALTERNATIVE ROUTES TO NATIONALIST MOBILISATION (1997).

Danspeckgruber, Wolfgang (ed.), THE SELF-DETERMINATION OF PEOPLES: COMMUNITY, NATION AND THE STATE IN AN INTER-DEPENDENT WORLD (2002).

Elon, Menachem NEW HORIZONS IN MEDICAL ETHICS: DECISION OF THE SUPREME COURT OF ISRAEL IN THE SHEFER CASE, CIVIL APPEAL 88/506, YAEL SHEFER V. THE STATE OF ISRAEL 48 (1) P.D. 87 (1997).

Friedman, Thomas L. THE WORLD IS FLAT (2005).

Gans, Chaim A JUST ZIONISM (2008).

Geisler, Michael E. (ed.), NATIONAL SYMBOLS, FRACTURED IDENTITIES (2005).

Gellner, Ernest NATIONS AND NATIONALISM (2nd ed., 2006).

Gutman, Amy (ed.), MULTICULTURALISM: EXAMINING THE POLITICS OF RECOGNITION (1994).

Hargreaves, John FREEDOM FOR CATALONIA? CATALAN NATIONALISM, SPANISH IDENTITY AND THE BARCELONA OLYMPIC GAMES (2000).

Hobsbawm, Eric NATIONS AND NATIONALISM SINCE 1780 (1990).

Jacobsohn, Garry J. CONSTITUTIONAL IDENTITY (2010).

Kedourie, Elie NATIONALISM (1993).

Kohn, Hans THE IDEA OF NATIONALISM, A STUDY IN ITS ORIGINS AND BACKGROUND (1961).

Kymlicka, Will MULTICULTURAL CITIZENSHIP: A LIBERAL THEORY OF MINORITY RIGHTS (1995).

Kymlicka, Will (ed.), THE RIGHTS OF MINORITY CULTURES (1995).

Kymlicka, Will and Bashir Bashir (eds.), THE POLITICS OF RECONCILIATION IN MULTICULTURAL SOCIETIES (2008).

Larson, Colleen L. and Ovando Carlos J. THE COLOR OF BUREAUCRACY: THE POLITICS OF EQUITY IN MULTICULTURAL SCHOOL COMMUNITIES (2001).

Lerner, Hana MAKING CONSTITUTIONS IN DEEPLY DIVIDED SOCIETIES (2013).

Lopez, Mark THE ORIGINS OF MULTICULTURALISM IN AUSTRALIAN POLITICS (2000).

MacIntyre, Alsadir AFTER VIRTUE: A STUDY IN MORAL THEORY (1984).

Maoz, Asher (ed.), ISRAEL AS A JEWISH AND DEMOCRATIC STATE (2011).

Miller, David ON NATIONALITY (1995).

Peled, Yoav THE CHALLENGE OF ETHNIC DEMOCRACY (2014).

Phillips, Anne THE POLITICS OF PRESENCE (1995).

Recchia, Stefano and Urbinati Nadia (eds.), A COSMOPOLITANISM OF NATIONS: GIUSEPPE MAZZINI'S WRITINGS ON DEMOCRACY, NATION BUILDING, AND INTERNATIONAL RELATIONS (2010).

Sand, Shlomo THE INVENTION OF THE JEWISH PEOPLE (translated by Yael Lotan) (2009).

Sandel, Michael LIBERALISM AND THE LIMITS OF JUSTICE (1998).

Schachter, Oscar and Joyner Christopher (eds.), 1 *Self Determination*, *in* UNITED NATIONS LEGAL ORDER 349 (1995).

Sellers, Mortimer N. (ed.), THE NEW WORLD ORDER: SOVEREIGNTY, HUMAN RIGHTS AND THE SELF-DETERMINATION OF PEOPLES (1996).

Smooha, Sammy AUTONOMY FOR ARABS IN ISRAEL? (1999) [Hebrew].

Summers, James PEOPLES AND INTERNATIONAL LAW: HOW NATIONALISM AND SELF-DETERMINATION SHAPE A CONTEMPORARY LAW OF THE NATIONS (1974).

Shafir, Gershon and Peled Yoav, BEING ISRAELI: THE DYNAMICS OF MULTIPLE CITIZENSHIP (2002).

Shaw, Malcolm N. INTERNATIONAL LAW (7th ed., 2014).

Shoham, Hizky LET'S CELEBRATE! FESTIVALS AND CIVIC CULTURE IN ISRAEL (2014) [Hebrew].

Simoni, Marcella AT THE MARGINS OF CONFLICT: SOCIAL PERSPECTIVES ON ARABS AND JEWS IN BRITISH PALESTINE (2010).

Smith, Anthony D. NATIONAL IDENTITY (1991).

Smith, Anthony D. ETHNO-SYMBOLISM AND NATIONALISM: A CULTURAL APPROACH (2009).

Spencer, Philip and Wollman Howard, NATIONALISM: A CRITICAL INTRODUCTION (2002).

Tamir, Yael LIBERAL NATIONALISM (1993).

Tully, James STRANGE MULTIPLICITY: CONSTITUTIONALISM IN AN AGE OF DIVERSITY (1995).

Walzer, Michael THINKING POLITICALLY (2007).

Wilson, Thomas M. and Donnan Hastings (eds.), BORDER IDENTITIES: NATION AND STATE AT INTERNATIONAL FRONTIERS (1988).

Yacobson, Alexander and Rubinstein Amnon, ISRAEL AND THE FAMILY OF NATIONS (2010).

Young, Iris M. JUSTICE AND THE POLITICS OF DIFFERENCE (1990).

Young, Iris M. INCLUSION AND DEMOCRACY (2000).

Articles

Albinski, Henry S. *Politics and Biculturalism in Canada: The Flag Debate*, THE AUSTRALIAN JOURNAL OF POLITICS AND HISTORY 169 (1967).

Alexander, Jeffrey C. *On the Social Construction of Moral Universals: The "Holocaust" from War Crime to Trauma Drama, in* CULTURAL TRAUMA AND COLLECTIVE IDENTITY 196 (Jeffrey C. Alexander et al. eds., 2004).

Amar, Akhil R. *Of Sovereignty and Federalism*, 96 YALE L.J. 1425 (1987).

Amara, Muhammad and Mostafa Mohanad *The Impact of The Occupation of the West Bank and the Gaza Strip on The Political Discourse of the Palestinians In Israel, in* THE IMPACTS OF LASTING OCCUPATION 279 (Daniel Bar-Tal and Izhak Schnell eds., 2013).

Arslan, Hasan *Multicultural Education: Approaches, Dimensions and Principles, in* MULTICULTURAL EDUCATION: FROM THEORY TO PRACTICE 15 (Hasan Arslan and Georgeta Raţă eds., 2013).

Banks, James A. *Multicultural Education: Historical Development, Dimensions, and Practice*, 19 REVIEW OF RESEARCH IN EDUCATION 3 (1993).

——— *Diversity, Group Identity, and Citizenship Education in a Global Age Diversity, in* DEMOCRACY AND MULTICULTURAL EDUCATION 16 (Farideh Salili and Rumjahn Hoosain eds., 2010).

Barshack, Lior *Constituent Power as Body: Outline of a Constitutional Theology*, 56 U. TORONTO L.J. 185 (2006).

Bekerman, Zvi *Reshaping Conflict Through School Ceremonial Events in Israeli Palestinians-Jewish Coeducation*, 34(2) ANTHROPOLOGY & EDUCATION QUARTERLY 205 (2003).

Callan, Eamonn *Discrimination and Religious Schooling, in* CITIZENSHIP IN DIVERSE SOCIETIES 47 (Will Kymlicka and Wayne Norman eds., 2000).

Cerulo, Karen A. *Symbols and the World System: National Anthems and Flags*, 8 (2) SOCIOLOGICAL FORUM 243 (1993).

Crawford, James *The General Assembly, The International Court and Self-Determination*, *in* FIFTY YEARS OF THE INTERNATIONAL COURT OF JUSTICE 585 (Alan V. Lowe and Malgosia Fitzmaurice eds., 1996)

Delmartino, Frank Dumont Hugues, and Van Droghenbroeck Sébastian, *Kingdom of Belgium, in* 7 A GLOBAL DIALOGUE ON FEDERALISM: DIVERSITY AND UNITY IN FEDERAL COUNTRIES 48 (Luis Moreno and César Colino eds., 2010).

Donitsa-Schmidt, Smadar Inbar Ofra and Shohamy Elana, *The Effects of Teaching Spoken Arabic on Students' Attitudes and Motivation in Israel*, 88(2) THE MODERN LANGUAGE JOURNAL 217 (2004).

Ehrlich, Charles E. *Democratic Alternatives to Ethnic Conflict: Consociationalism and Neoseparatism*, 26 BROOKLYN J. INT'L L. 447 (2000).

Eisenberg, Avigail and Kymlicka Will, *Bringing Institutions Back In: How Public Institutions Assess Identity, in* IDENTITY POLITICS IN THE PUBLIC REALM: BRINGING INSTITUTIONS BACK IN 1(Avigail Eisenberg and Will Kymlicka eds., 2011).

Eldering, Lotty *Multiculturalism and Multicultural Education in an International Perspective*, 27(3) ANTHROPOLOGY & EDUCATION QUARTERLY 315 (1996).

Fossum, John Erik *Citizenship, Diversity, and Pluralism: The Case of the European Union, in* CITIZENSHIP, DIVERSITY AND PLURALISM 203 (Alan C. Cairns et al. eds., 1999).

Gay, Geneva *Curriculum Theory and Multicultural Education, in* HANDBOOK OF RESEARCH OF MULTICULTURAL EDUCATION (James A. Banks ed., 2nd ed., 2004).

Gagnon, Alain-G. *The Moral Foundations of Asymmetrical Federalism: A Normative Exploration of the Case of Quebec and Canada, in* MULTINATIONAL DEMOCRACIES 319 (Alain-G. Gagnon, James Tully eds., 2001).

Gaudreault-DesBiens, Jean-François *The Quebec Secession Reference and the Judicial Arbitration of Conflicting Narratives About Law, Democracy and Identity*, 23 VT. L. REV. 793 (1999).

Van Ginderachter, Maarten and Leerssen Joep, *Denied Ethnicism: on the Walloon Movement in Belgium*, 18(2) NATIONS AND NATIONALISM 230, 235 (2012).

Greenfeld, Liah *Etimology, Definitions, Types, in* 1 ENCYCLOPEDIA OF NATIONALISM 251 (Alexander J. Motyl ed., 2001).

Gutman, Amy *Unity and Diversity in Democratic Multicultural Education: Creative and Destructive Tensions, in* DIVERSITY AND CITIZENSHIP EDUCATION: GLOBAL PERSPECTIVES 71 (James A. Banks, ed., 2003).

Habermas, Jurgen *Struggles for Recognition in the Democratic Constitutional State*, (Translated by Shierry Weber Nicholsen), *in* MULTICULTURALISM: EXAMINING THE POLITICS OF RECOGNITION 107 (Amy Gutman ed., 1994).

Irving, R.E.M. *The Flemings and Walloons of Belgium*, MINORITY GROUP RIGHTS REPORT No. 46, 1980.

Jabareen, Yousef T. *Constitution Building and Equality in Deeply-Divided Societies: The Case of the Palestinian-Arab Minority in Israel*, 26 WIS. INT'L L.J. 345 (2008).

Karayanni, Michael M. *The Separate Nature of the Religious Accommodations for the Palestinian-Arab Minority in Israel*, 5 (1) JIHR 41 (2007).

Koskeniemmi, Martti *National Self-Determination Today: Problems of Legal Theory and Practice*, 43 ICLQ, 241 (1994).

Kymlicka, Will *Multicultural States and Intercultural Citizens*, 1(2) THEORY AND RESEARCH IN EDUCATION 147 (2003).

——— *Justice and Security*, *in* ETHNICITY, NATIONALISM, AND MINORITY RIGHTS 144 (Stephen May, Tariq Modood, and Judith Squires eds., 2004).

Lerner, Natan *The Minorities Treaties System*, *in* GROUP RIGHTS AND DISCRIMINATION IN INTERNATIONAL LAW 10 (2003).

Luchtenberg, Sigrid *Multicultural Education: Challenges and Responses*, 4(1) JOURNAL OF SOCIAL SCIENCE EDUCATION 31 (2005).

McGlynn, Claire, Bekerman Zvi, *The Management of Pupil Difference in Catholic-Protestant and Palestinian-Jewish Integrated Education in Northern Ireland and Israel*, 37(5) COMPARE 689 (2007).

Mecham, J. Lloyd *The Origins of Federalism in Mexico*, 18(2) THE HISPANIC AMERICAN HISTORICAL REVIEW 164 (1938).

Medhurst, Kenneth *The Basques and Catalans*, THE MINORITY RIGHTS GROUP, Report no. 9, 1987.

Miller, David *Nationality in Divided Societies*, *in* MULTINATIONAL DEMOCRACIES 299 (Alain G. Gagnon, James Tully eds., 2001).

Moreno, Luis and Colino César, *Kingdom of Spain in Global Dialogue*, *in* 7 A GLOBAL DIALOGUE ON FEDERALISM: DIVERSITY AND UNITY IN FEDERAL COUNTRIES, 289 (Luis Moreno and César Colino eds., 2010).

Mnookin, Robert and Verbeke Alain, *Group-Conflict Resolution: Sources of Resistance to Reconciliation: Persistent Nonviolent Conflict with No Reconciliation: The Flemish and Walloons in Belgium*, 72 LAW & CONTEMP. PROB., 151 (2009).

Patten, Alan *Liberal Citizenship in Multinational Societies*, *in* MULTINATIONAL DEMOCRACIES 279 (Alain-G. Gagnon, James Tully eds., 2001).

Protsyk, Oleh Majority-Minority Relations in Ukraine, 1 EUR. ETHNOPOLITICS & MINORITY ISSUES 8 (2008).

Puppinck, Gregor *The Case of Lautsi v. Italy: A Synthesis*, 3 B.Y.U.L REV. 873 (2012).

Renan, Ernest *What is a Nation, in*, MODERN POLITICAL DOCTRINES (A Zimmern ed., 1939)

Roth, Brad R. *The Virtues of Bright Lines: Self-Determination, Secession and External Intervention*, 16(3) GERMAN LAW JOURNAL 384 (2015).

Rouhana, Nadim N. *Reconciling History and Equal Citizenship in Israel: Democracy and the Politics of Historical Denial, in* THE POLITICS OF RECONCILIATION IN MULTICULTURAL SOCIETIES 70 (Will Kymlicka and Bashir Bashir eds., 2008).

Roznai, Yaniv and Suteu Silvia, *The Eternal Territory? The Crimean Crisis and Ukraine's Territorial Integrity as an Unamendable Constitutional Principle*, 16(3) GERMAN LAW JOURNAL 542 (2015).

Saban, Ilan *Minority Rights in Deeply Divided Societies: A Framework for Analysis and the Case of the Arab-Palestinian Minority in Israel*, 36 N.Y.U. J. INT'L L. & POL. 885 (2004).

Shachar, Ayelet *Whose Republic? Citizenship and Membership in the Israeli Polity*, 13 GEO. IMMIGR. L.J. 233 (1999).

Schnell, Izhak *Geographical Ramifications of the Occupation for Israeli Society, in* THE IMPACTS OF LASTING OCCUPATION 93 (Daniel Bar-Tal and Izhak Schnell eds., 2013).

Schofield, Janet W. *Fostering Positive Intergroup Relations in Schools, in* HANDBOOK OF RESEARCH OF MULTICULTURAL EDUCATION 799 (James A. Banks ed., 2nd ed., 2004).

Simeon, Richard and Conway Daniel-Patrick, *Federalism and the Management of Conflict in Multinational Societies, in* MULTINATIONAL DEMOCRACIES, 338 (Alain-G. Gagnon, James Tully eds., 2001).

Sieyes, Emmanuel J. *What is the Third Estate?* [1789], *in* POLITICAL WRITINGS 97 (2003).

Sleeter, Christine E. and McLaren Peter L., *in* MULTICULTURAL EDUCATION, CRITICAL PEDAGOGY, AND THE POLITICS OF DIFFERENCE 11 (Christine E. Sleeter and Peter L. McLaren eds., 1995).

Smith, Anthony D. *The Rites of Nations: Elites, Masses and the Re-enactment of the 'National Past' in* THE RITES OF NATIONS IN THE CULTURAL POLITICS OF NATIONALISM AND NATION-BUILDING: RITUAL AND PERFORMANCE IN THE FORGING OF NATIONS 21 (Rachel Tsang, Eric Taylor Woods eds., 2014).

Smith, Whitney *National Symbols, in* ENCYCLOPEDIA OF NATIONALISM 521 (Alexander J. Motyl ed., 2001).

Stephan, Walter G. and Stephan Cookie White, *Intergroup Relations in Multicultural Education Programs, in* HANDBOOK OF RESEARCH OF MULTICULTURAL EDUCATION 782 (James A. Banks ed., 2nd ed., 2004).

Sterio, Milena *On the Right to External Self-Determination: 'Selfistans', Secessions, and the Great Power Rule*, 19 MINN. J. INT'L. L. 137 (2010).

Summers, James *The Internal and External Aspects of Self-Determination Reconsidered, in* STATEHOOD AND SELF-DETERMINATION: RECONCILING TRADITION AND MODERNITY IN INTERNATIONAL LAW 229 (Duncan French ed., 2013).

Sunstein, Cass *Constitutionalism and Secession*, 58 UNI. CHI. L. REV. 633 (1991).

Taylor, Charles *Cross-Purposes: the liberal-Communitarian Debate, in* LIBERALISM AND THE MORAL LIFE, (Nancy Rosenbaum ed., 1989).

——— *Shared and Divergent Values, in* OPTIONS FOR A NEW CANADA 53 (Ronald. L. Watts and Douglas M. Brown eds., 1991).

——— *The Politics of Recognition,* in MULTICULTURALISM: EXAMINING THE POLITICS OF RECOGNITION (Amy Gutman, ed., 1994).

Weintal, Sharon *The Inherent Authority of Judges in a Three-Track Democracy to Recognise Unenumerated Constitutional Rights: The Israeli Story of a Judicial Mission with No Ammunition, in* ISRAELI CONSTITUTIONAL LAW IN THE MAKING 292 (Gideon Sapir, Daphne Barak-Erez and Aharon Barak eds., 2013).

Vos, Louis *Reconstructions of the Past in Belgium and Flanders, in* SECESSION, HISTORY AND THE SOCIAL SCEINCES 179 (Bruno Coppieters and Michel Huysseune eds., 2002).

Yuval-Davis, Nira *Borders, Boundaries, and the Politics of Belonging, in* ETHNICITY, NATIONALISM AND MINORITY RIGHTS 214 (Stephen May, Tariq Modood, Judith Squires eds., 2004).

Yuksel, Edip *Yes, I am a Kurd,* 7 D.C.L.J. INT'L L. & PRAC. 359 (1998).

Zembylas, Michalinos *Negotiating Co-Existence in Divided Societies: Teachers, Students and Parents' Perspectives at a Shared School in Cyprus,* 25(4) RESEARCH PAPERS IN EDUCATION 433 (2010).

Zikmund II, Joseph *National Anthems as Political Symbols,* XIII(3) THE AUSTRALIAN JOURNAL OF POLITICS AND HISTORY 73 (1989).

Dissertations

Robert, Mark *The Construction of Culture in Multicultural Education: Classroom Participation and Teacher-student Interaction in a Jewish-Arab School,* Thesis submitted for the degree of Doctor of Philosophy, April 2013.

United Nations Documents

United Nations General Assembly Documents

Declaration on the Granting of Independence to Colonial Countries and Peoples, G.A. res. 1514 (XV), 15 U.N. GAOR Supp. (No. 16) U.N. Doc. A/4684, at 66 (14 Dec. 1960).

Declaration on Principles of international Law Concerning Friendly Relations and Cooperation Among States, G.A. Res. 2625 (XXV), Annex, 25 UN GAOR, Supp. (No. 28), U.N. Doc. A/5217, at 121 (24 Oct. 1970).

United Nations Committees Documents

Committee on the Elimination of Racial Discrimination, General Recommendation 21, The right to self-determination (Forty-eighth session, 1996), U.N. Doc. A/51/18, annex VIII at 125 (1996), 4.

Other United Nations Documents

The Hague Recommendations Regarding the Education Rights of National Minorities, High Commissioner on National Minorities, 1 October 1996.

International Conferences and Other International Documents

The Final Act of the Conference on Security and Cooperation in Europe, Aug. 1, 1975, 14 I.L.M. 1292.

Venice Comm'n for Democracy Through Law, *Self-Determination and Secession in Constitutional Law*, COUNCIL OF EUR. (Jan. 12, 2000).

Websites

<http://www.bbc.com/news/world-europe-13038095>.

<http://www.nytimes.com/2009/11/30/world/europe/30swiss.html?_r=0>.

<http://www.bbc.com/news/uk-scotland-29270441>.

<http://plato.stanford.edu/entries/communitarianism/>.

<http://education.uky.edu/OFE/sites/education.uky.edu.OFE/files/documents/CultureGram-Belgium1.pdf>.

<http://www.economist.com/node/21552564>.

<http://ida.com.np/upload_files/ncps4.pdf.>.

<http://www.nationalanthems.info/gt.htm>.

<http://www.national-anthems.org/history.php#s-africa>.

<http://www.theguardian.com/world/2014/feb/03/new-zealand-plans-flag-referendum>.

<http://adalah.org/newsletter/eng/dec06/tasawor-mostaqbali.pdf>.

<http://www.jpost.com/Diplomacy-and-Politics/Kerry-says-Netanyahu-wrong-to-insist-Palestinians-recognize-Israel-as-Jewish-state-345341>.

<http://nationalinterest.org/commentary/why-palestine-must-recognize-israel-jewish-state-10174>.

Index

www.ingramcontent.com/pod-product-compliance
Lightning Source LLC
LaVergne TN
LVHW010626300926
849162LV00001B/81